GEN

GEN

KAMEN VOLUME 1

KAMEN™, GEN™ & GEN MANGA™ ARE TRADEMARKS OF GEN MANGA ENTERTAINMENT, INC./
© 2014 GEN MANGA ENTERTAINMENT, INC. ALL RIGHTS RESERVED.

FOR INFORMATION, CONTACT GEN MANGA ENTERTAINMENT, INC.

COVER ART . . . . HARVEY TOLIBAO
COVER AND INTERIOR DESIGN . . . . RICHARD RODRIGUEZ
ART AND STORY . . . . GUNYA MIHARA

PUBLISHED BY
GEN MANGA ENTERTAINMENT, INC.
250 PARK AVENUE, SUITE 7002
NEW YORK, NY 10117 USA
WWW.GENMANGA.COM

PRINTED IN CANADA

MANGA

Kamen

volume 1

mihara gunya

Japanese Style

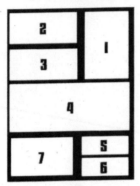

**Remember to read
from right to left**

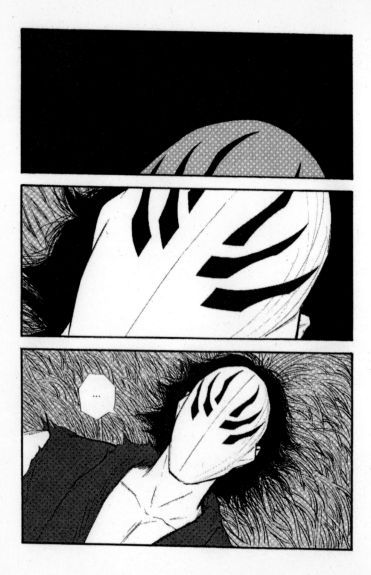

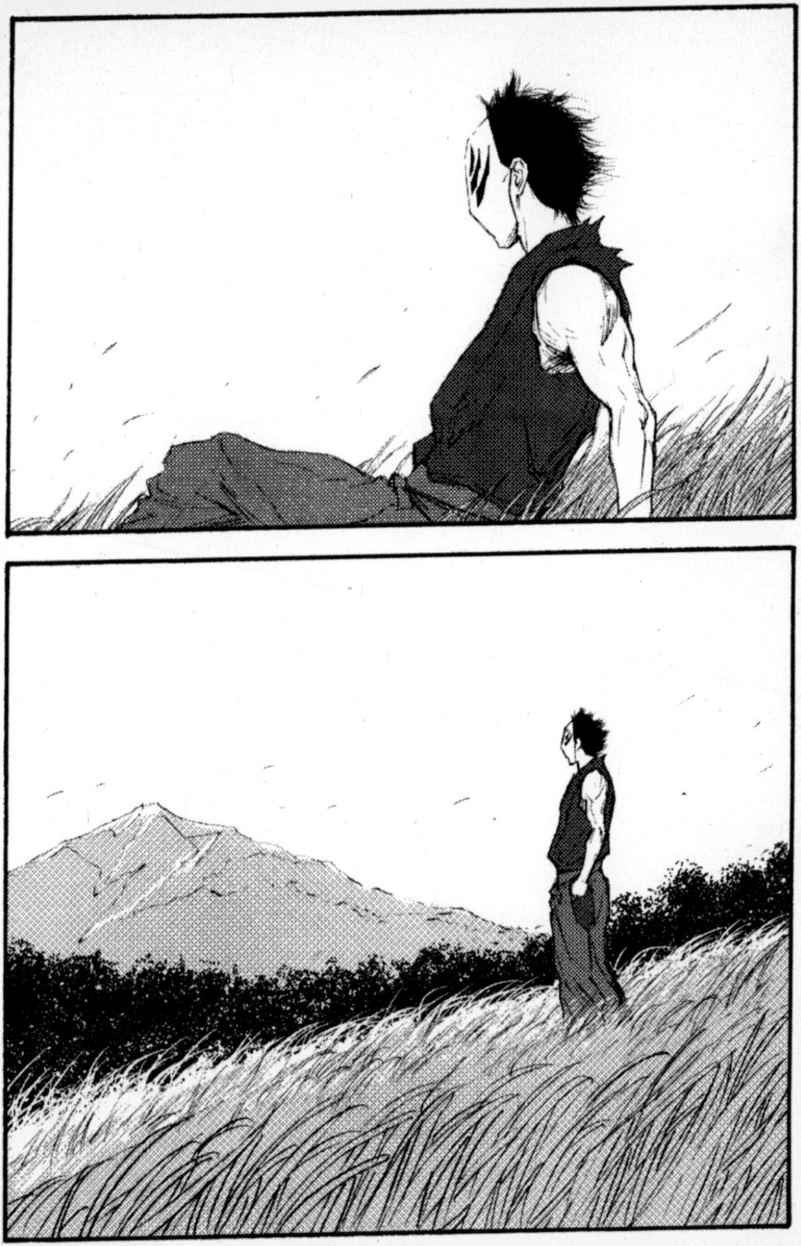

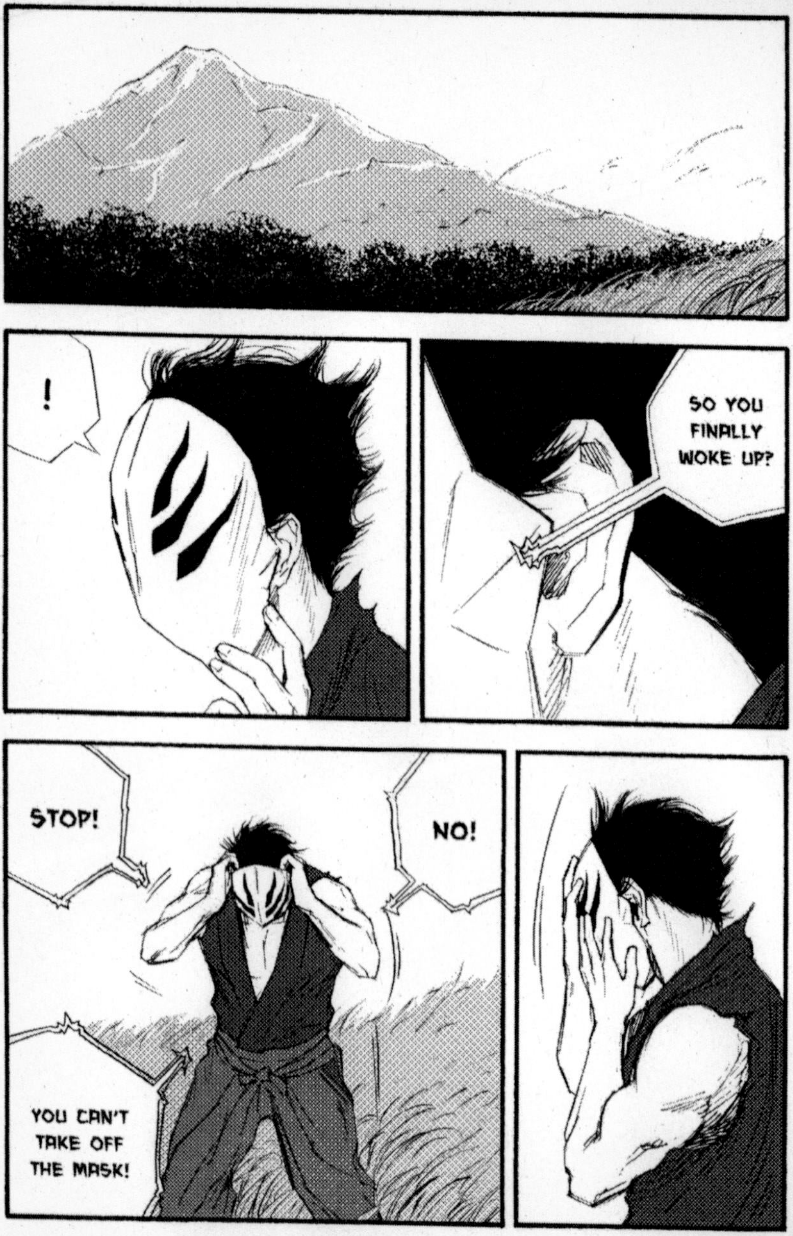
SO YOU FINALLY WOKE UP?
!
NO!
STOP!
YOU CAN'T TAKE OFF THE MASK!

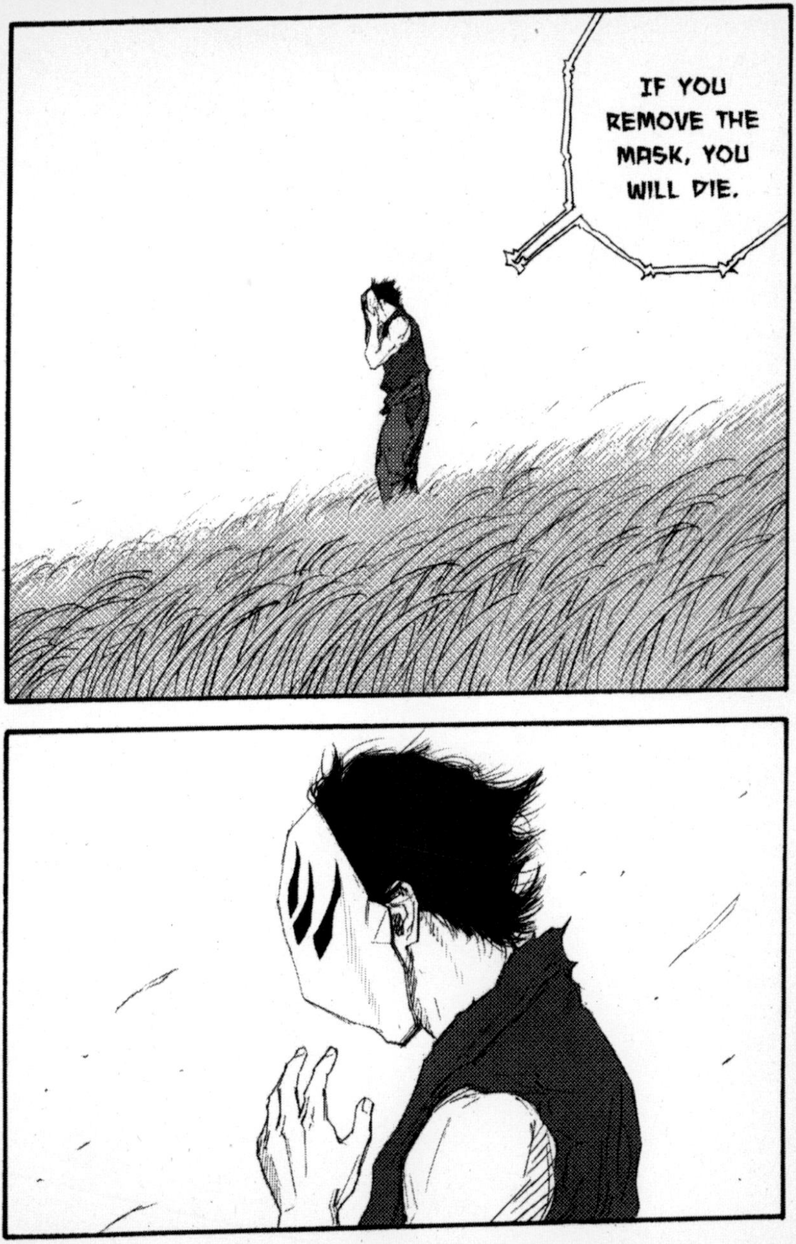
IF YOU REMOVE THE MASK, YOU WILL DIE.

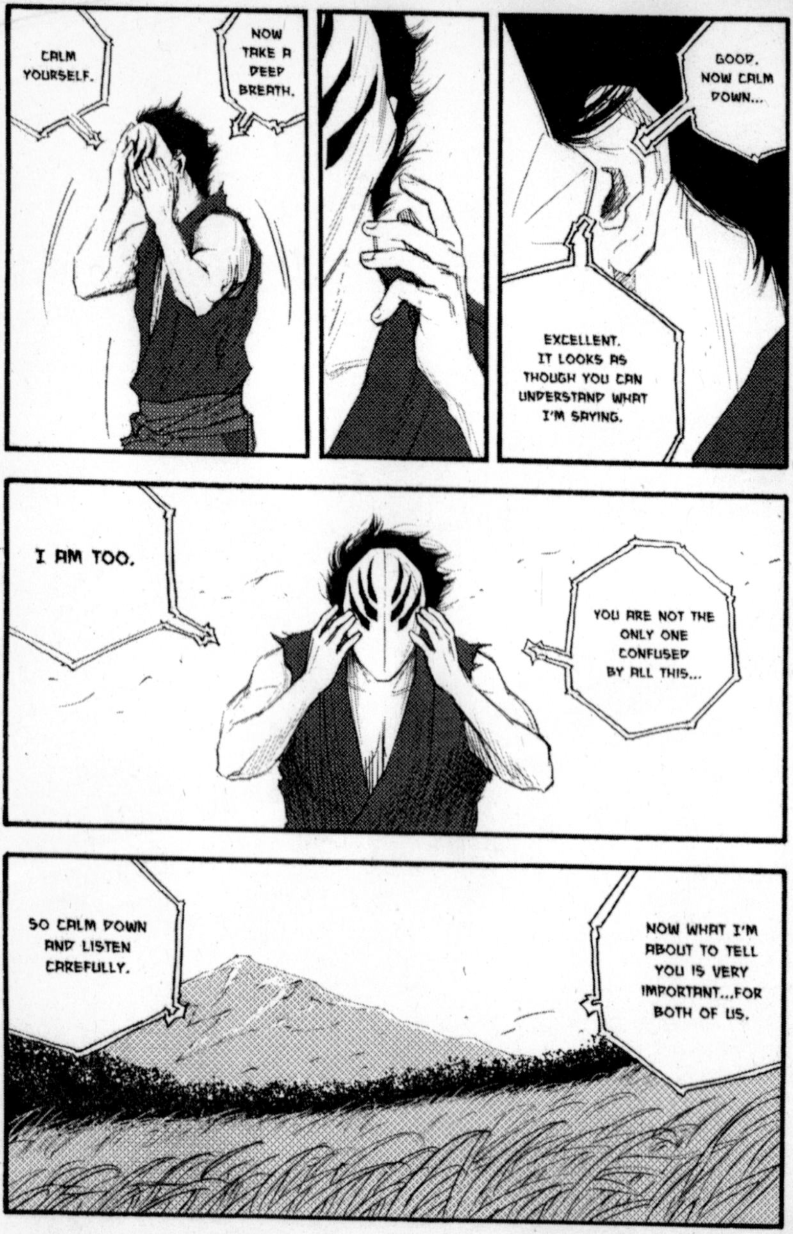
GOOD. NOW CALM DOWN...
EXCELLENT. IT LOOKS AS THOUGH YOU CAN UNDERSTAND WHAT I'M SAYING.
NOW TAKE A DEEP BREATH.
CALM YOURSELF.
YOU ARE NOT THE ONLY ONE CONFUSED BY ALL THIS...
I AM TOO.
NOW WHAT I'M ABOUT TO TELL YOU IS VERY IMPORTANT...FOR BOTH OF US.
SO CALM DOWN AND LISTEN CAREFULLY.

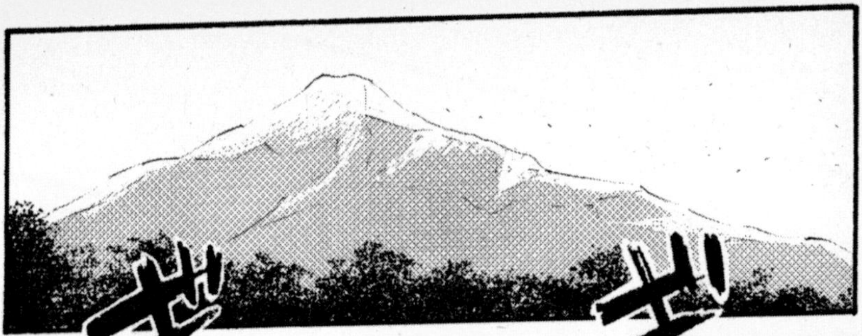

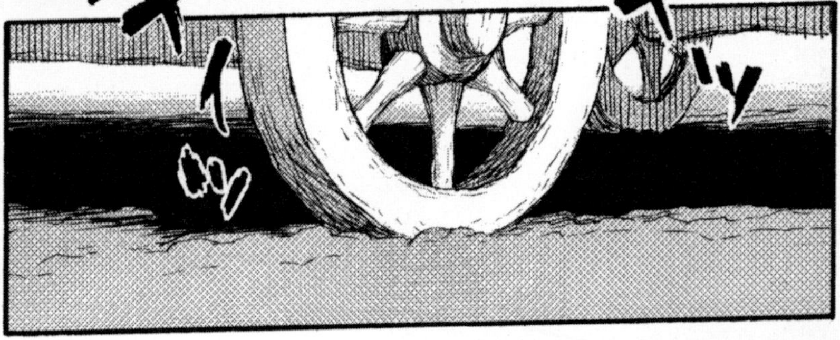
ギギッ
ギイッ

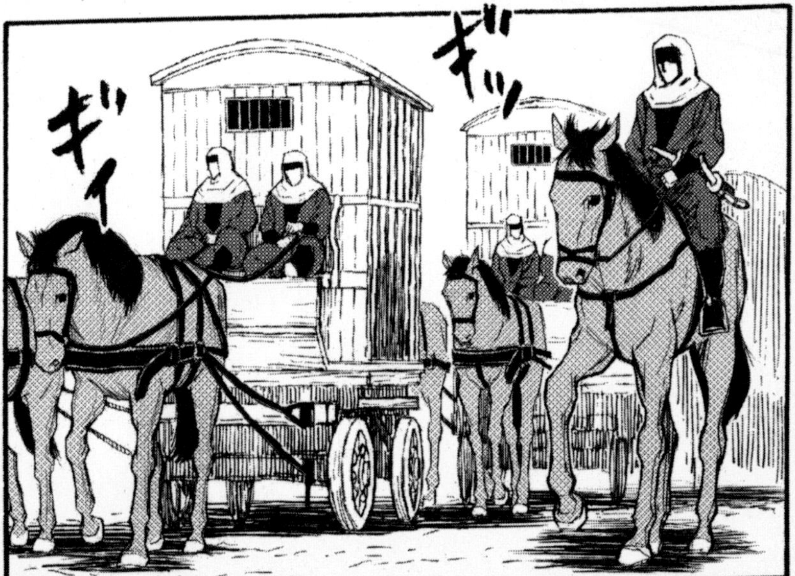
ギッ
ギイ

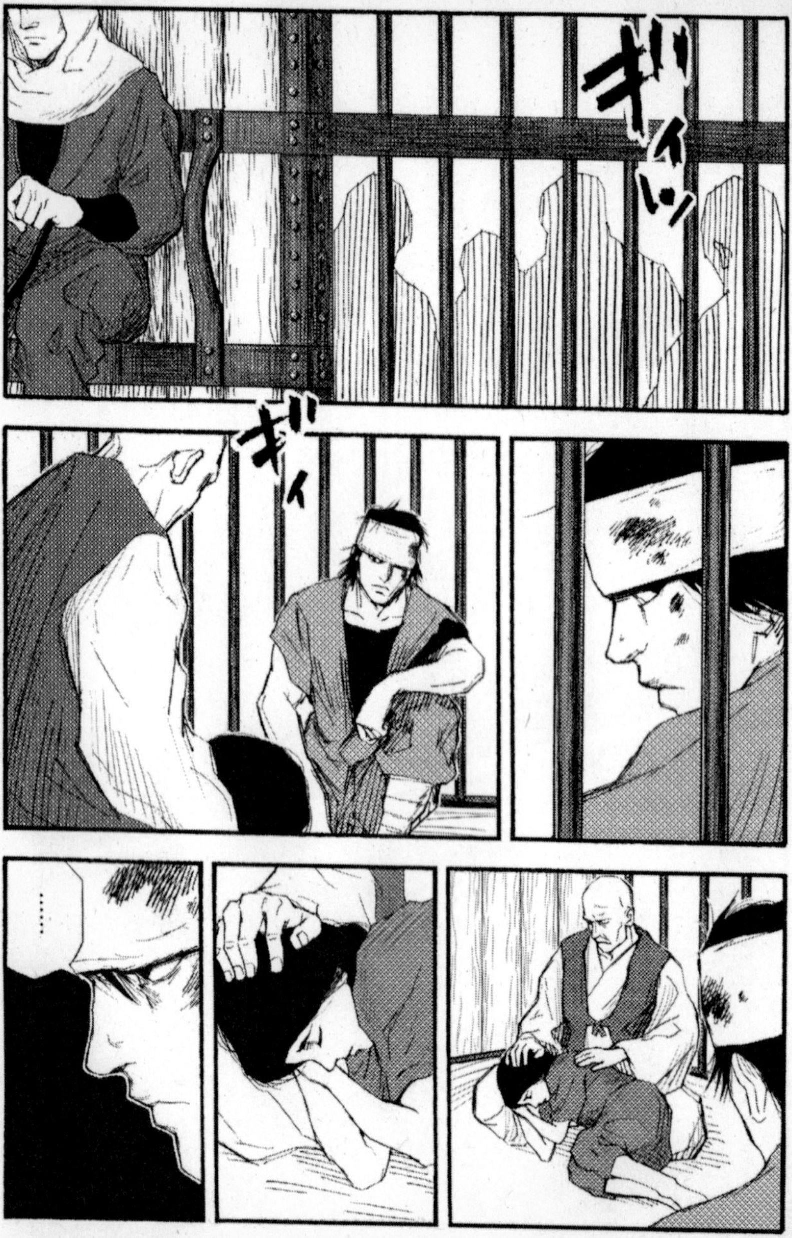
ギィィン
ギィ
……

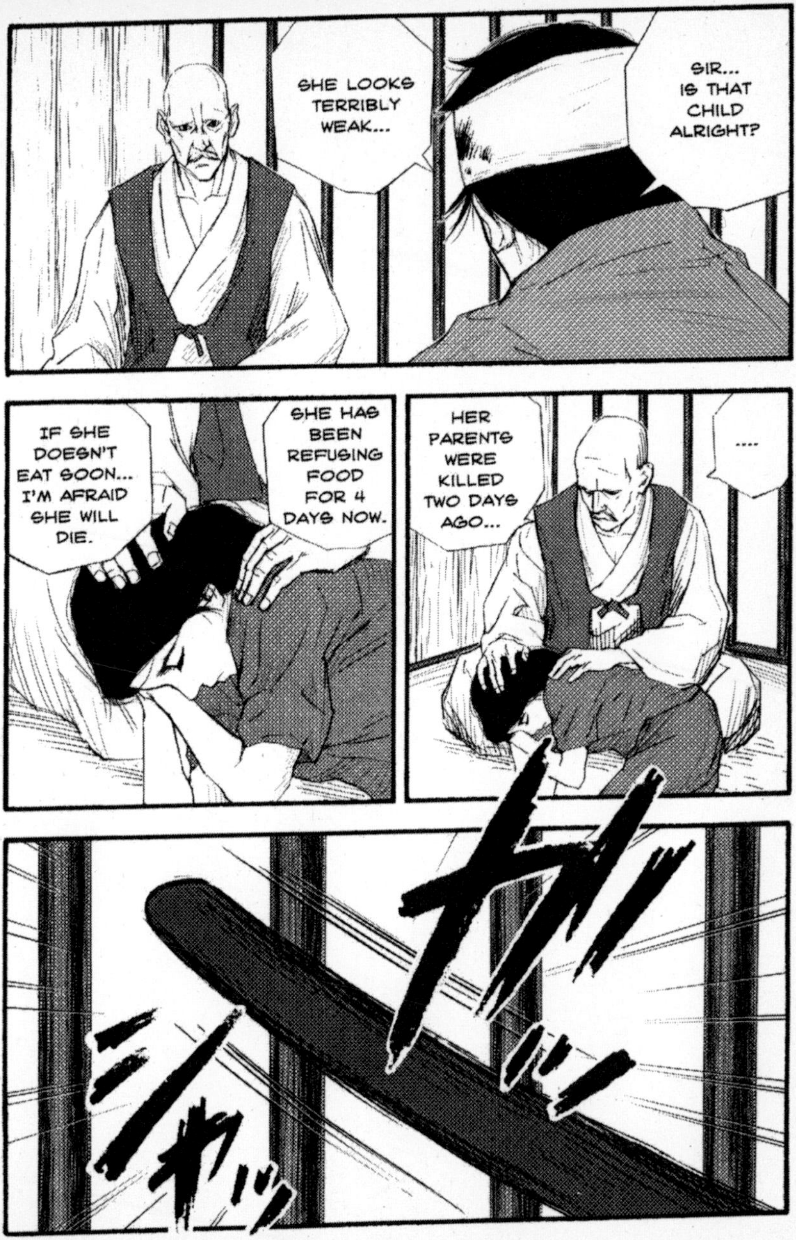
SIR... IS THAT CHILD ALRIGHT?
SHE LOOKS TERRIBLY WEAK...
....
HER PARENTS WERE KILLED TWO DAYS AGO...
SHE HAS BEEN REFUSING FOOD FOR 4 DAYS NOW.
IF SHE DOESN'T EAT SOON... I'M AFRAID SHE WILL DIE.

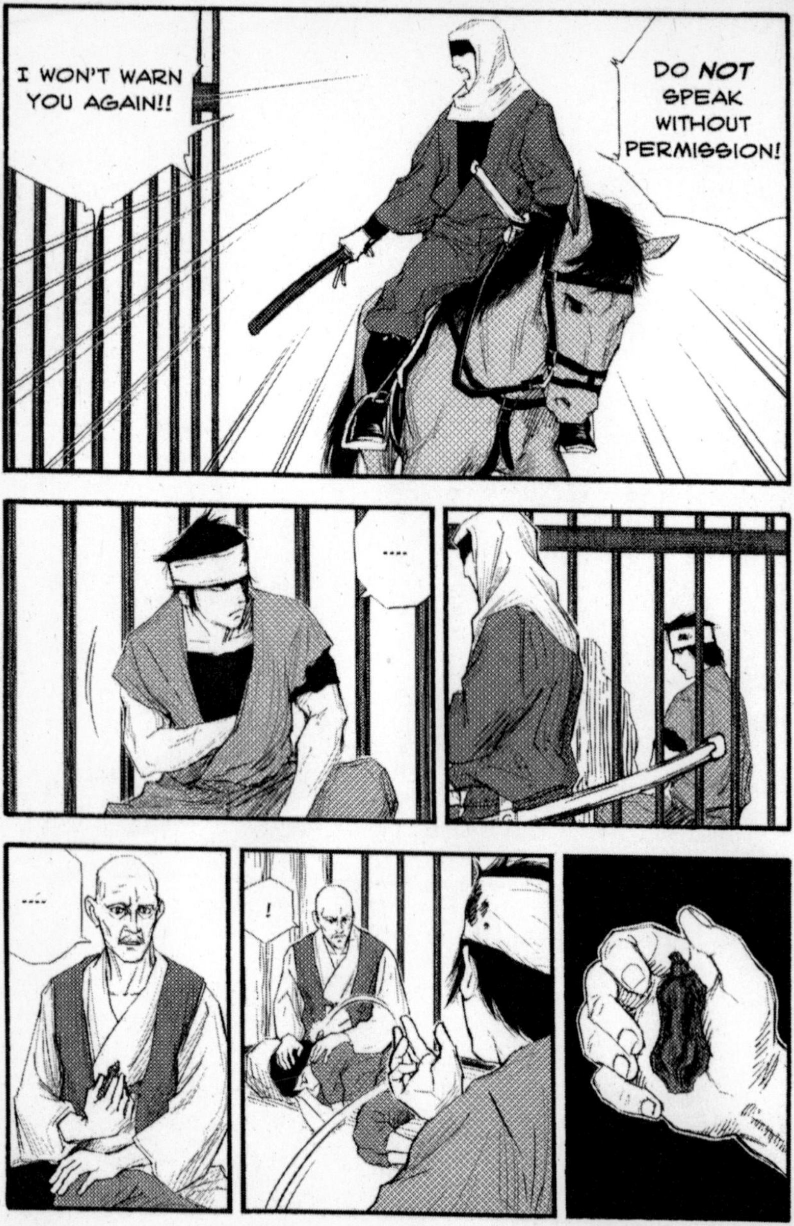
DO NOT SPEAK WITHOUT PERMISSION!
I WON'T WARN YOU AGAIN!!
....
!
....

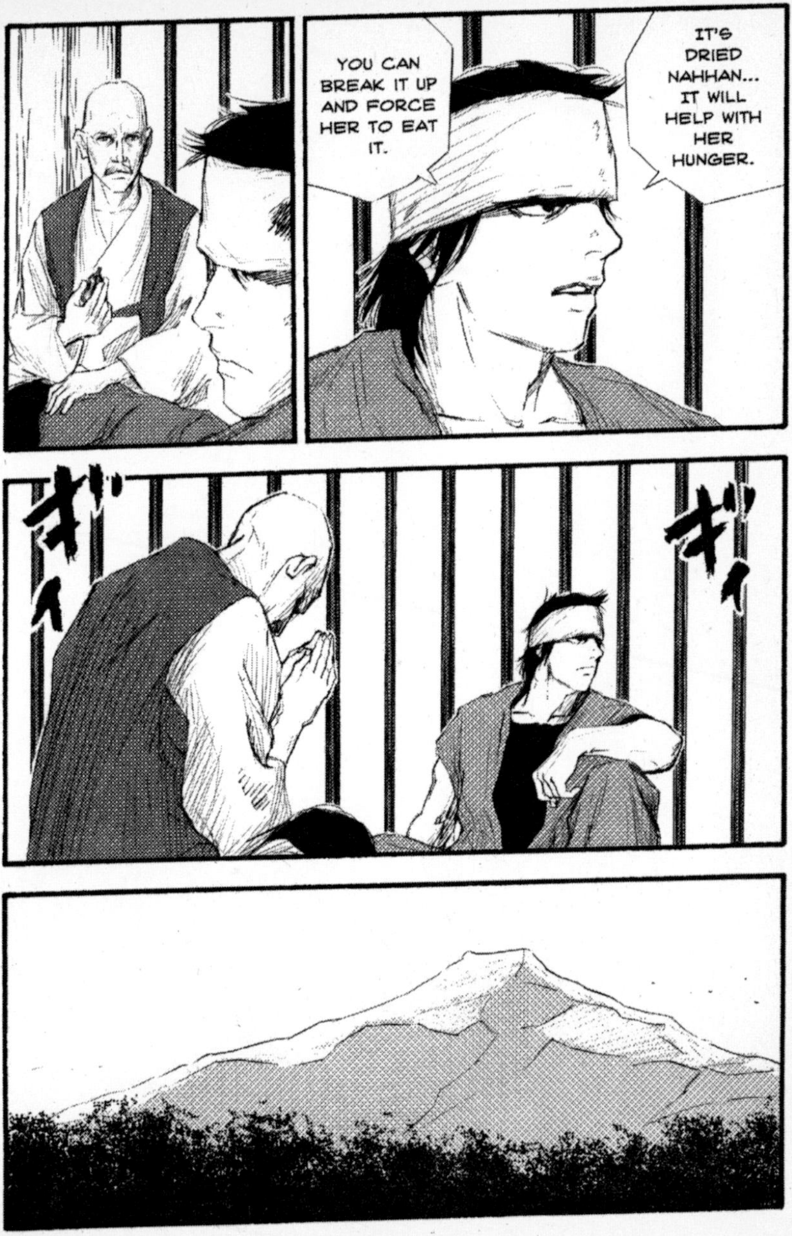
IT'S DRIED NAHHAN... IT WILL HELP WITH HER HUNGER.
YOU CAN BREAK IT UP AND FORCE HER TO EAT IT.
ギィ
ギィ

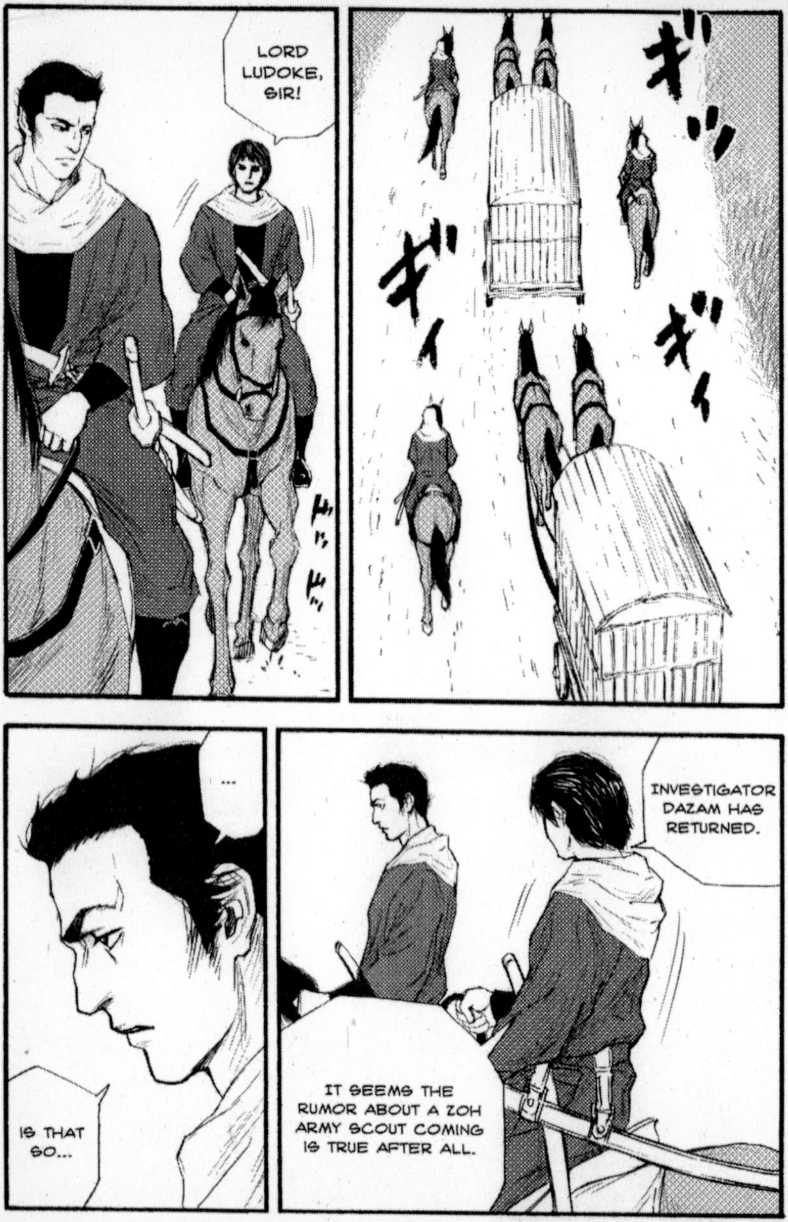

ギッ
ギィ
ギィ
LORD LUDOKE, SIR!
ドッドッ
INVESTIGATOR DAZAM HAS RETURNED.
IT SEEMS THE RUMOR ABOUT A ZOH ARMY SCOUT COMING IS TRUE AFTER ALL.
...
IS THAT SO...

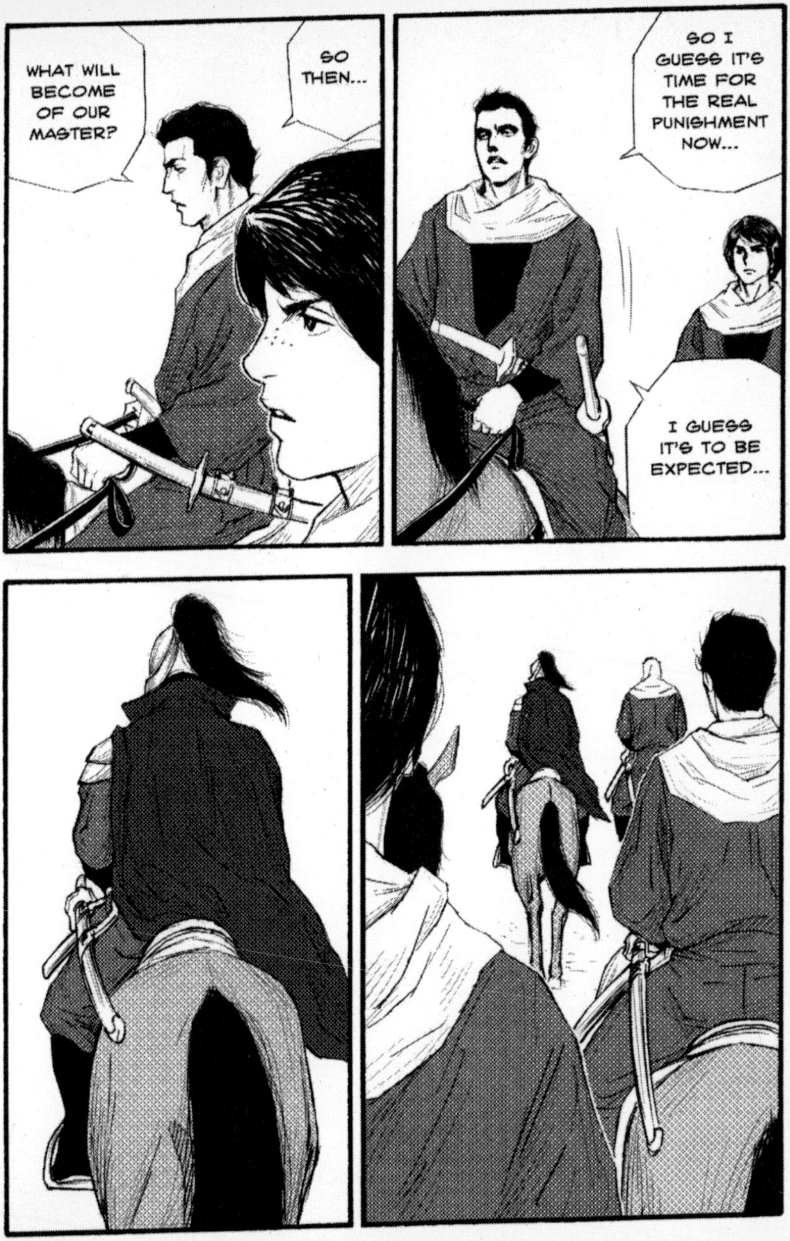
SO I GUESS IT'S TIME FOR THE REAL PUNISHMENT NOW...
I GUESS IT'S TO BE EXPECTED...
SO THEN...
WHAT WILL BECOME OF OUR MASTER?

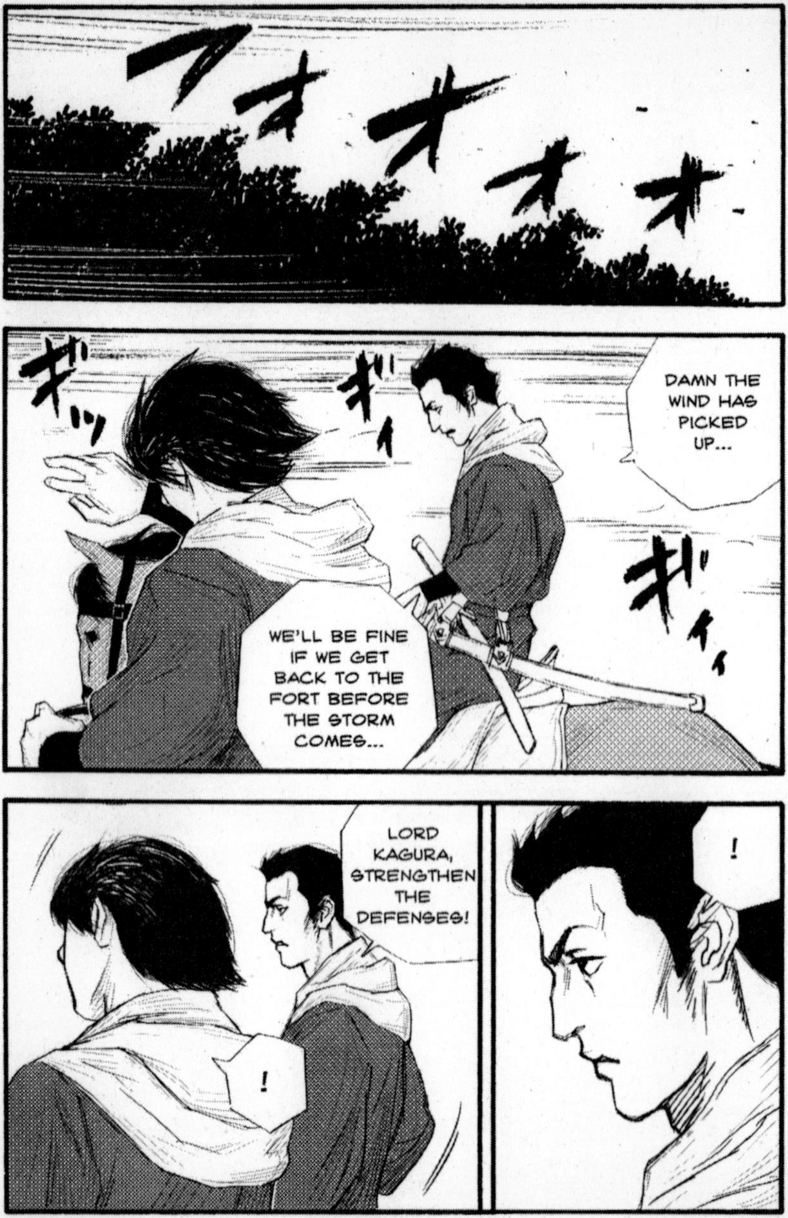
フオオオオ
DAMN THE WIND HAS PICKED UP...
ギイィ
WE'LL BE FINE IF WE GET BACK TO THE FORT BEFORE THE STORM COMES...
ギイ
ギッ
!
LORD KAGURA, STRENGTHEN THE DEFENSES!
!

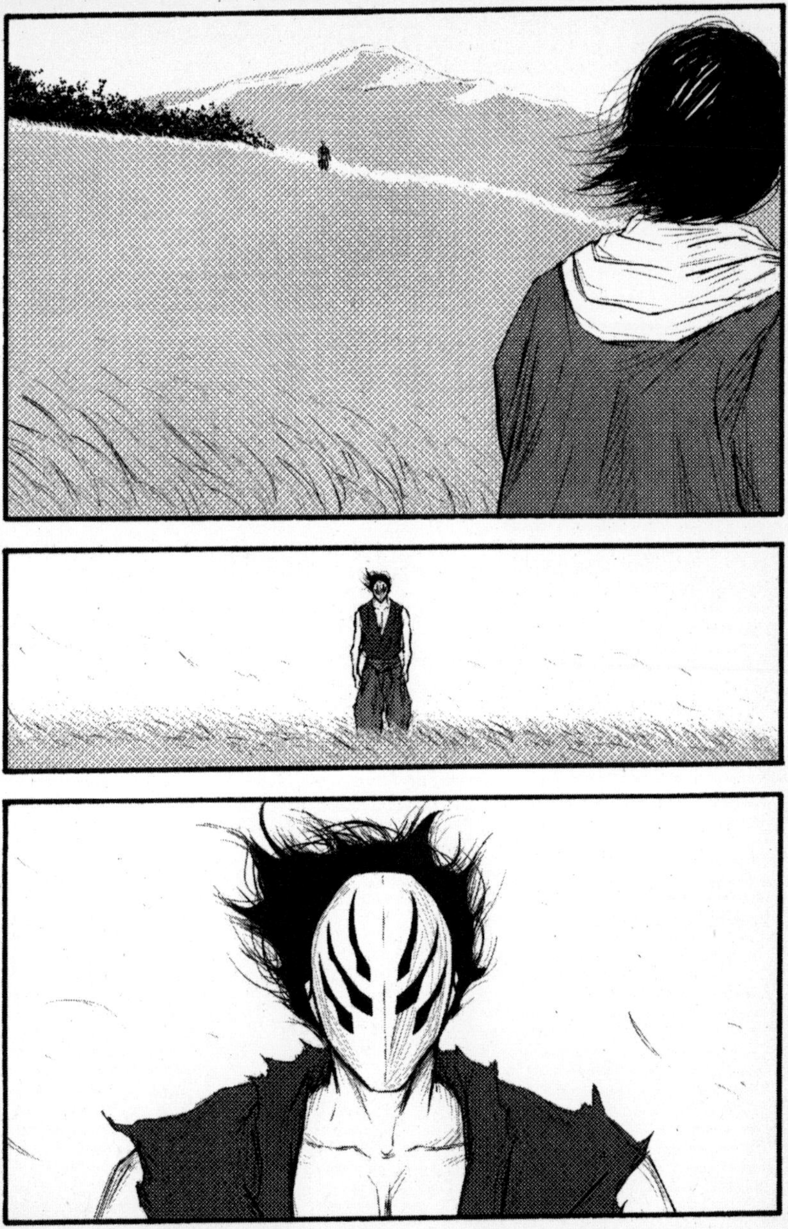

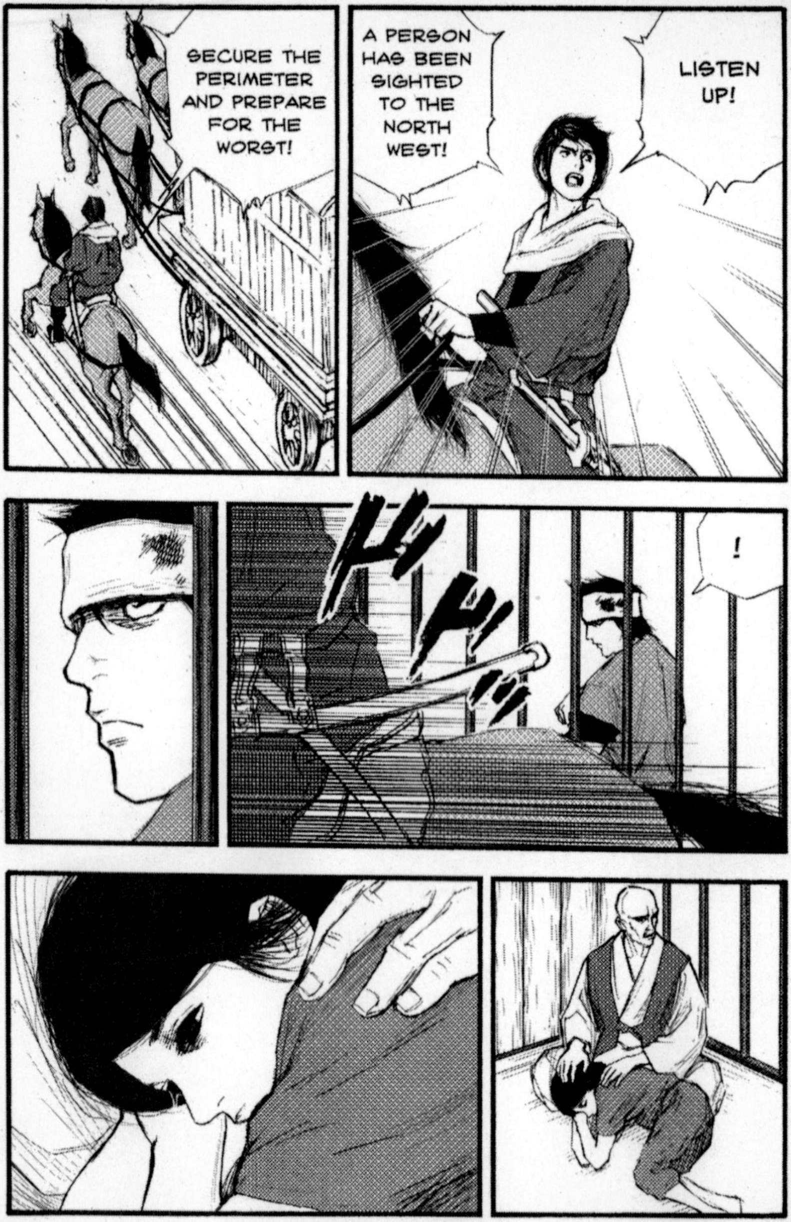
LISTEN UP!
A PERSON HAS BEEN SIGHTED TO THE NORTH WEST!
SECURE THE PERIMETER AND PREPARE FOR THE WORST!
!

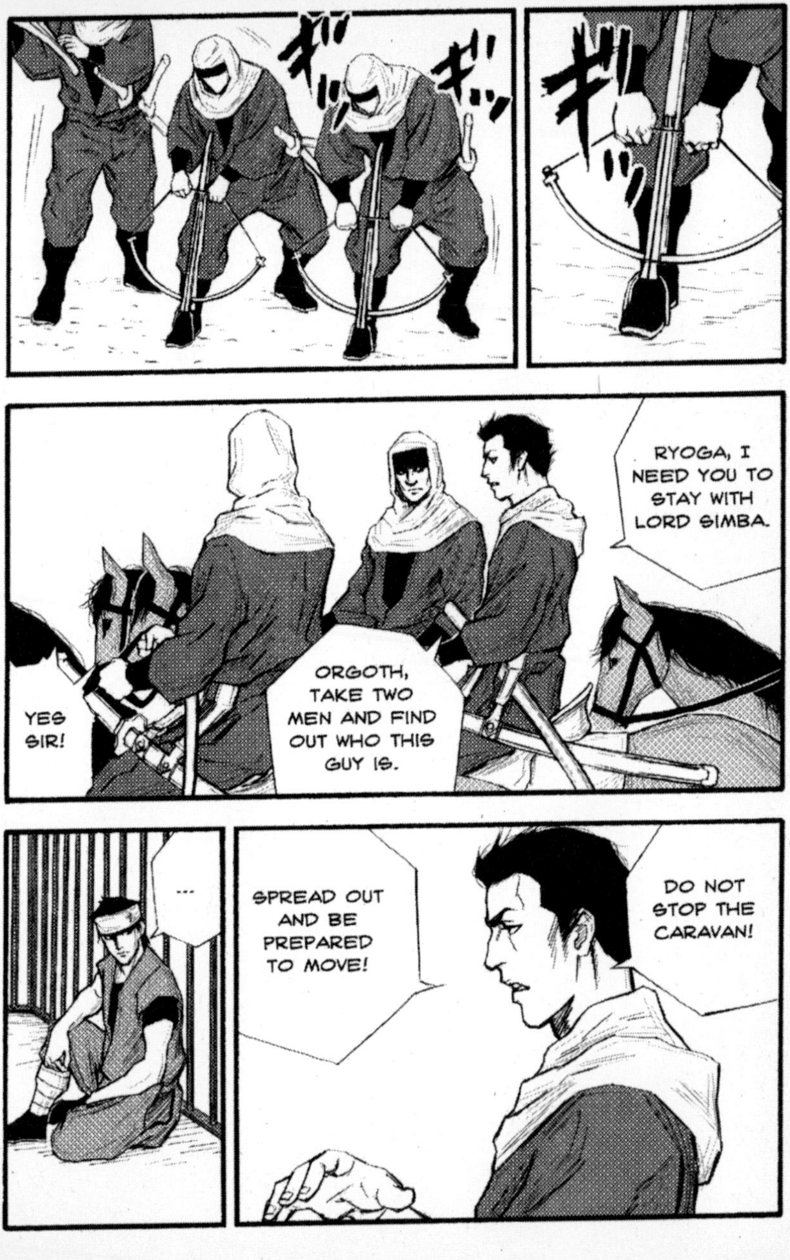
RYOGA, I NEED YOU TO STAY WITH LORD SIMBA.
ORGOTH, TAKE TWO MEN AND FIND OUT WHO THIS GUY IS.
YES SIR!
DO NOT STOP THE CARAVAN!
SPREAD OUT AND BE PREPARED TO MOVE!
...

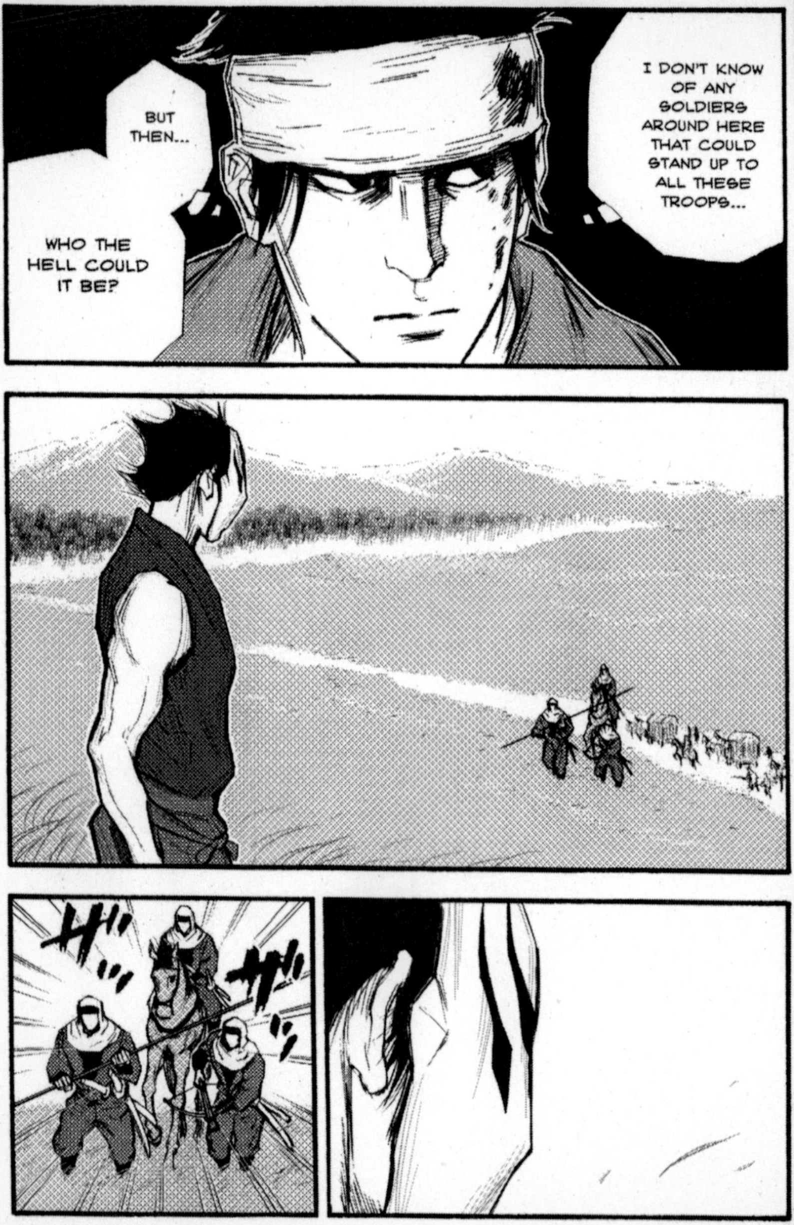
I DON'T KNOW OF ANY SOLDIERS AROUND HERE THAT COULD STAND UP TO ALL THESE TROOPS...
BUT THEN...
WHO THE HELL COULD IT BE?
ザッ
ザッ

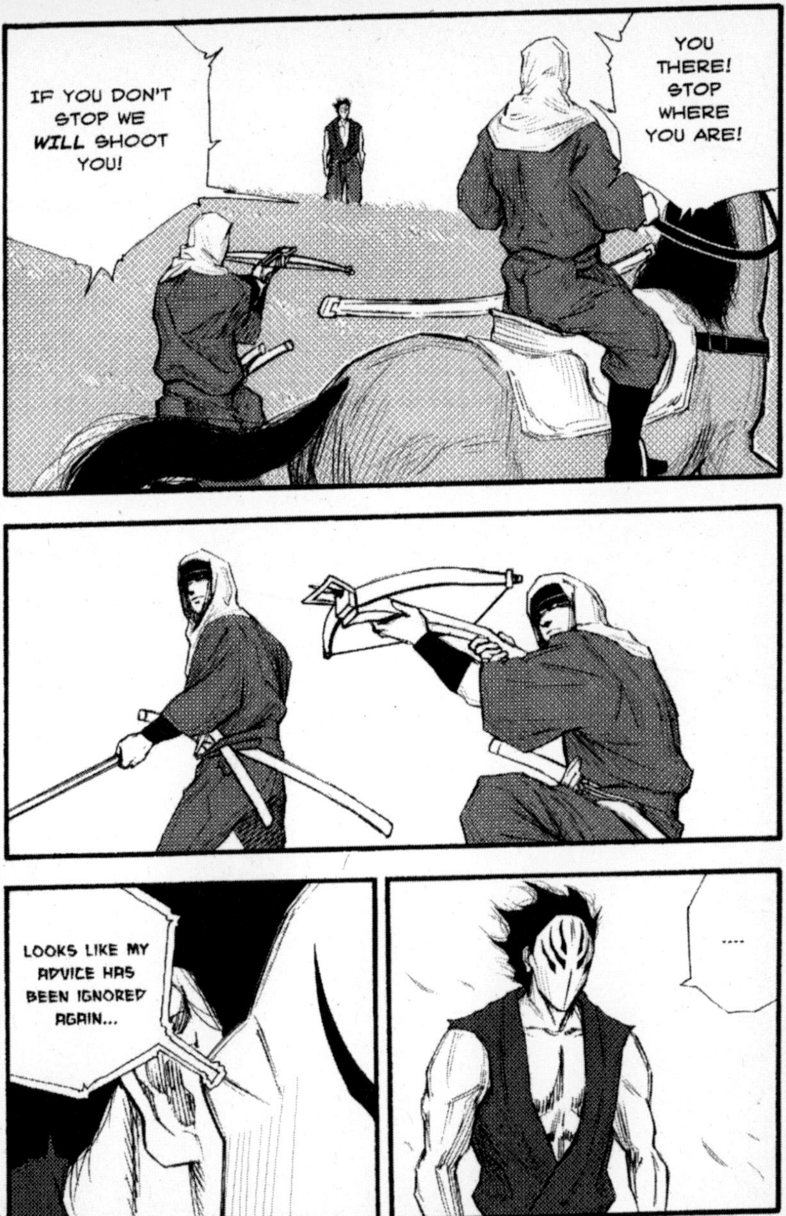
YOU THERE! STOP WHERE YOU ARE!
IF YOU DON'T STOP WE WILL SHOOT YOU!
....
LOOKS LIKE MY ADVICE HAS BEEN IGNORED AGAIN...

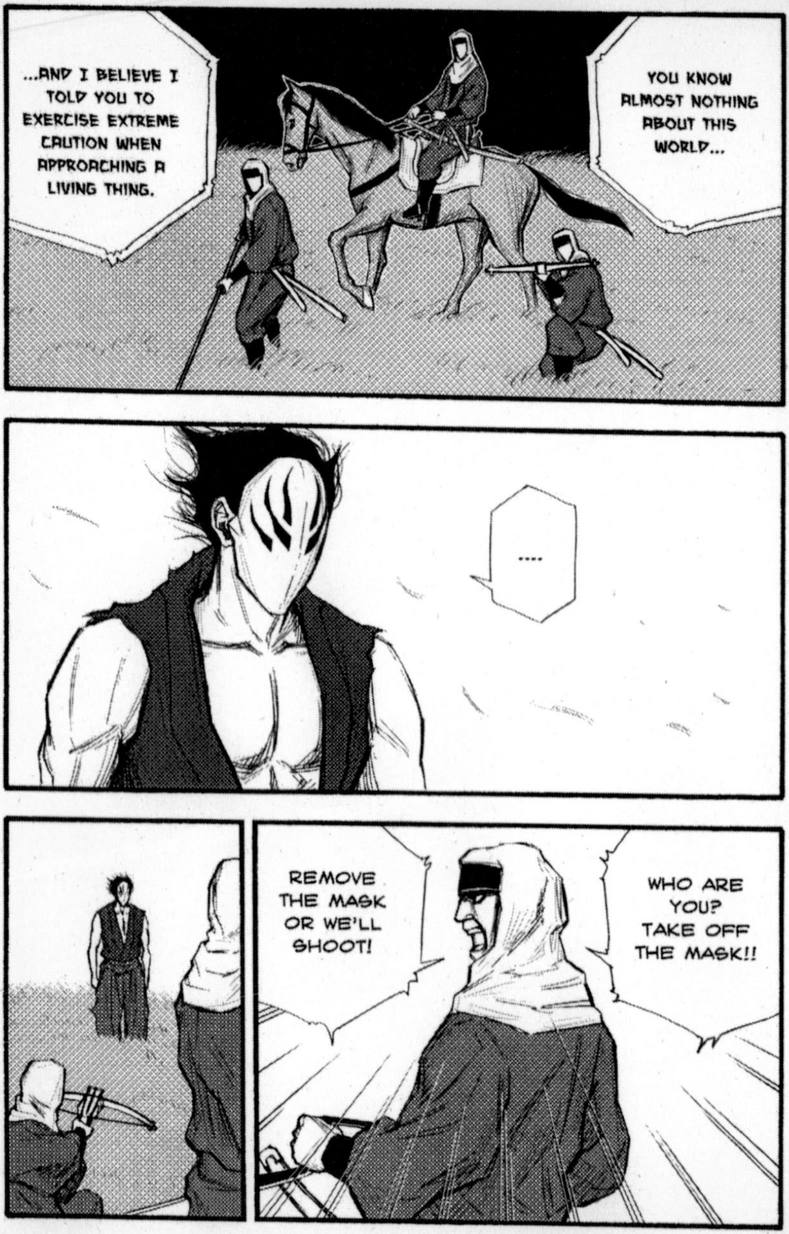
YOU KNOW ALMOST NOTHING ABOUT THIS WORLD...
...AND I BELIEVE I TOLD YOU TO EXERCISE EXTREME CAUTION WHEN APPROACHING A LIVING THING.
....
WHO ARE YOU? TAKE OFF THE MASK!!
REMOVE THE MASK OR WE'LL SHOOT!

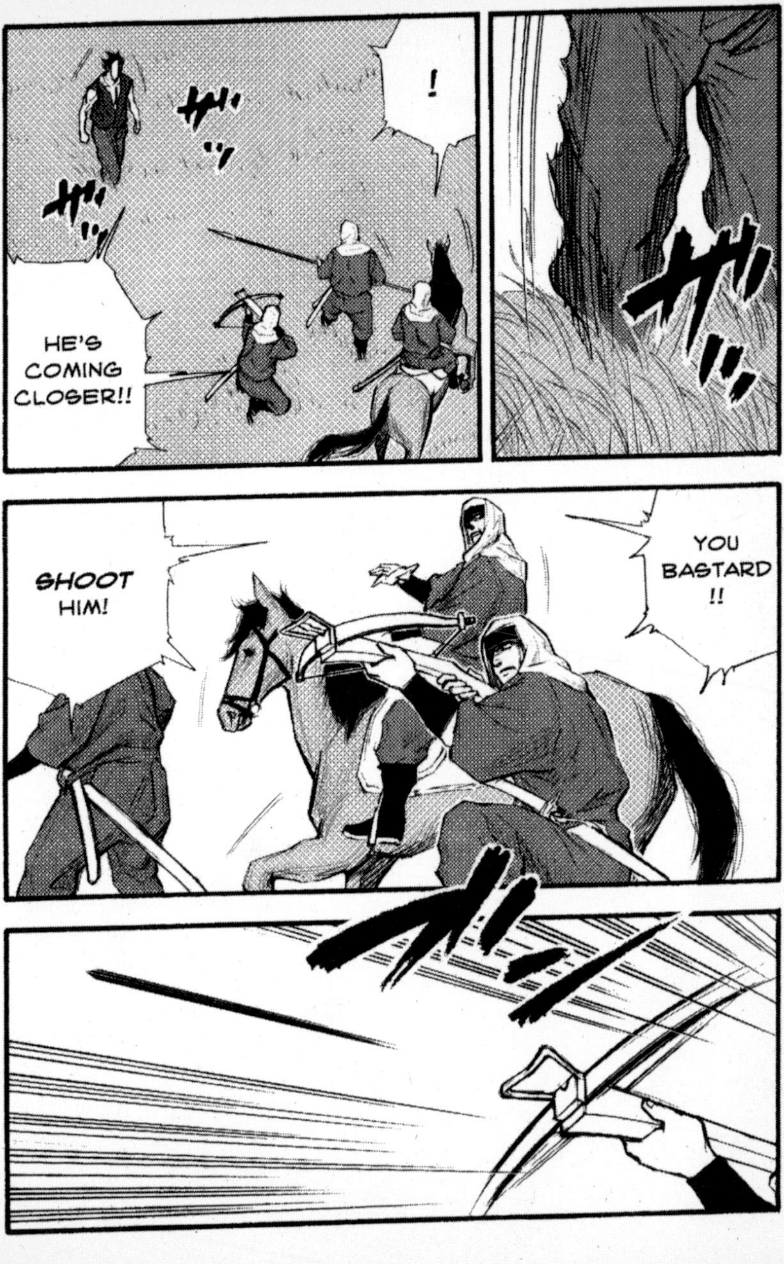
!
HE'S COMING CLOSER!!
YOU BASTARD !!
SHOOT HIM!

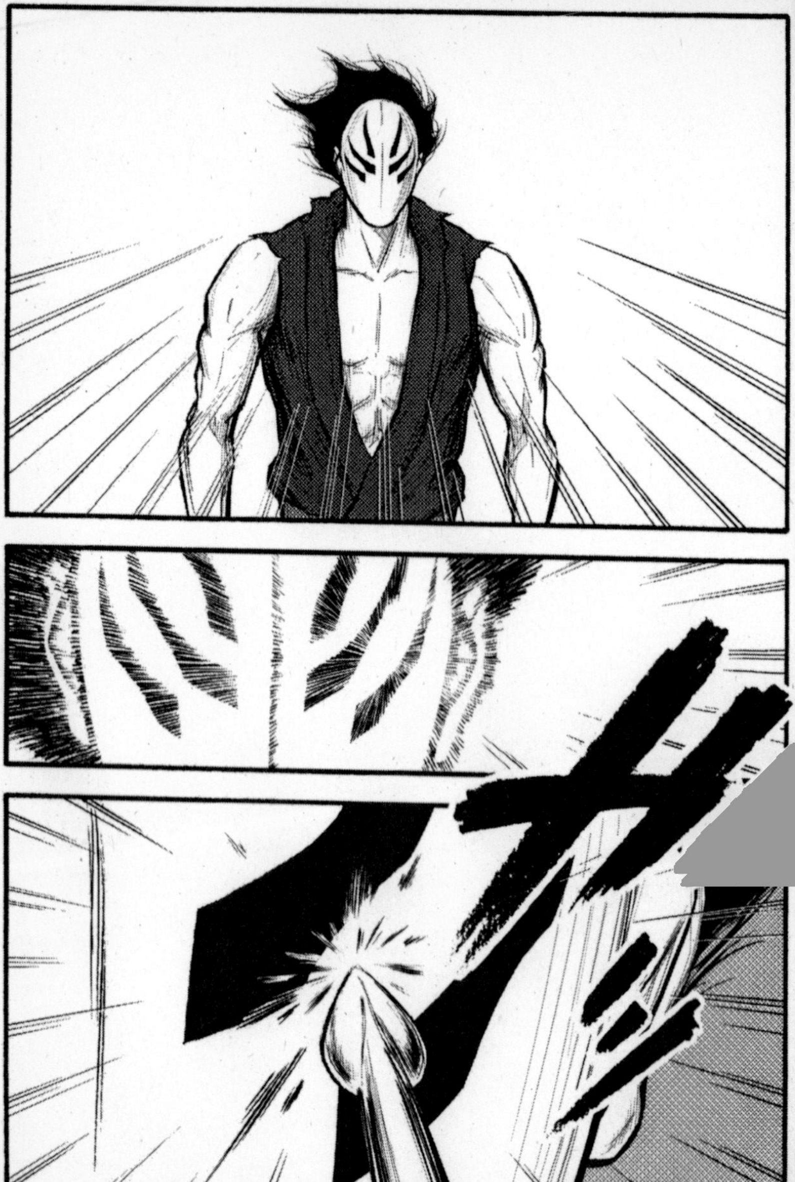

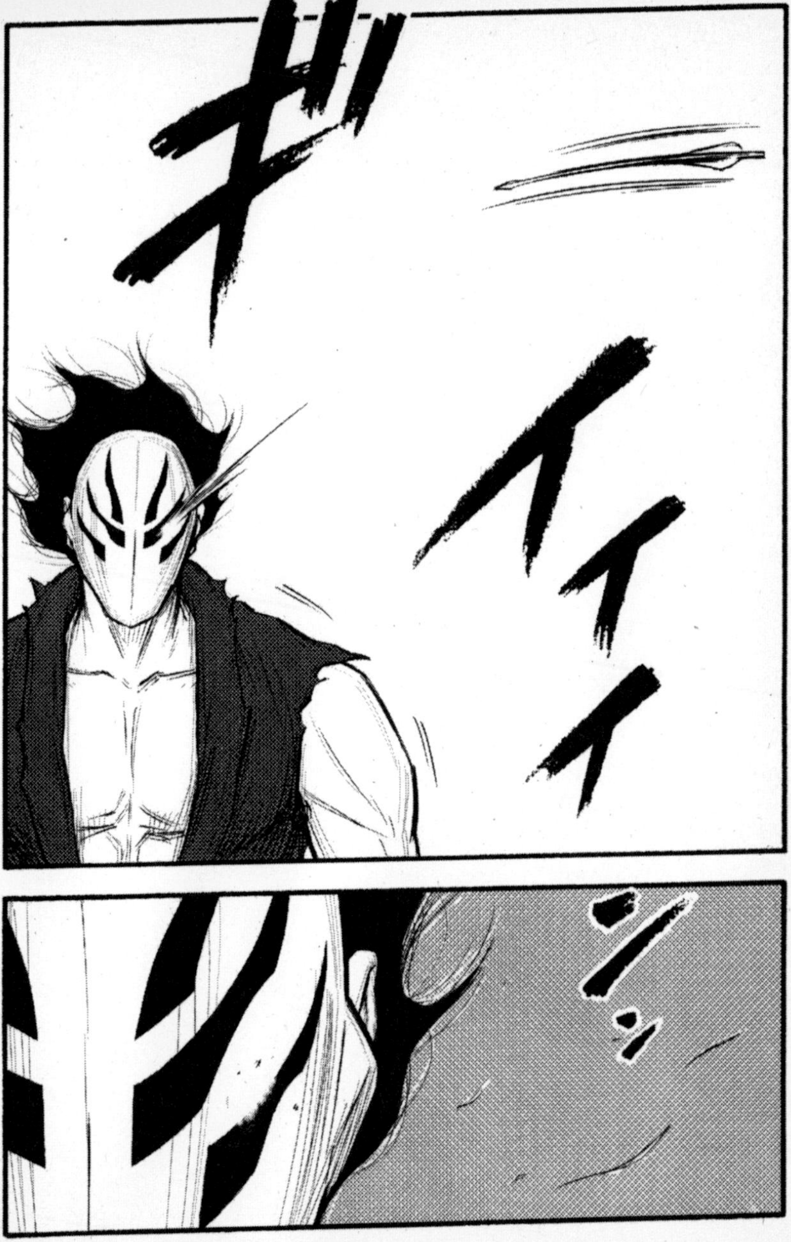
ズイイイ

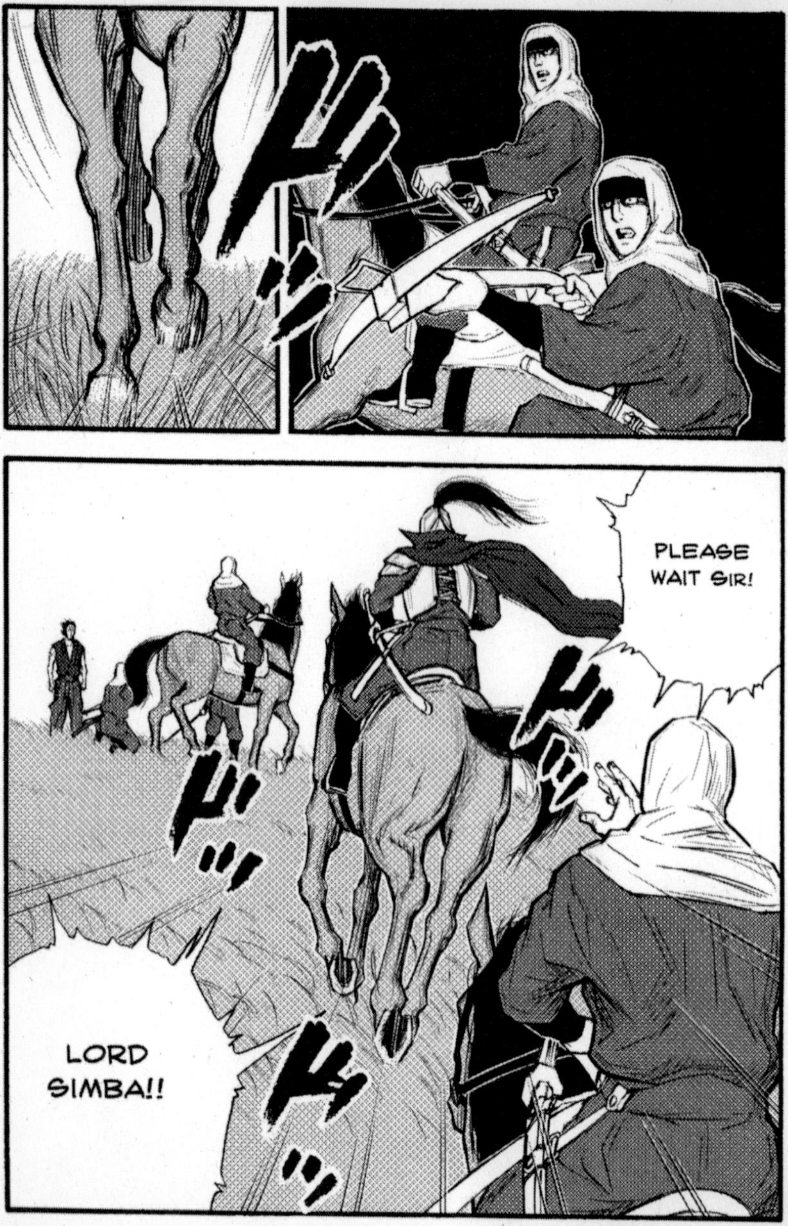
PLEASE WAIT SIR!
LORD SIMBA!!

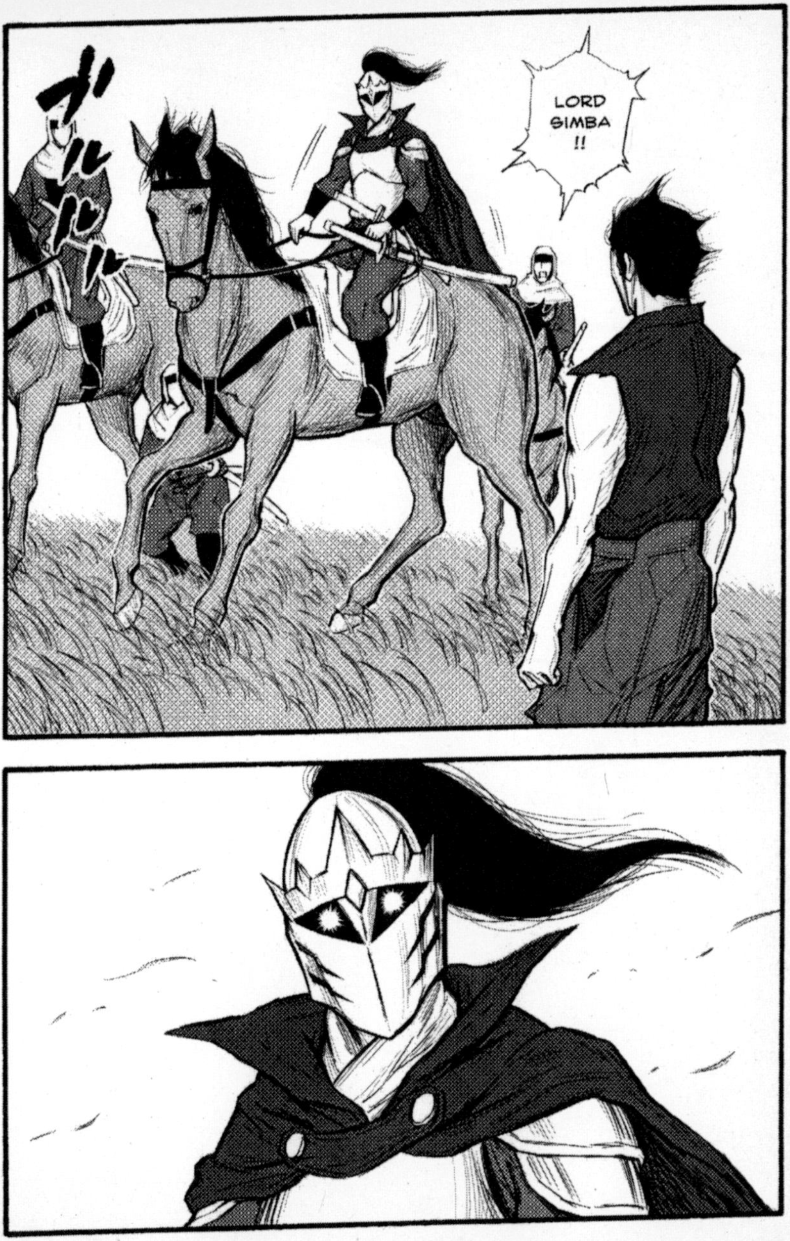
ブルルル
LORD SIMBA !!

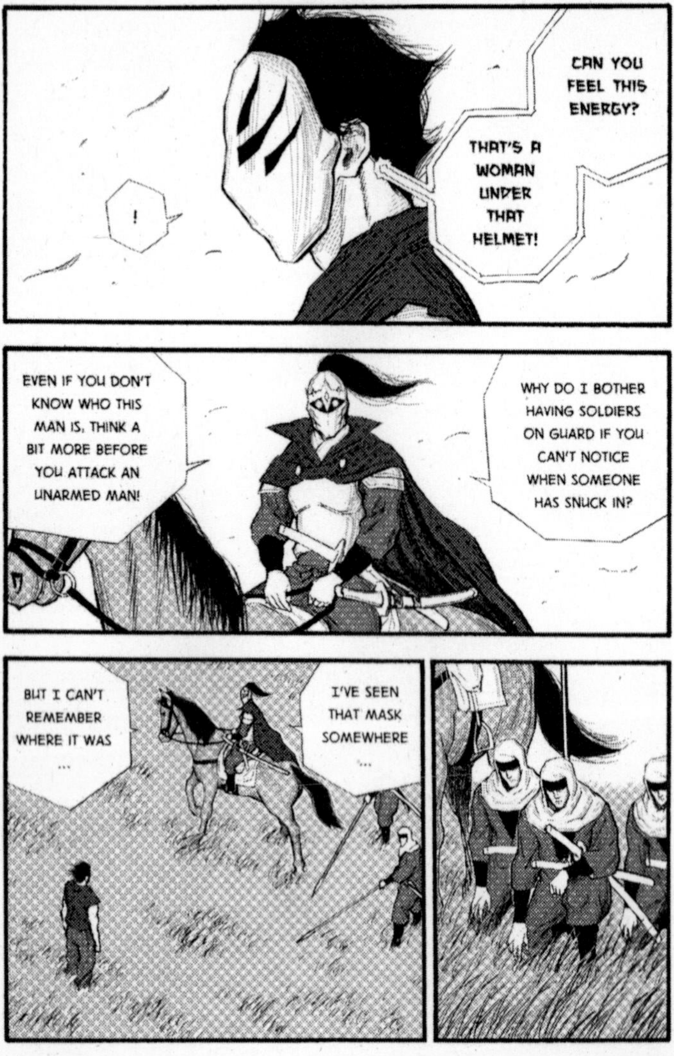
CAN YOU FEEL THIS ENERGY?
THAT'S A WOMAN UNDER THAT HELMET!
!
WHY DO I BOTHER HAVING SOLDIERS ON GUARD IF YOU CAN'T NOTICE WHEN SOMEONE HAS SNUCK IN?
EVEN IF YOU DON'T KNOW WHO THIS MAN IS, THINK A BIT MORE BEFORE YOU ATTACK AN UNARMED MAN!
I'VE SEEN THAT MASK SOMEWHERE ...
BUT I CAN'T REMEMBER WHERE IT WAS ...

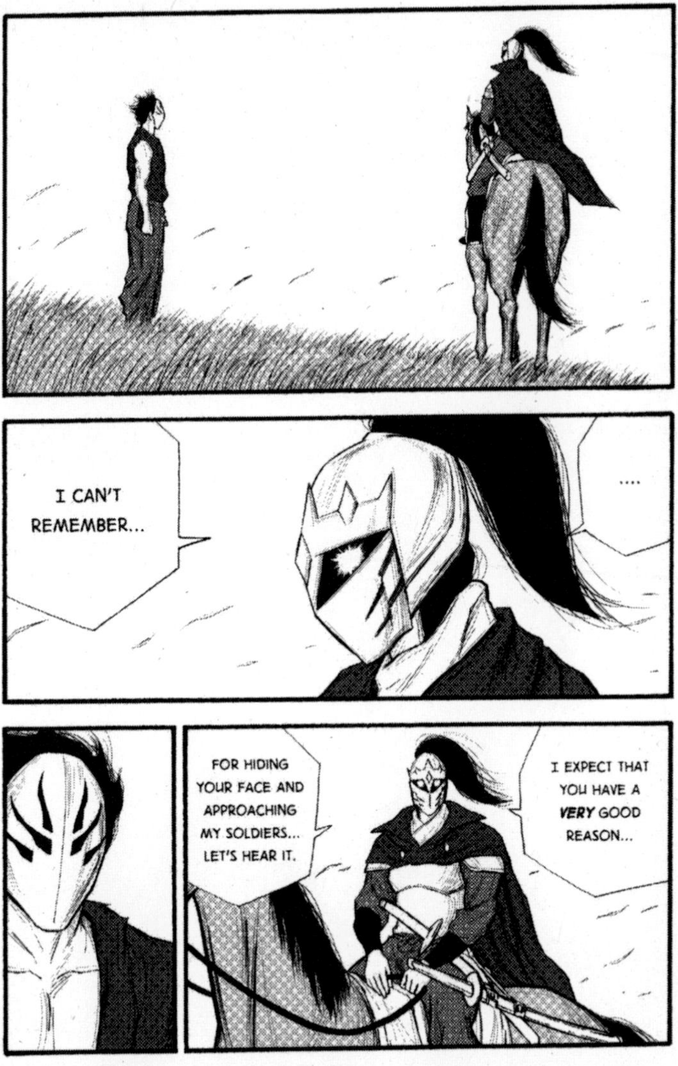
....
I CAN'T REMEMBER...
I EXPECT THAT YOU HAVE A *VERY* GOOD REASON...
FOR HIDING YOUR FACE AND APPROACHING MY SOLDIERS... LET'S HEAR IT.

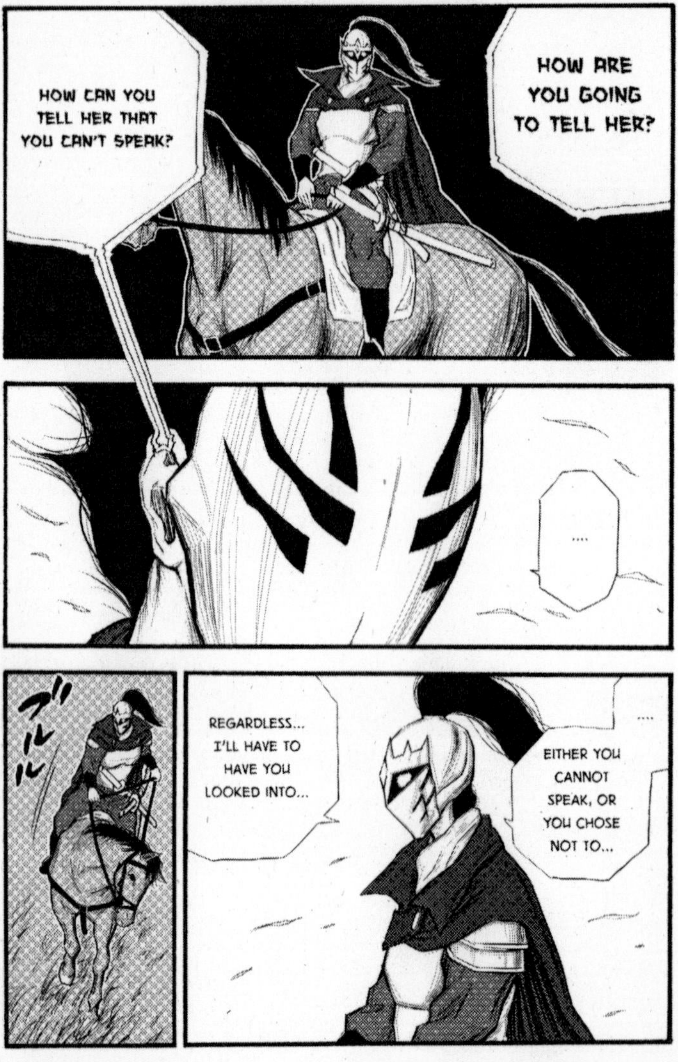
HOW ARE YOU GOING TO TELL HER?
HOW CAN YOU TELL HER THAT YOU CAN'T SPEAK?
....
....
EITHER YOU CANNOT SPEAK, OR YOU CHOSE NOT TO...
REGARDLESS... I'LL HAVE TO HAVE YOU LOOKED INTO...
ブルル

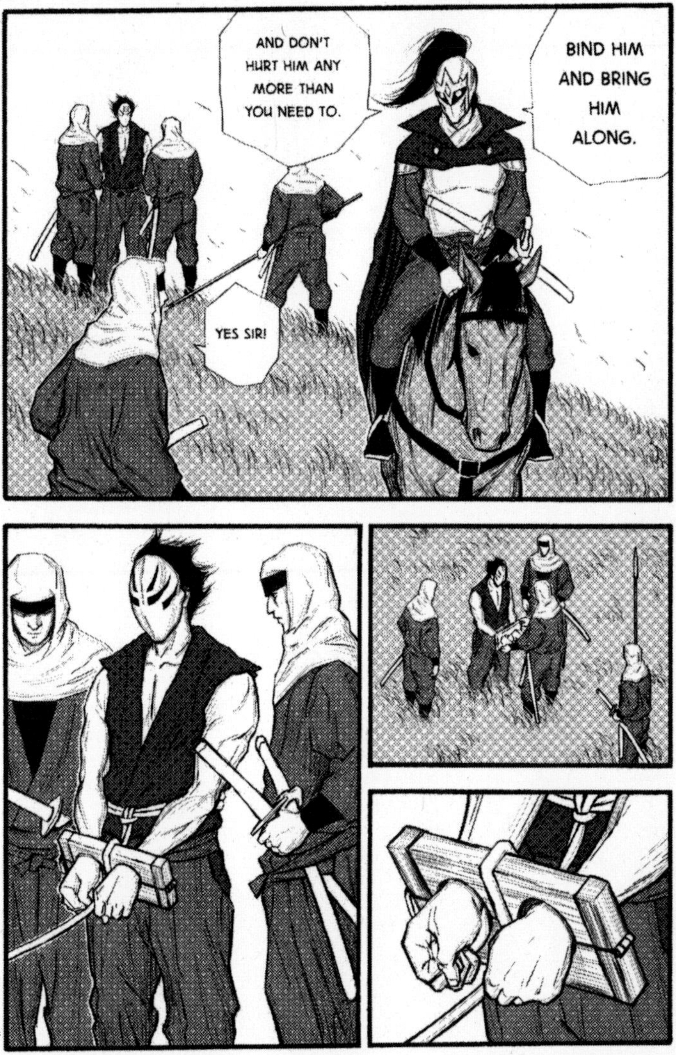
BIND HIM AND BRING HIM ALONG.
AND DON'T HURT HIM ANY MORE THAN YOU NEED TO.
YES SIR!

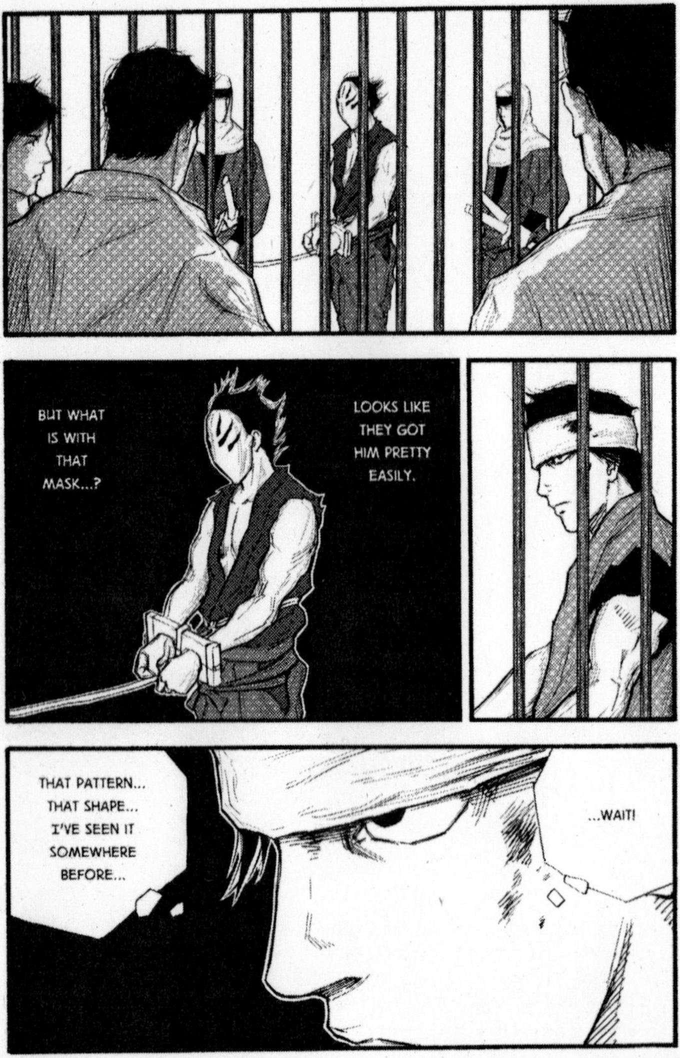
LOOKS LIKE THEY GOT HIM PRETTY EASILY.
BUT WHAT IS WITH THAT MASK...?
THAT PATTERN... THAT SHAPE... I'VE SEEN IT SOMEWHERE BEFORE...
...WAIT!

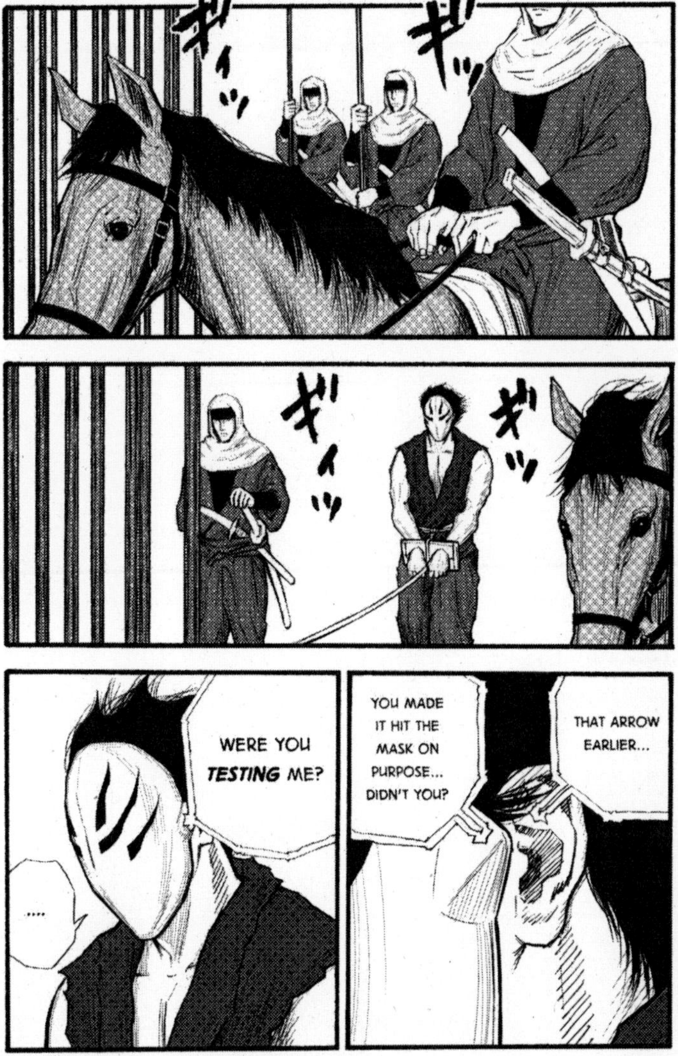
ギッ
ギイッ
ギッ
ギイッ
THAT ARROW EARLIER...
YOU MADE IT HIT THE MASK ON PURPOSE... DIDN'T YOU?
WERE YOU *TESTING* ME?
.....

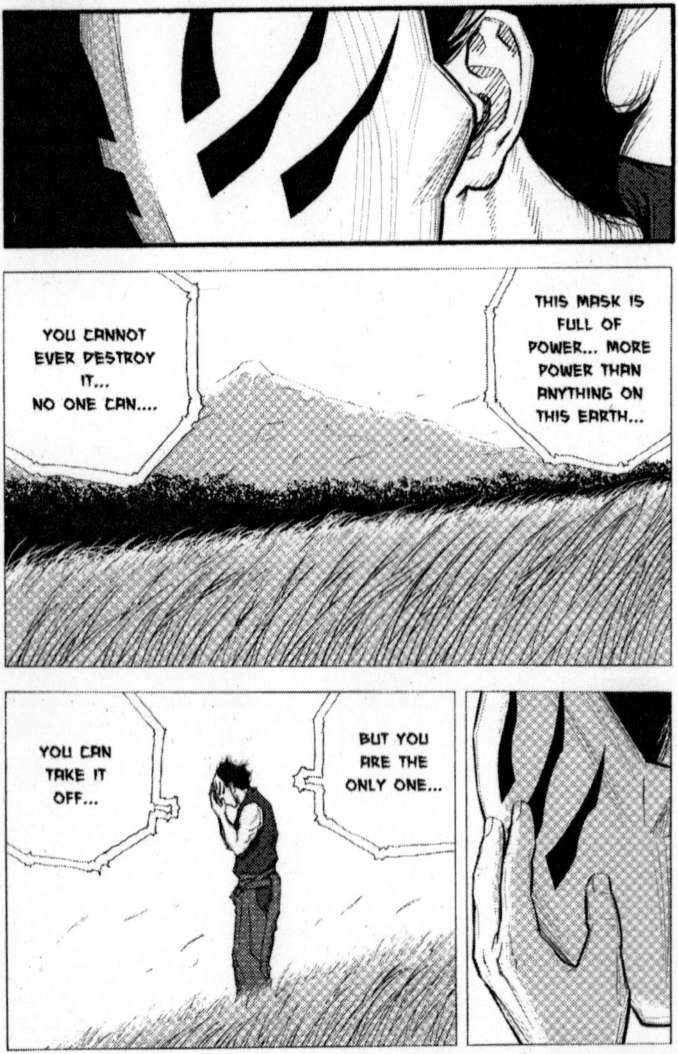
THIS MASK IS FULL OF POWER... MORE POWER THAN ANYTHING ON THIS EARTH...
YOU CANNOT EVER DESTROY IT... NO ONE CAN....
BUT YOU ARE THE ONLY ONE...
YOU CAN TAKE IT OFF...

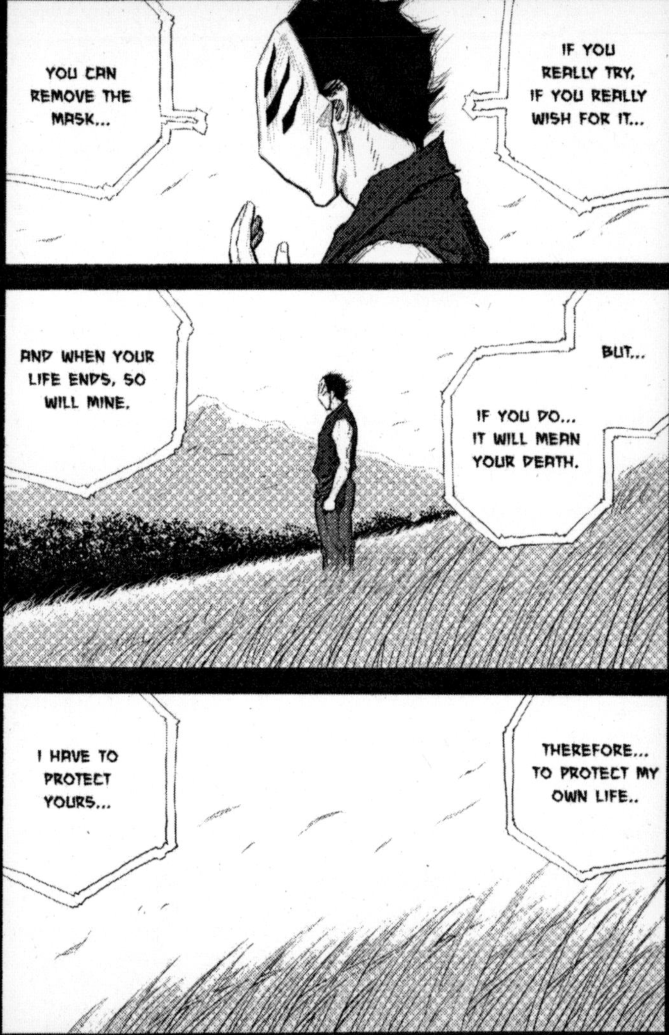
IF YOU REALLY TRY, IF YOU REALLY WISH FOR IT...
YOU CAN REMOVE THE MASK...
BUT...
IF YOU DO... IT WILL MEAN YOUR DEATH.
AND WHEN YOUR LIFE ENDS, SO WILL MINE.
THEREFORE... TO PROTECT MY OWN LIFE..
I HAVE TO PROTECT YOURS...

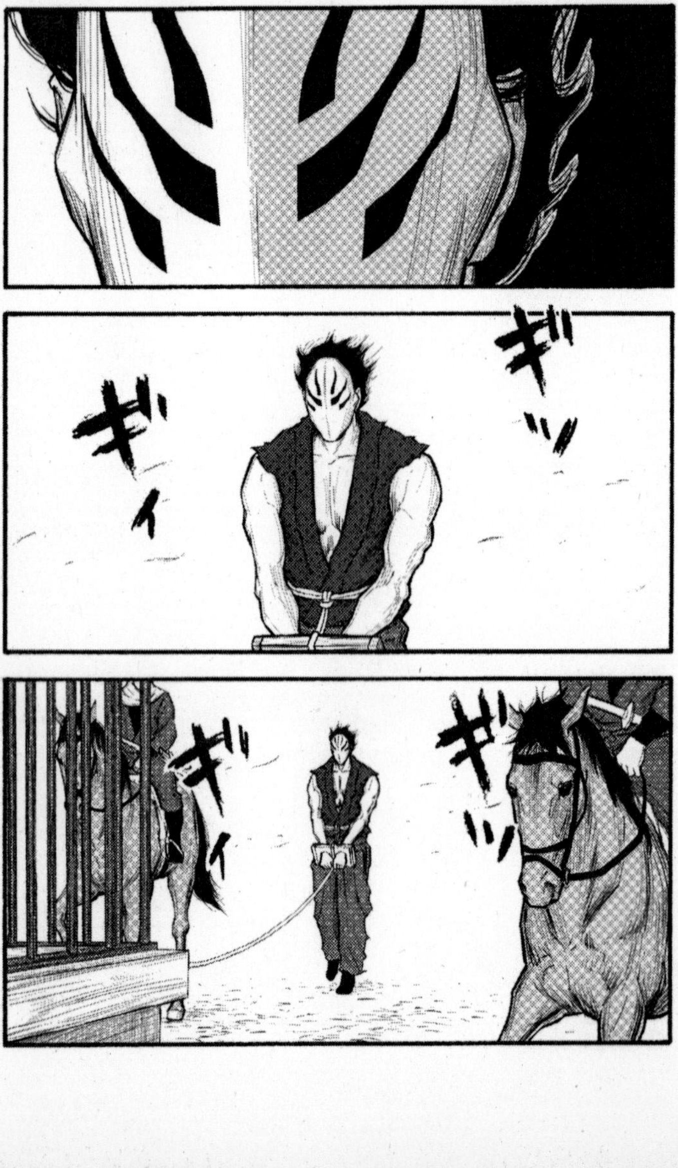
ギッ
ギィ
ギッ
ギィ

LORD SIMBA.

AN URGENT MESSAGE ARRIVED FROM LORD DAZAM.

!

LORD GAILAS WILL BE ARRIVING FROM THE FORTRESS.

MY UNCLE WILL...

.....

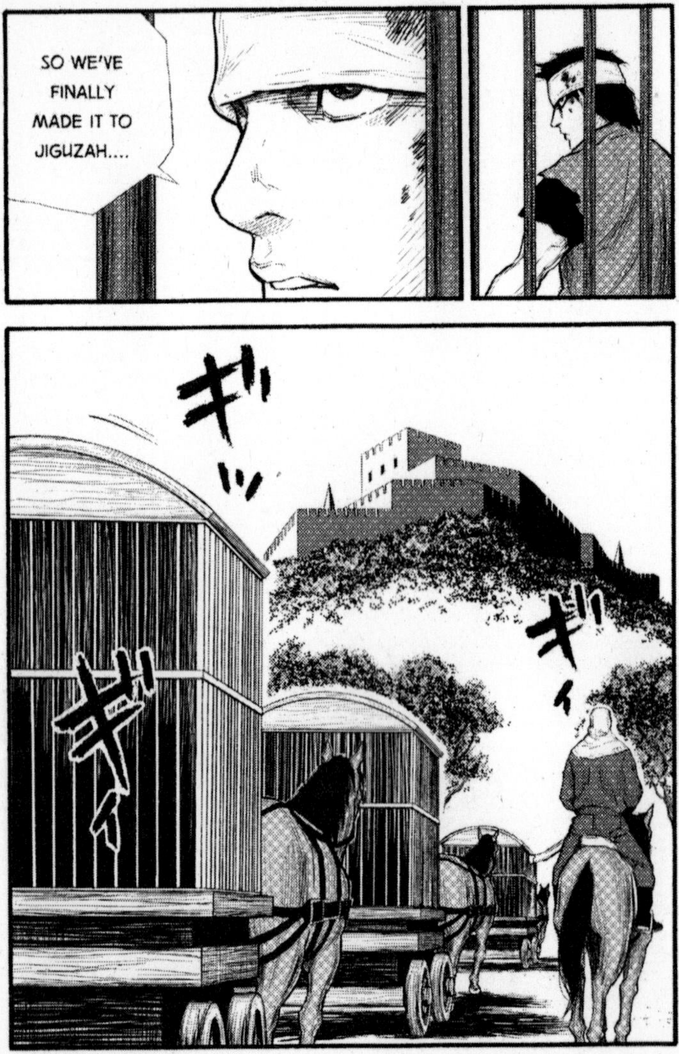
SO WE'VE FINALLY MADE IT TO JIGUZAH....
ギッ
ギィ
ギィ

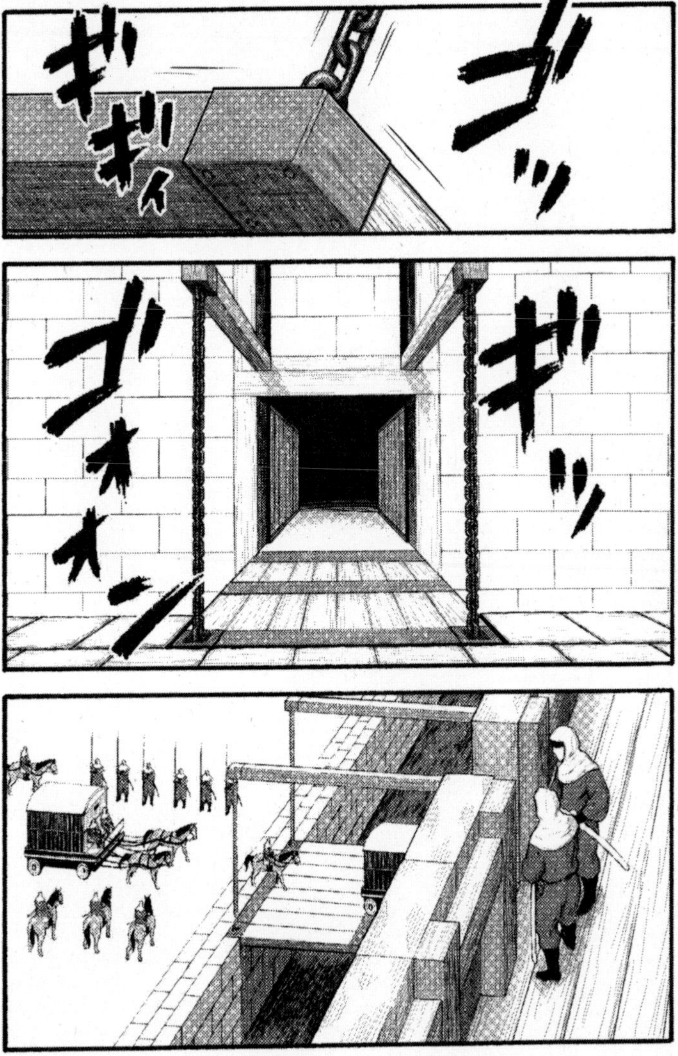
ゴッ
ギギイ
ギッ
ゴオオン

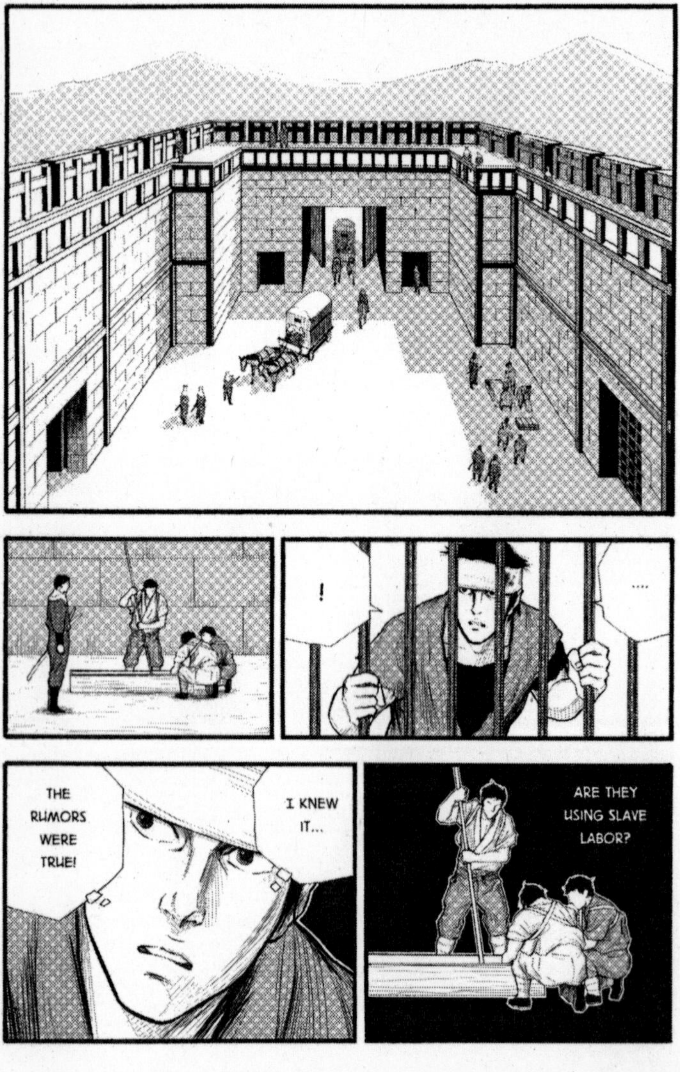
....
!
ARE THEY USING SLAVE LABOR?
I KNEW IT...
THE RUMORS WERE TRUE!

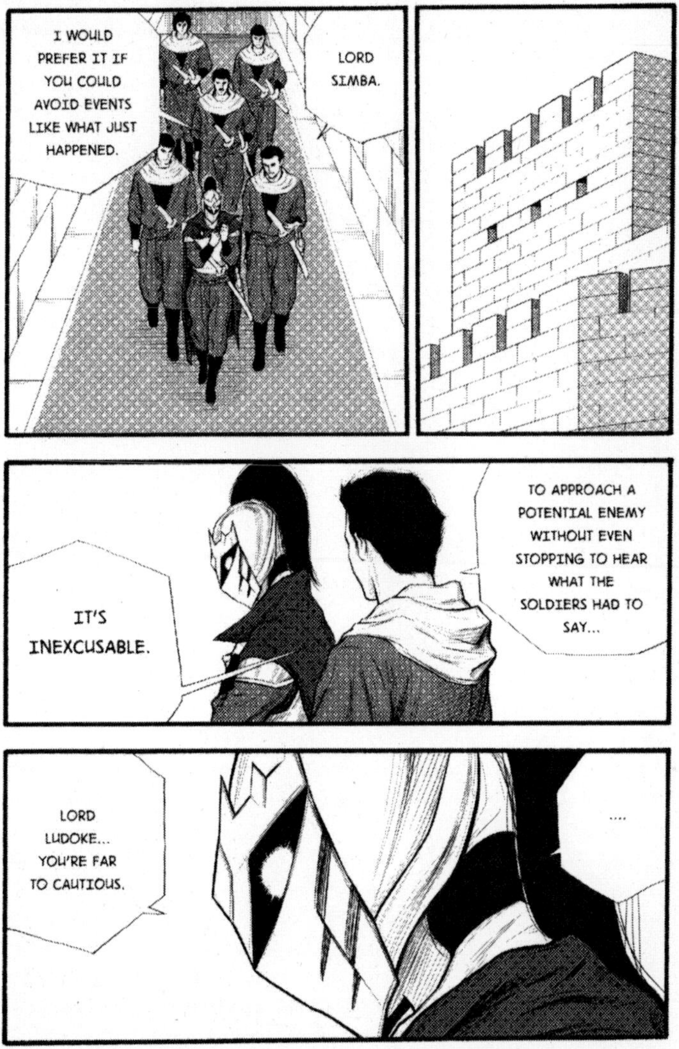
LORD SIMBA.
I WOULD PREFER IT IF YOU COULD AVOID EVENTS LIKE WHAT JUST HAPPENED.
TO APPROACH A POTENTIAL ENEMY WITHOUT EVEN STOPPING TO HEAR WHAT THE SOLDIERS HAD TO SAY...
IT'S INEXCUSABLE.
....
LORD LUDOKE... YOU'RE FAR TO CAUTIOUS.

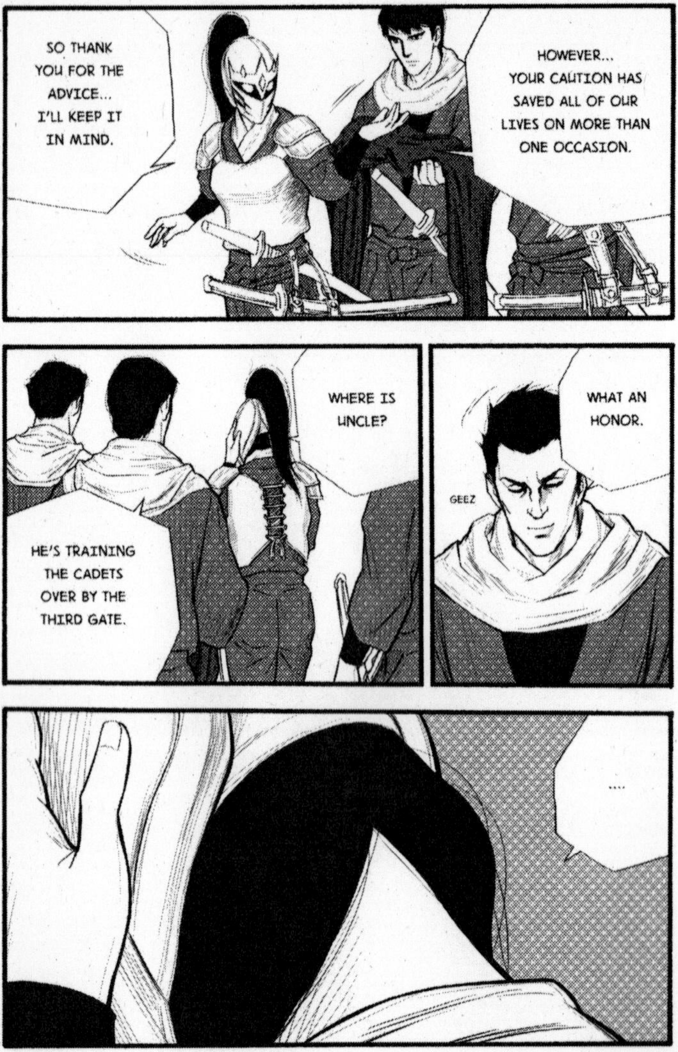
HOWEVER... YOUR CAUTION HAS SAVED ALL OF OUR LIVES ON MORE THAN ONE OCCASION.
SO THANK YOU FOR THE ADVICE... I'LL KEEP IT IN MIND.
WHAT AN HONOR.
GEEZ
WHERE IS UNCLE?
HE'S TRAINING THE CADETS OVER BY THE THIRD GATE.
....

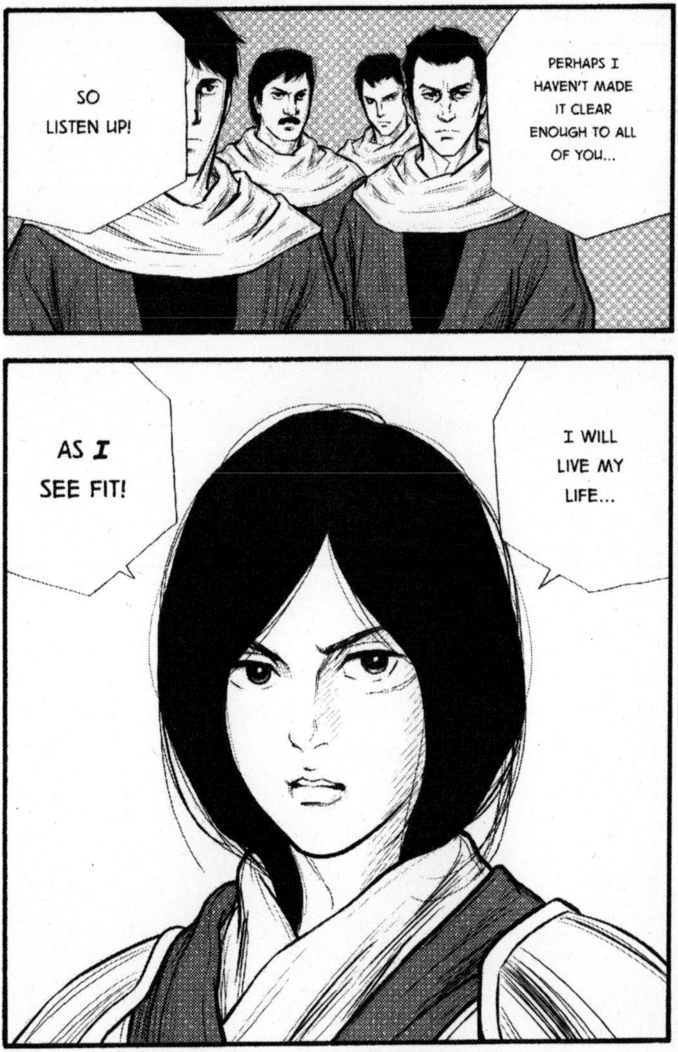
PERHAPS I HAVEN'T MADE IT CLEAR ENOUGH TO ALL OF YOU...
SO LISTEN UP!
I WILL LIVE MY LIFE...
AS *I* SEE FIT!

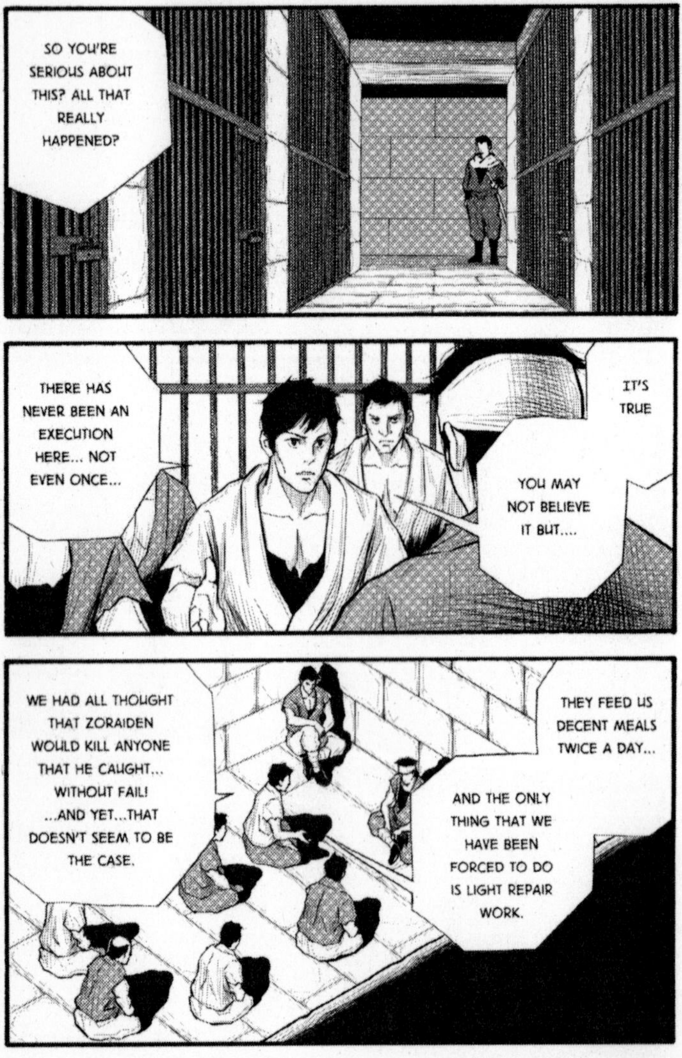
SO YOU'RE SERIOUS ABOUT THIS? ALL THAT REALLY HAPPENED?
IT'S TRUE
YOU MAY NOT BELIEVE IT BUT....
THERE HAS NEVER BEEN AN EXECUTION HERE... NOT EVEN ONCE...
THEY FEED US DECENT MEALS TWICE A DAY...
AND THE ONLY THING THAT WE HAVE BEEN FORCED TO DO IS LIGHT REPAIR WORK.
WE HAD ALL THOUGHT THAT ZORAIDEN WOULD KILL ANYONE THAT HE CAUGHT... WITHOUT FAIL! ...AND YET...THAT DOESN'T SEEM TO BE THE CASE.

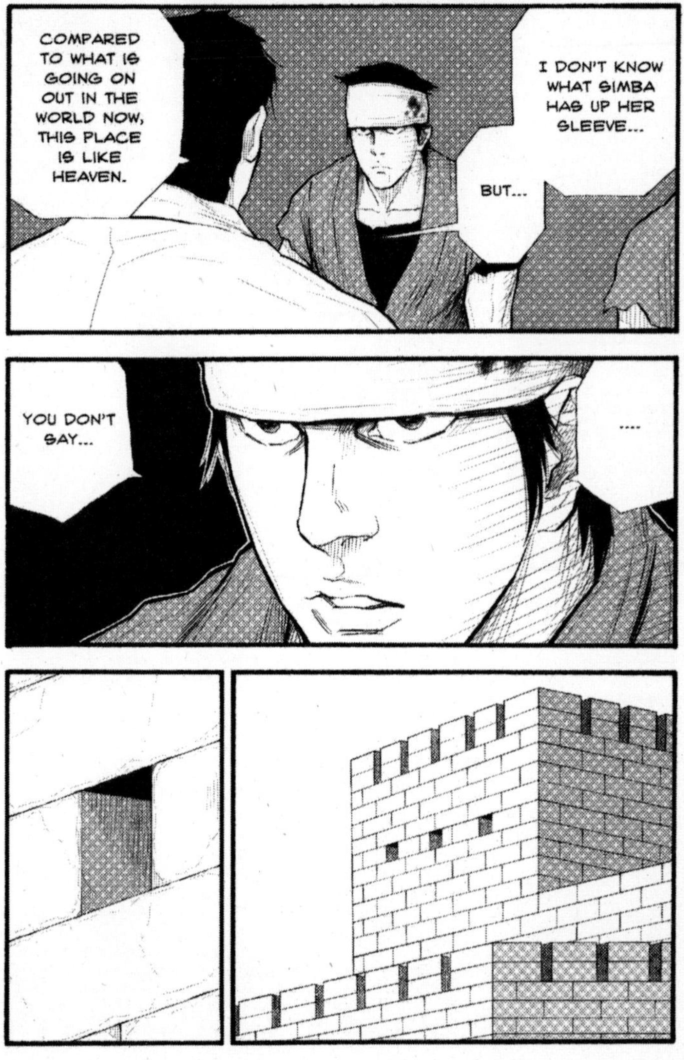
I DON'T KNOW WHAT SIMBA HAS UP HER SLEEVE...
BUT...
COMPARED TO WHAT IS GOING ON OUT IN THE WORLD NOW, THIS PLACE IS LIKE HEAVEN.
....
YOU DON'T SAY...

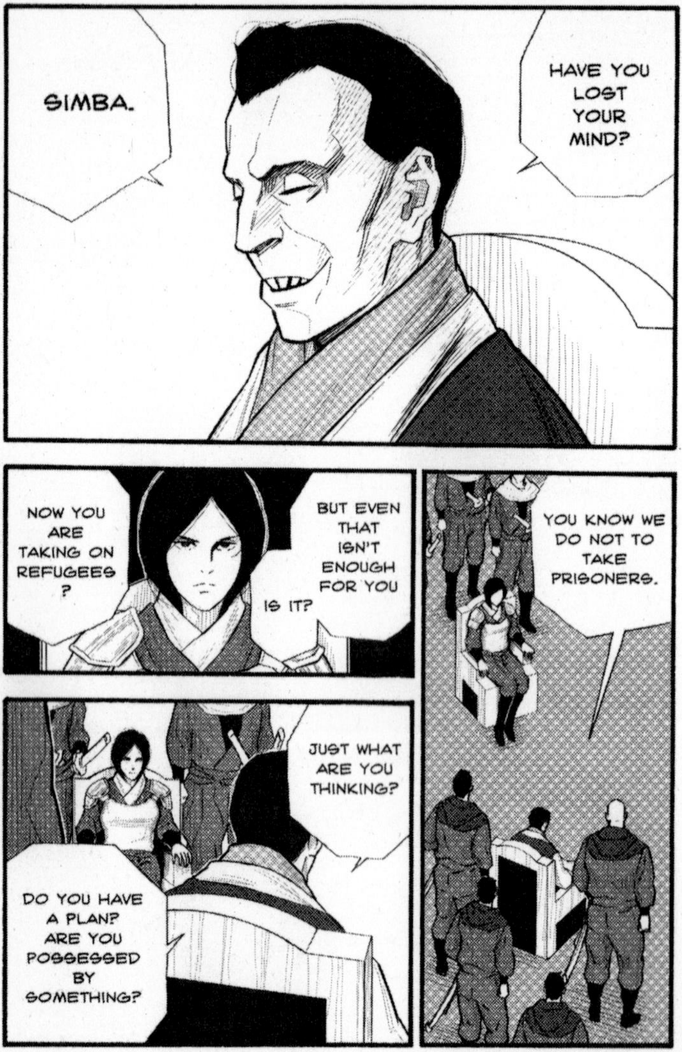
HAVE YOU LOST YOUR MIND?
SIMBA.
YOU KNOW WE DO NOT TO TAKE PRISONERS.
BUT EVEN THAT ISN'T ENOUGH FOR YOU
IS IT?
NOW YOU ARE TAKING ON REFUGEES ?
JUST WHAT ARE YOU THINKING?
DO YOU HAVE A PLAN? ARE YOU POSSESSED BY SOMETHING?

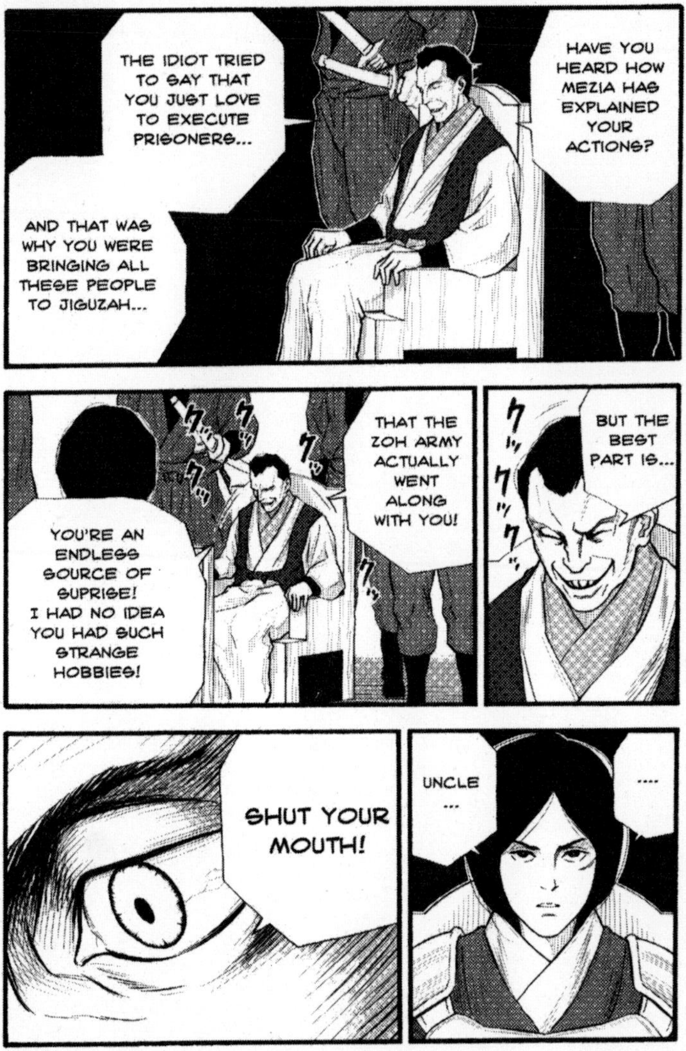
HAVE YOU HEARD HOW MEZIA HAS EXPLAINED YOUR ACTIONS?
THE IDIOT TRIED TO SAY THAT YOU JUST LOVE TO EXECUTE PRISONERS...
AND THAT WAS WHY YOU WERE BRINGING ALL THESE PEOPLE TO JIGUZAH...
BUT THE BEST PART IS...
THAT THE ZOH ARMY ACTUALLY WENT ALONG WITH YOU!
YOU'RE AN ENDLESS SOURCE OF SUPRISE! I HAD NO IDEA YOU HAD SUCH STRANGE HOBBIES!
....
UNCLE ...
SHUT YOUR MOUTH!

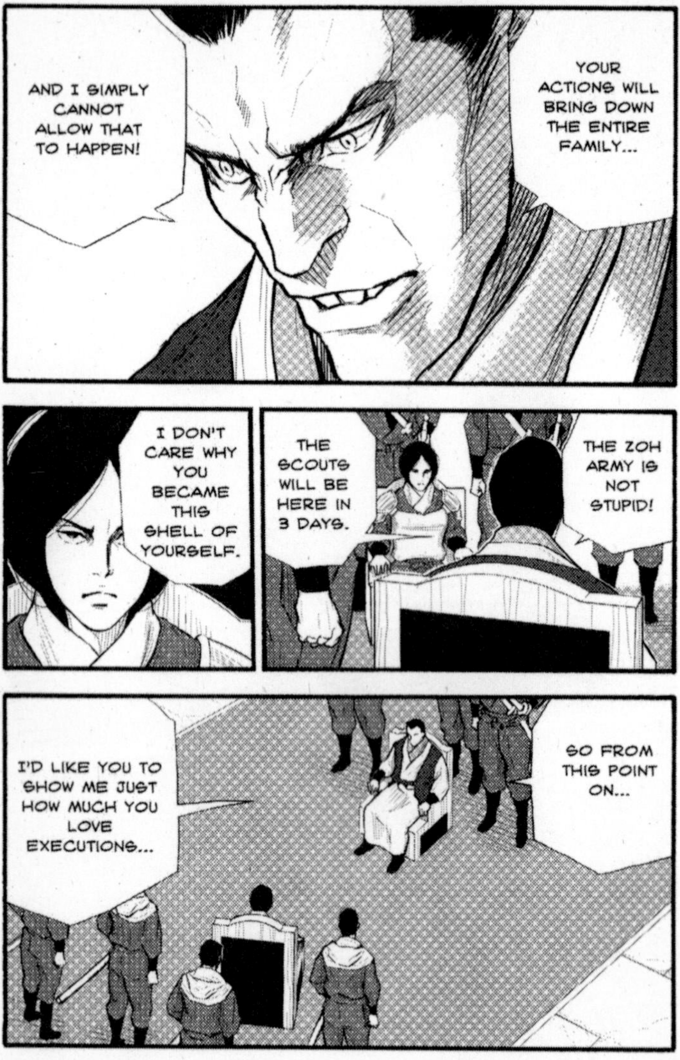
YOUR ACTIONS WILL BRING DOWN THE ENTIRE FAMILY...
AND I SIMPLY CANNOT ALLOW THAT TO HAPPEN!
THE ZOH ARMY IS NOT STUPID!
THE SCOUTS WILL BE HERE IN 3 DAYS.
I DON'T CARE WHY YOU BECAME THIS SHELL OF YOURSELF.
SO FROM THIS POINT ON...
I'D LIKE YOU TO SHOW ME JUST HOW MUCH YOU LOVE EXECUTIONS...

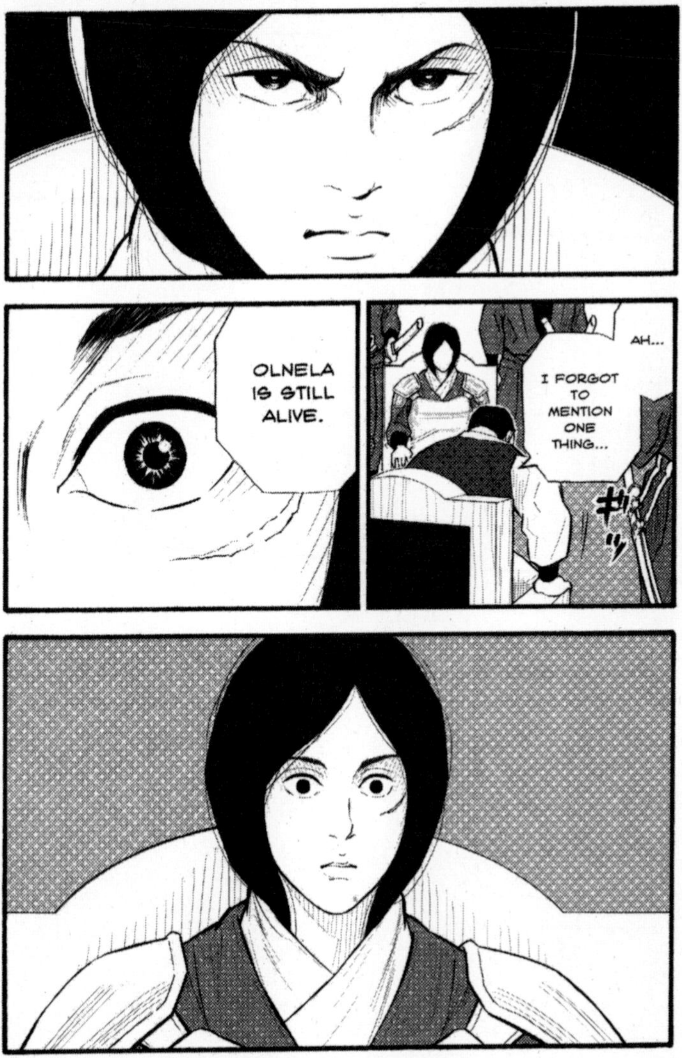
AH...
I FORGOT TO MENTION ONE THING...
ギッ
OLNELA IS STILL ALIVE.

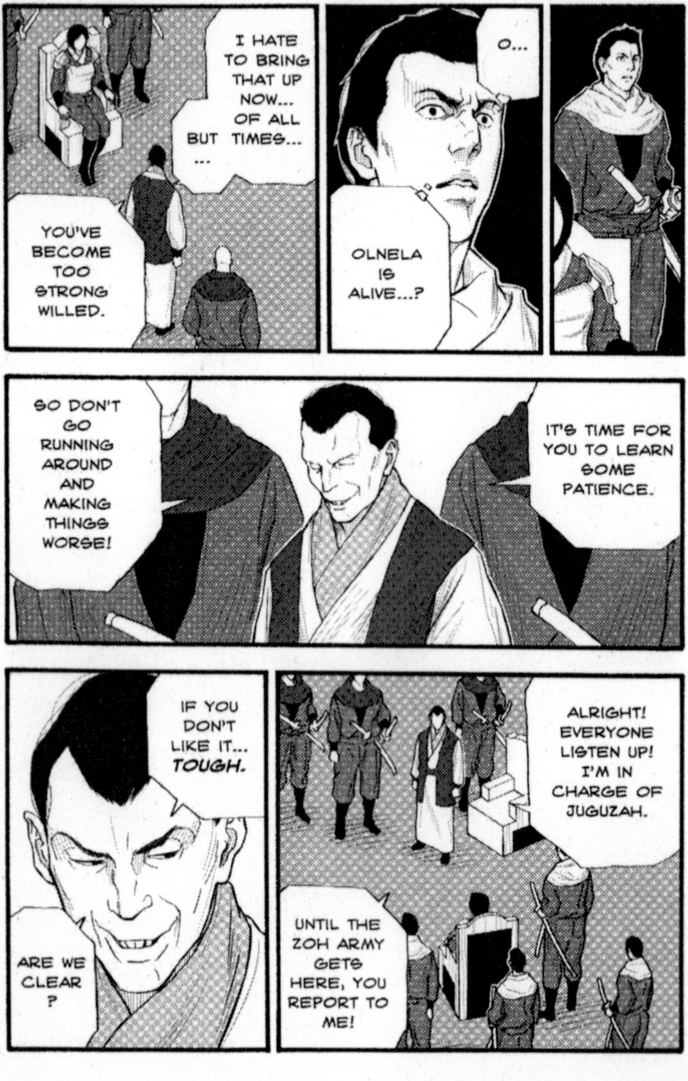

O...
OLNELA IS ALIVE...?
I HATE TO BRING THAT UP NOW... OF ALL BUT TIMES... ...
YOU'VE BECOME TOO STRONG WILLED.
IT'S TIME FOR YOU TO LEARN SOME PATIENCE.
SO DON'T GO RUNNING AROUND AND MAKING THINGS WORSE!
ALRIGHT! EVERYONE LISTEN UP! I'M IN CHARGE OF JUGUZAH.
UNTIL THE ZOH ARMY GETS HERE, YOU REPORT TO ME!
IF YOU DON'T LIKE IT... *TOUGH.*
ARE WE CLEAR ?

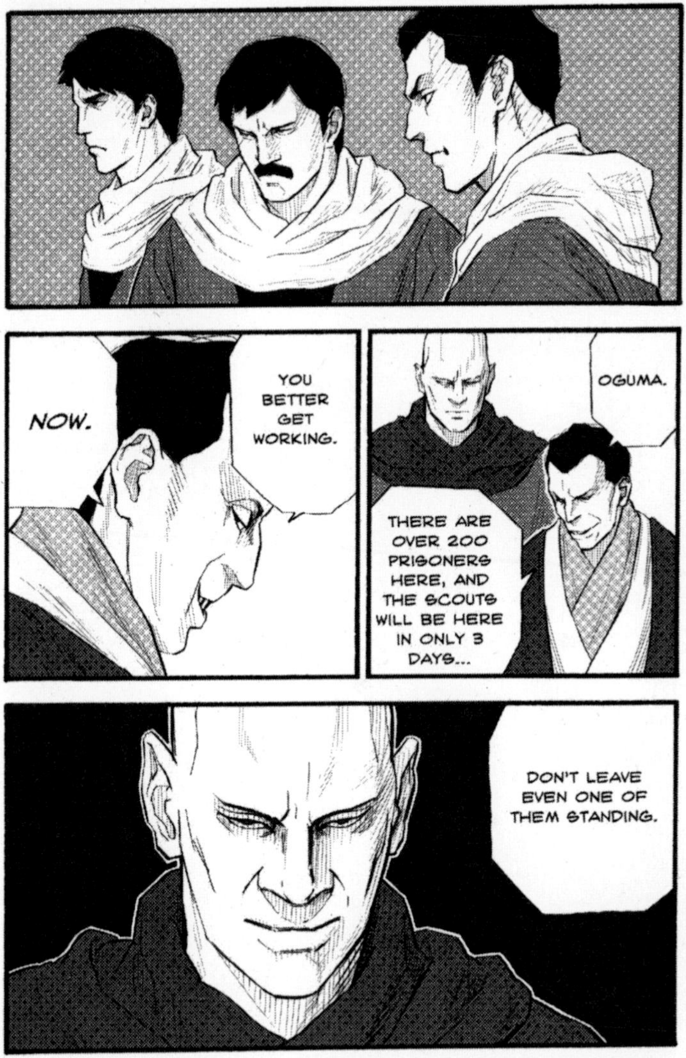
OGUMA.
THERE ARE OVER 200 PRISONERS HERE, AND THE SCOUTS WILL BE HERE IN ONLY 3 DAYS...
YOU BETTER GET WORKING.
NOW.
DON'T LEAVE EVEN ONE OF THEM STANDING.

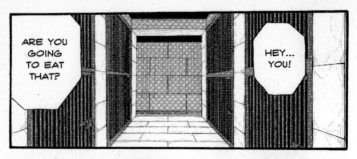

ARE YOU GOING TO EAT THAT?

HEY... YOU!

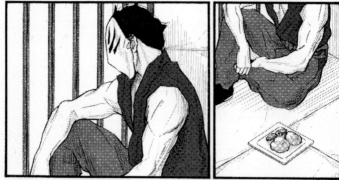

IF YOU DON'T WANT IT... COULD YOU GIVE IT TO US?

I HATE TO BE A BURDEN...

....

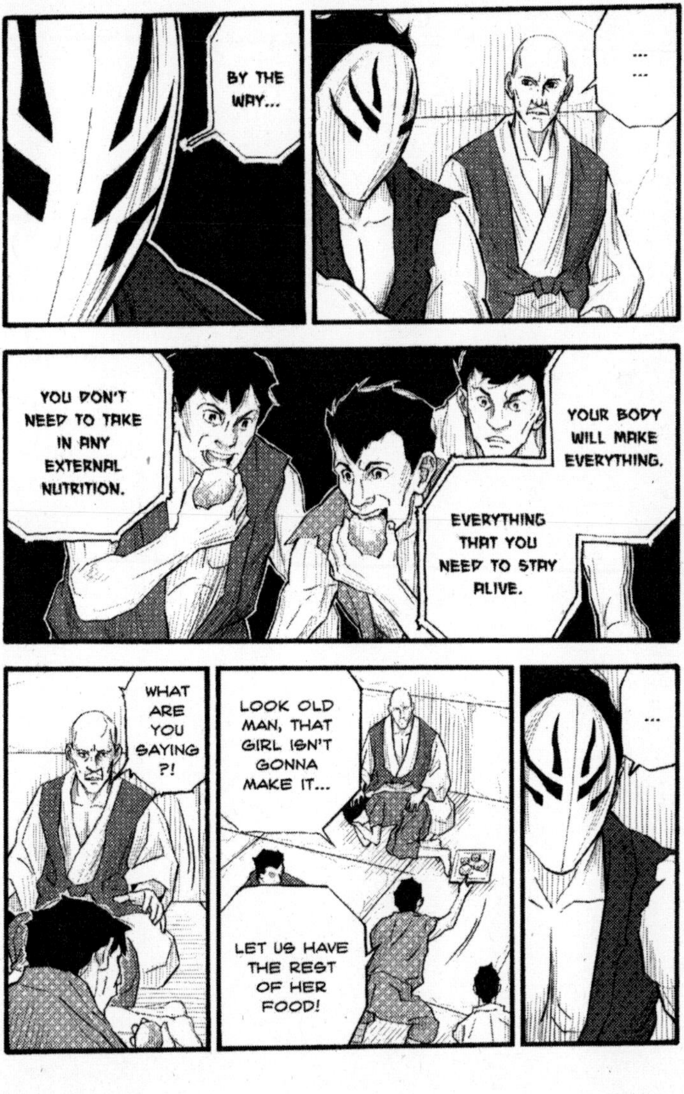
...
...
BY THE WAY...
YOUR BODY WILL MAKE EVERYTHING.
YOU DON'T NEED TO TAKE IN ANY EXTERNAL NUTRITION.
EVERYTHING THAT YOU NEED TO STAY ALIVE.
...
LOOK OLD MAN, THAT GIRL ISN'T GONNA MAKE IT...
LET US HAVE THE REST OF HER FOOD!
WHAT ARE YOU SAYING?!

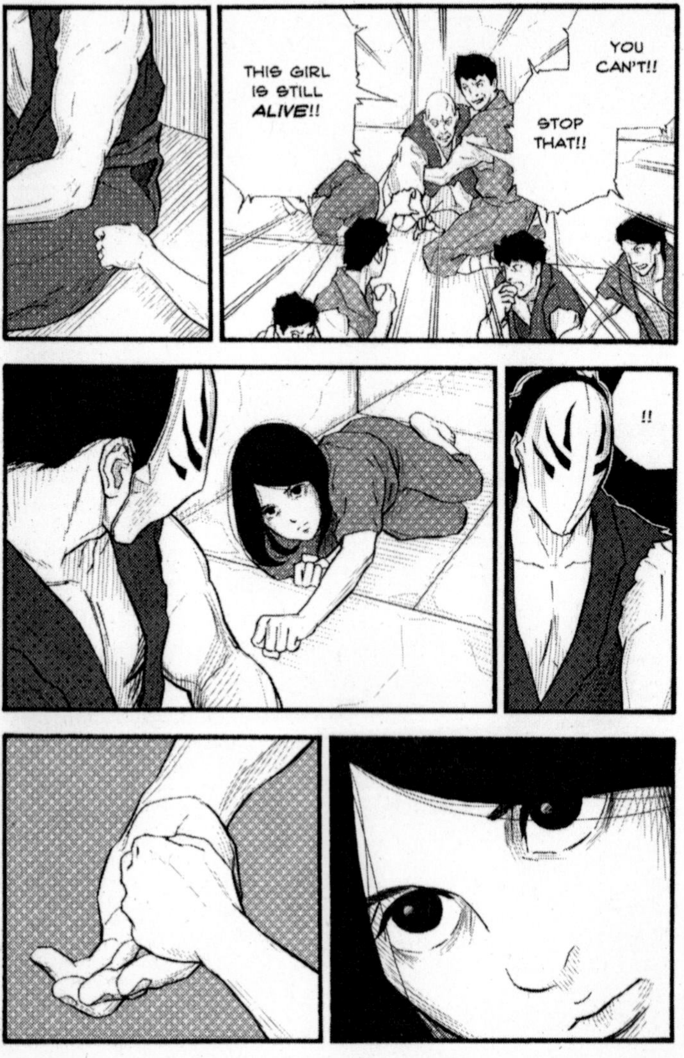
YOU CAN'T!!
THIS GIRL IS STILL ALIVE!!
STOP THAT!!
!!

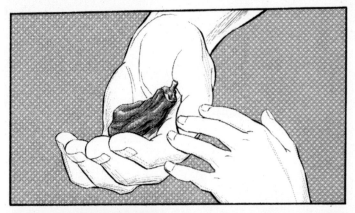

THIS GIRL
IS...

!!!

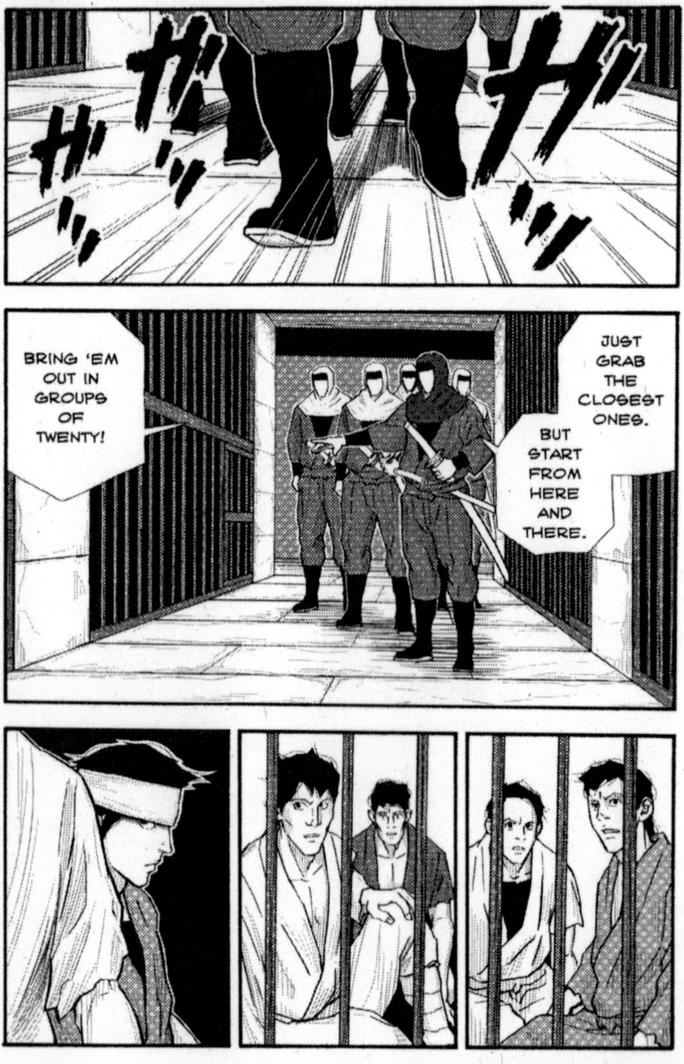
ザッ
ザッ
ザッ
JUST GRAB THE CLOSEST ONES.
BUT START FROM HERE AND THERE.
BRING 'EM OUT IN GROUPS OF TWENTY!

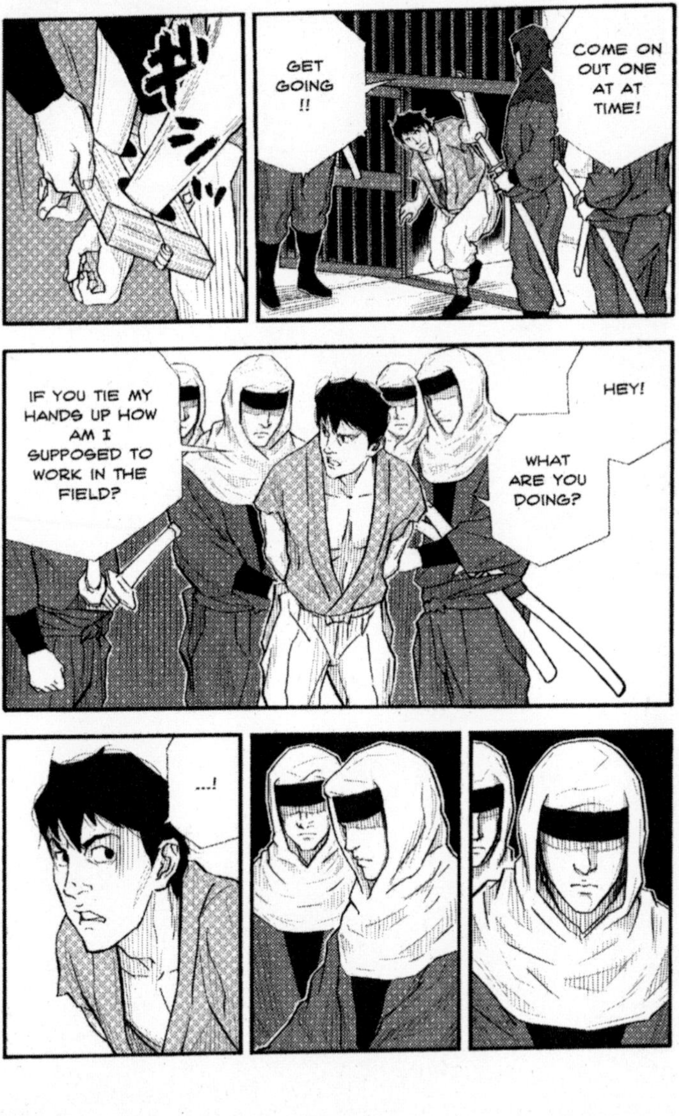
COME ON OUT ONE AT AT TIME!
GET GOING !!
HEY!
WHAT ARE YOU DOING?
IF YOU TIE MY HANDS UP HOW AM I SUPPOSED TO WORK IN THE FIELD?
...!

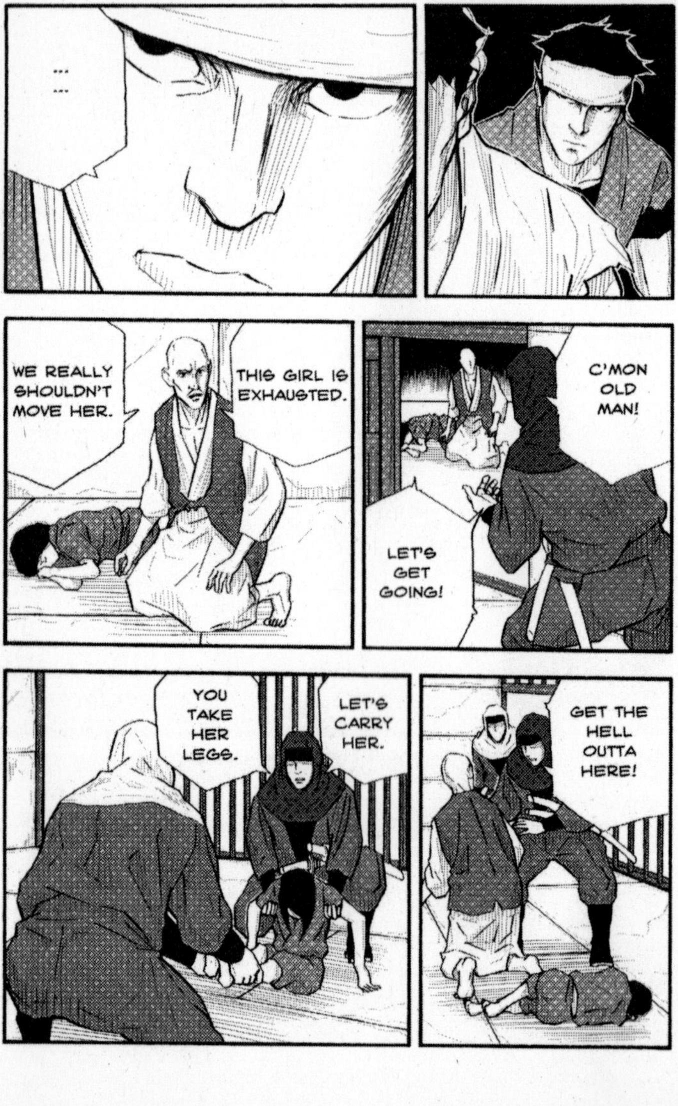
...
...
C'MON OLD MAN!
LET'S GET GOING!
THIS GIRL IS EXHAUSTED.
WE REALLY SHOULDN'T MOVE HER.
GET THE HELL OUTTA HERE!
LET'S CARRY HER.
YOU TAKE HER LEGS.

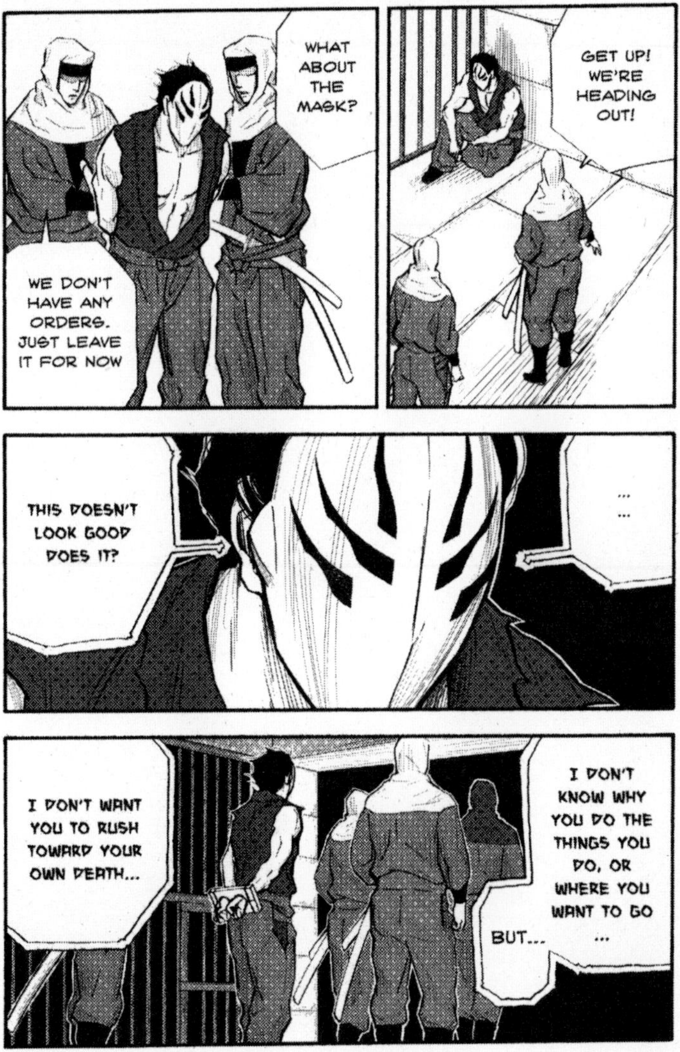
GET UP! WE'RE HEADING OUT!
WHAT ABOUT THE MASK?
WE DON'T HAVE ANY ORDERS. JUST LEAVE IT FOR NOW
… …
THIS DOESN'T LOOK GOOD DOES IT?
I DON'T KNOW WHY YOU DO THE THINGS YOU DO, OR WHERE YOU WANT TO GO …
BUT…
I DON'T WANT YOU TO RUSH TOWARD YOUR OWN DEATH…

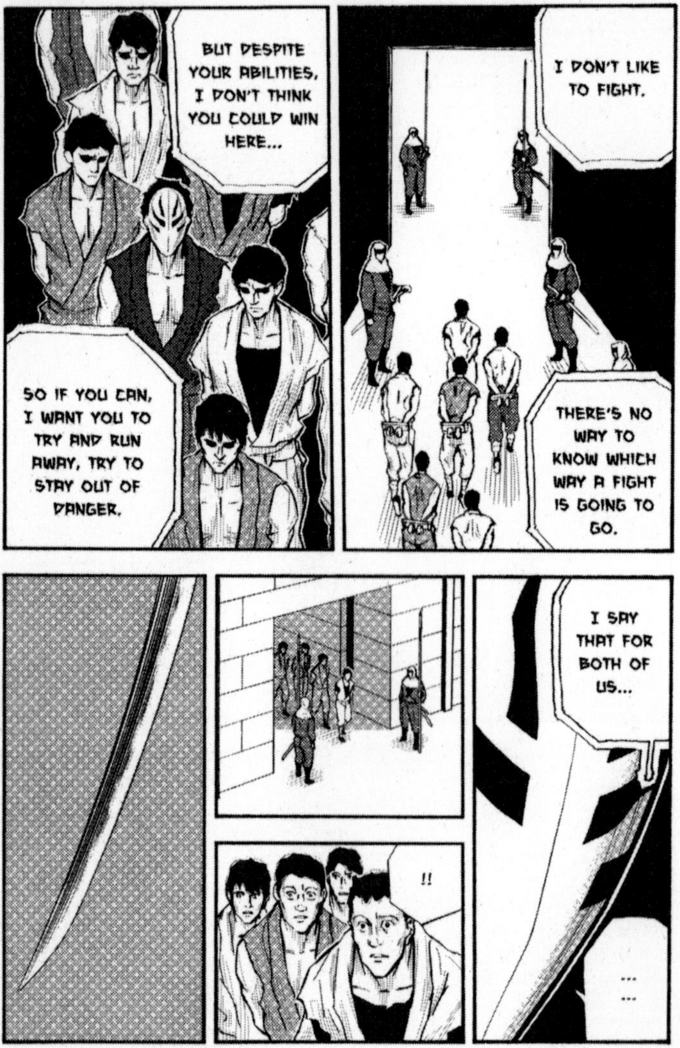
I DON'T LIKE TO FIGHT.
THERE'S NO WAY TO KNOW WHICH WAY A FIGHT IS GOING TO GO.
BUT DESPITE YOUR ABILITIES, I DON'T THINK YOU COULD WIN HERE...
SO IF YOU CAN, I WANT YOU TO TRY AND RUN AWAY, TRY TO STAY OUT OF DANGER.
I SAY THAT FOR BOTH OF US...
...
...
!!

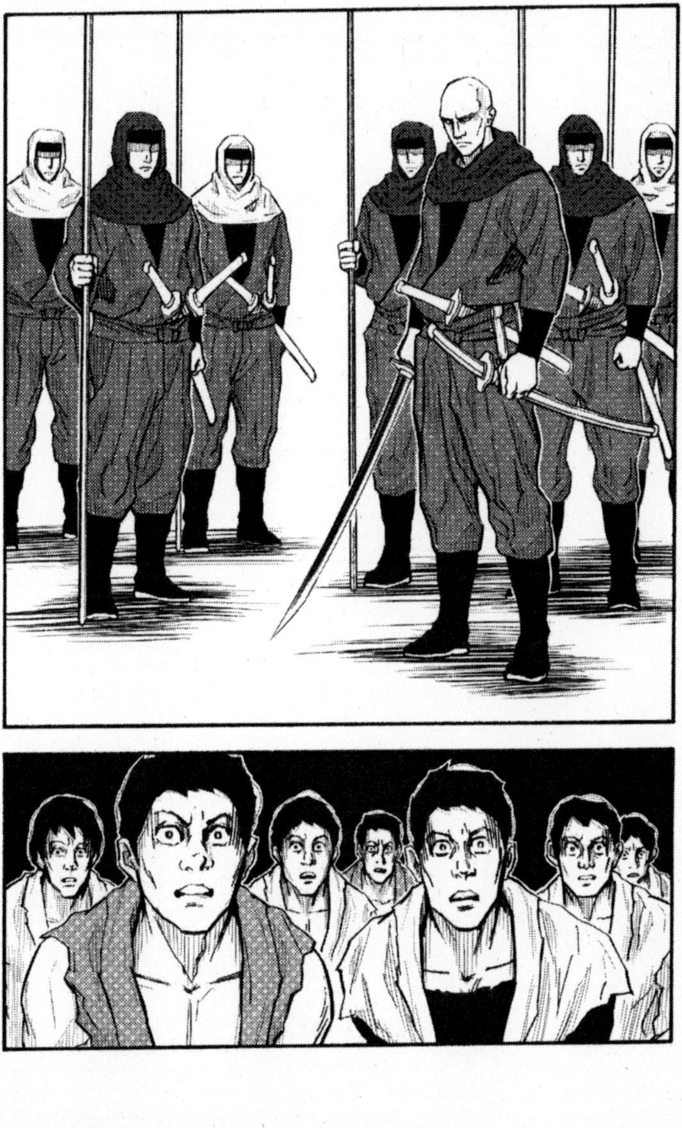

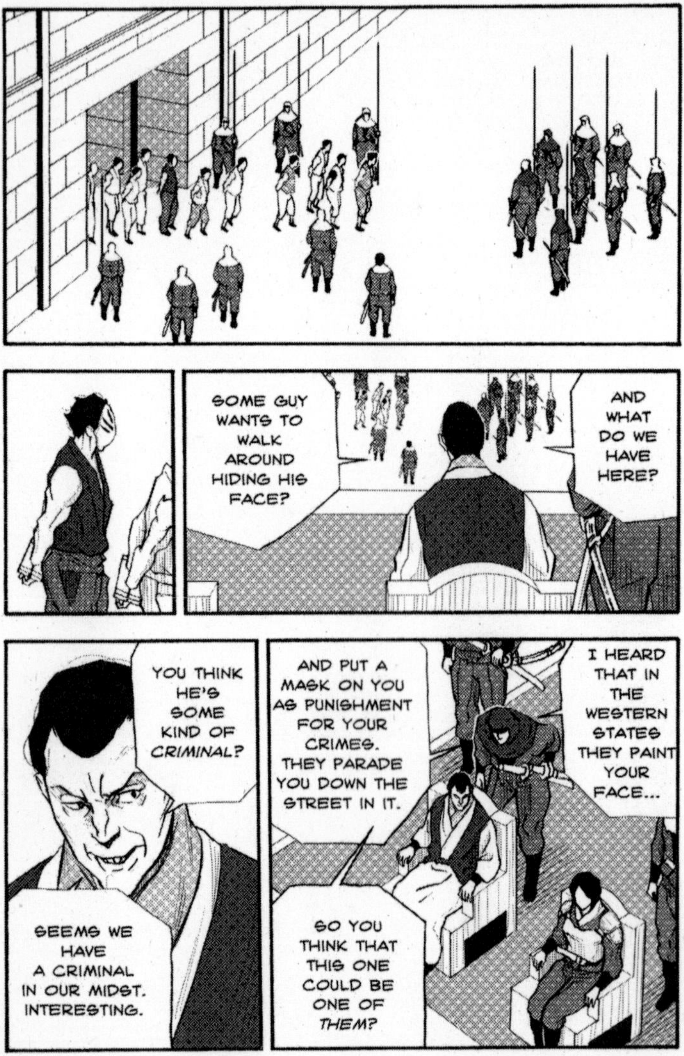
AND WHAT DO WE HAVE HERE?
SOME GUY WANTS TO WALK AROUND HIDING HIS FACE?
I HEARD THAT IN THE WESTERN STATES THEY PAINT YOUR FACE...
AND PUT A MASK ON YOU AS PUNISHMENT FOR YOUR CRIMES. THEY PARADE YOU DOWN THE STREET IN IT.
SO YOU THINK THAT THIS ONE COULD BE ONE OF *THEM*?
YOU THINK HE'S SOME KIND OF *CRIMINAL*?
SEEMS WE HAVE A CRIMINAL IN OUR MIDST. INTERESTING.

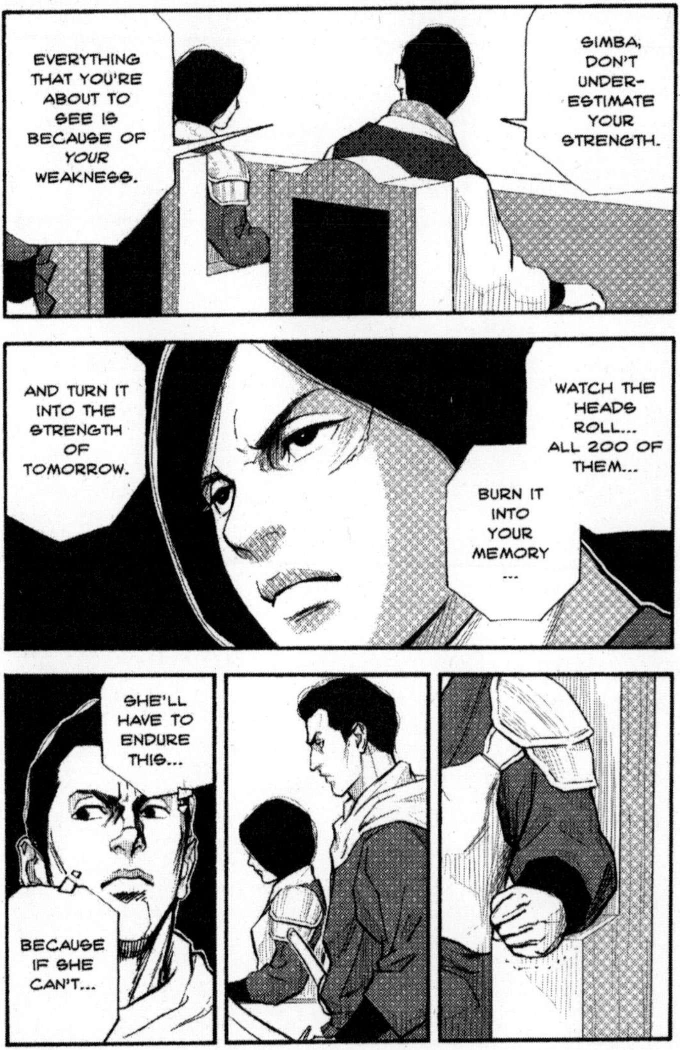
SIMBA, DON'T UNDER-ESTIMATE YOUR STRENGTH.
EVERYTHING THAT YOU'RE ABOUT TO SEE IS BECAUSE OF *YOUR* WEAKNESS.
WATCH THE HEADS ROLL... ALL 200 OF THEM...
BURN IT INTO YOUR MEMORY ...
AND TURN IT INTO THE STRENGTH OF TOMORROW.
SHE'LL HAVE TO ENDURE THIS...
BECAUSE IF SHE CAN'T...

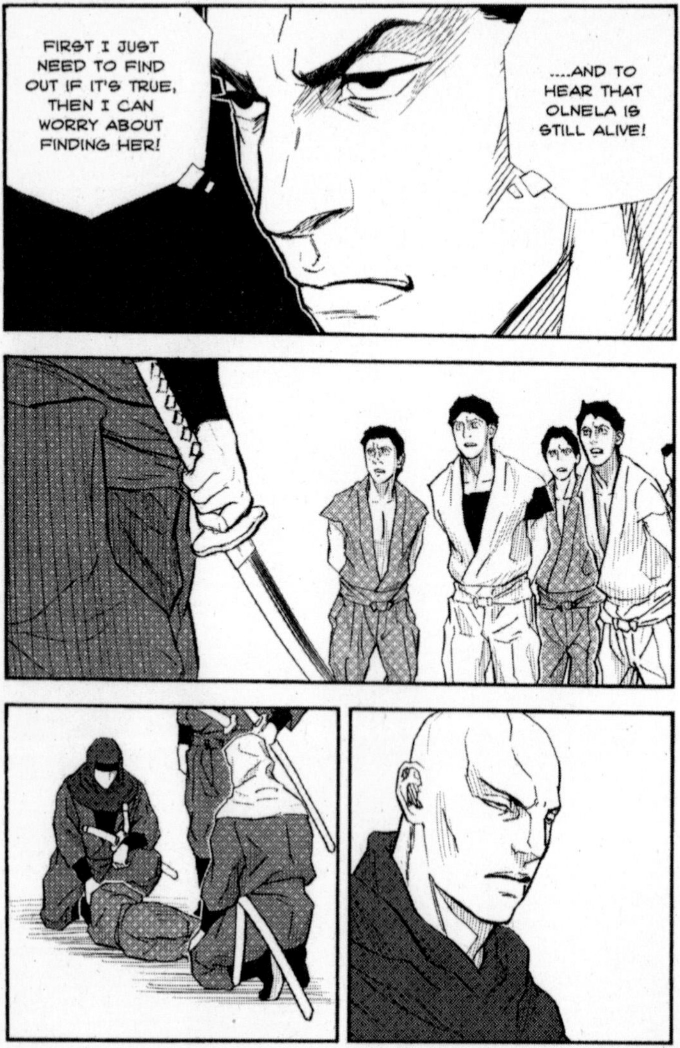
....AND TO HEAR THAT OLNELA IS STILL ALIVE!
FIRST I JUST NEED TO FIND OUT IF IT'S TRUE, THEN I CAN WORRY ABOUT FINDING HER!

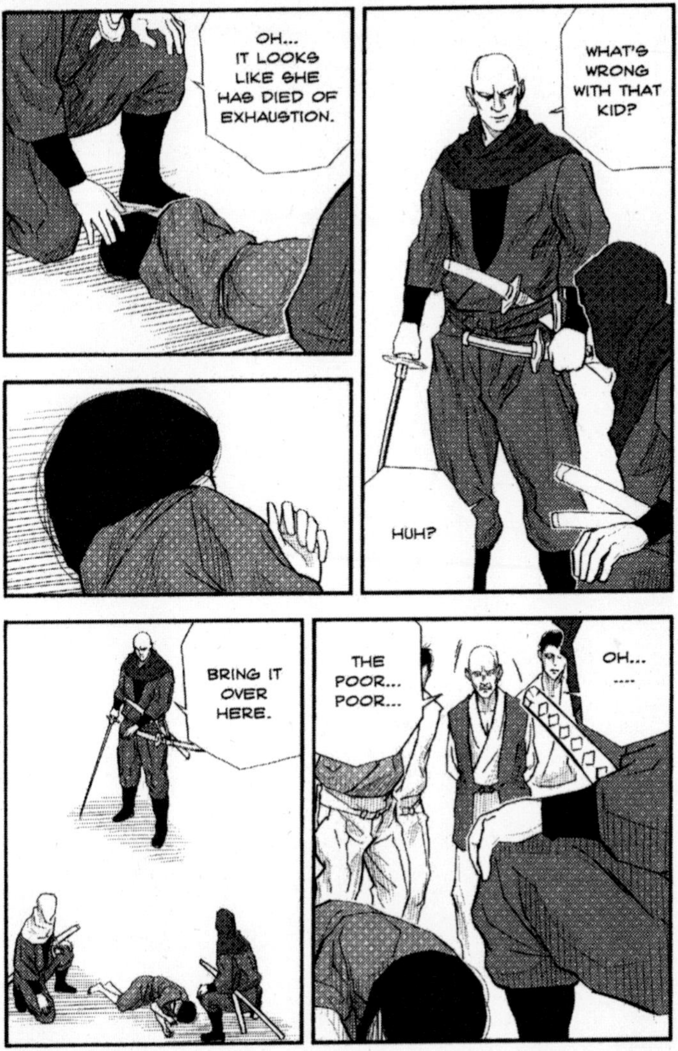
WHAT'S WRONG WITH THAT KID?
HUH?
OH... IT LOOKS LIKE SHE HAS DIED OF EXHAUSTION.
OH... ----
THE POOR... POOR...
BRING IT OVER HERE.

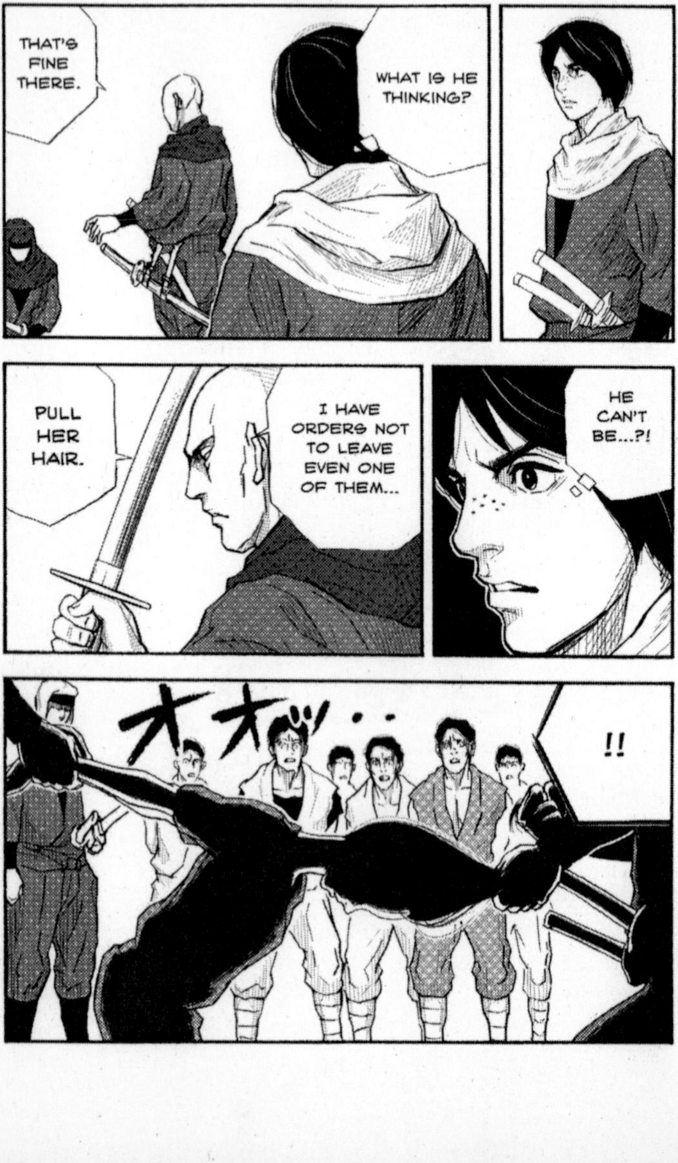
WHAT IS HE THINKING?
THAT'S FINE THERE.
HE CAN'T BE...?!
I HAVE ORDERS NOT TO LEAVE EVEN ONE OF THEM...
PULL HER HAIR.
!!

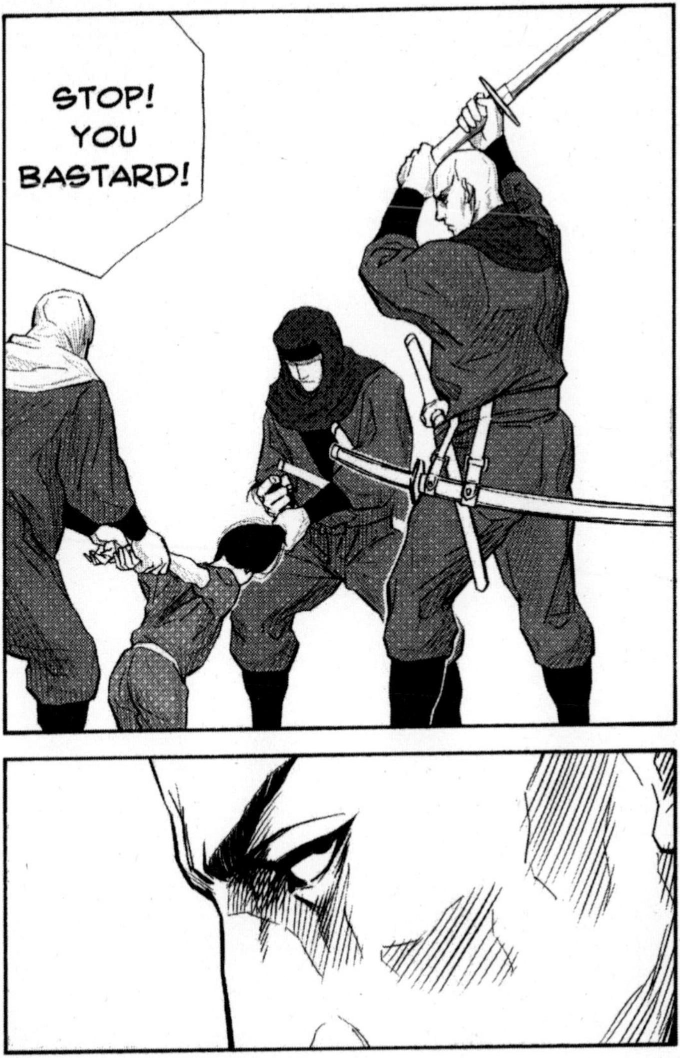
STOP! YOU BASTARD!

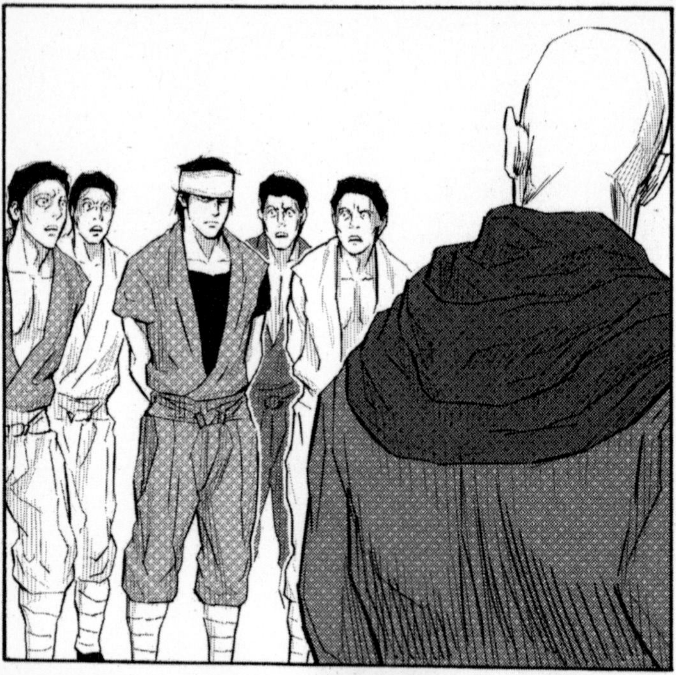

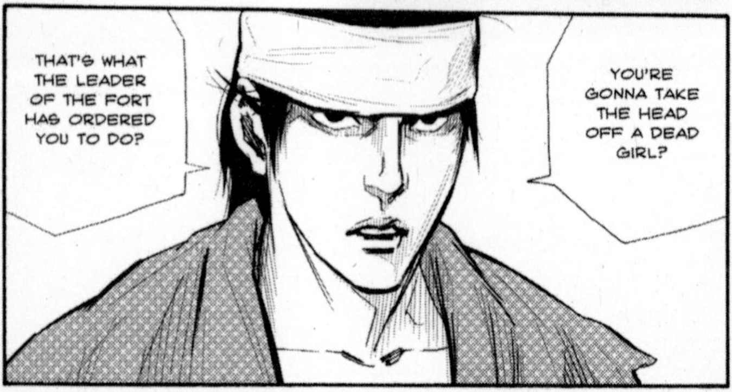
YOU'RE GONNA TAKE THE HEAD OFF A DEAD GIRL?
THAT'S WHAT THE LEADER OF THE FORT HAS ORDERED YOU TO DO?

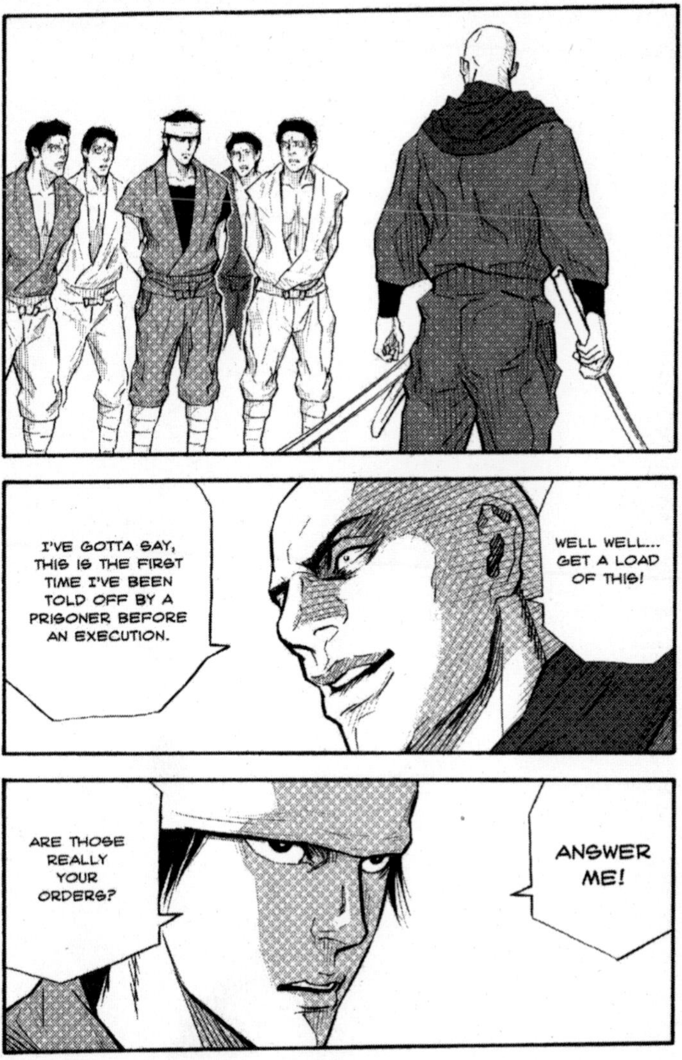
WELL WELL... GET A LOAD OF THIS!
I'VE GOTTA SAY, THIS IS THE FIRST TIME I'VE BEEN TOLD OFF BY A PRISONER BEFORE AN EXECUTION.
ANSWER ME!
ARE THOSE REALLY YOUR ORDERS?

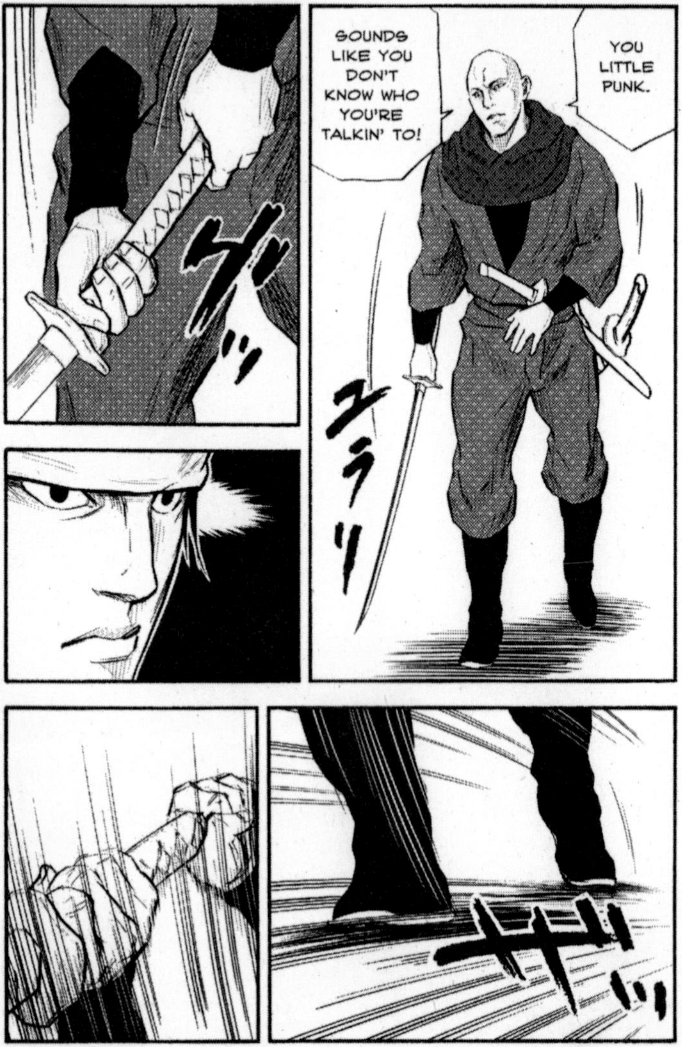
YOU LITTLE PUNK.
SOUNDS LIKE YOU DON'T KNOW WHO YOU'RE TALKIN' TO!
ユラリ
ザッ

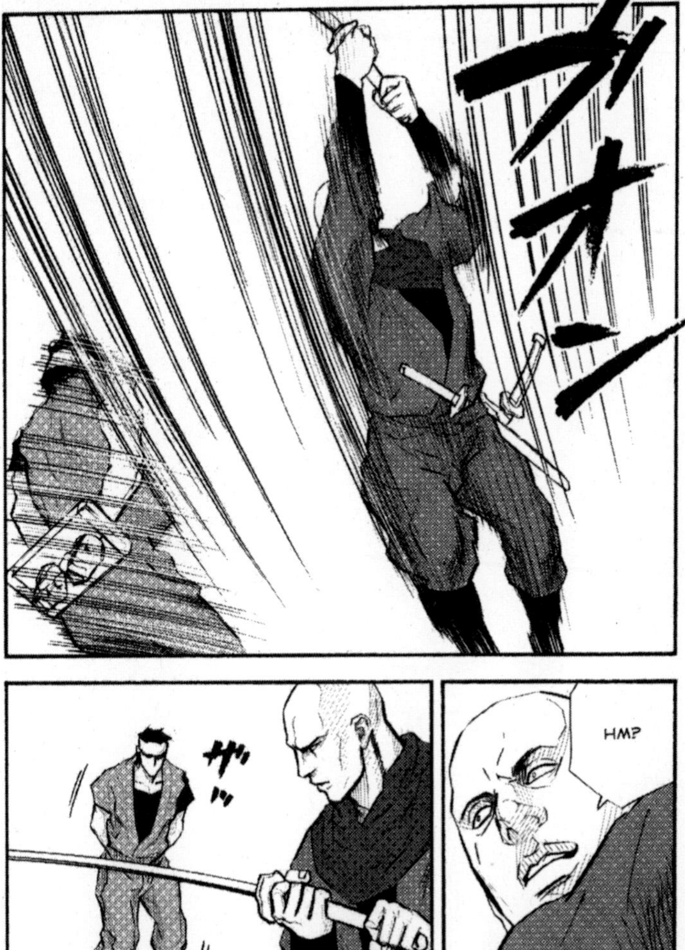
HM?
ザッ

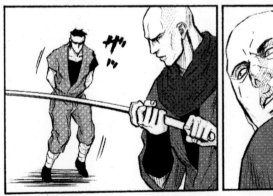

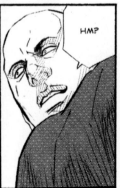

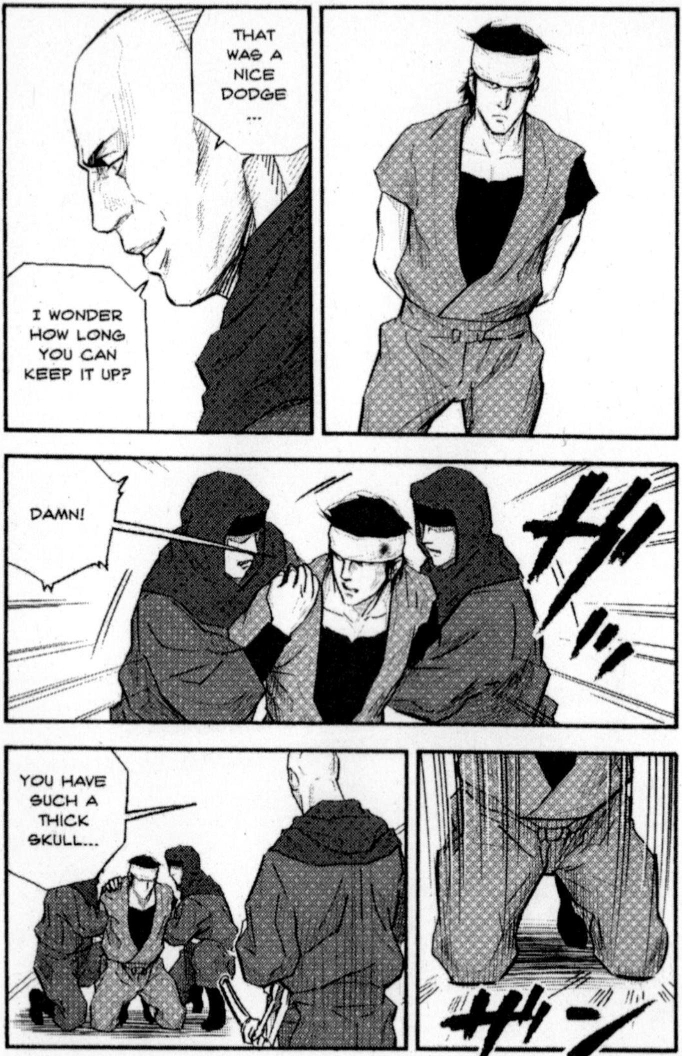
THAT WAS A NICE DODGE ...
I WONDER HOW LONG YOU CAN KEEP IT UP?
ザッ
DAMN!
ザーン
YOU HAVE SUCH A THICK SKULL...

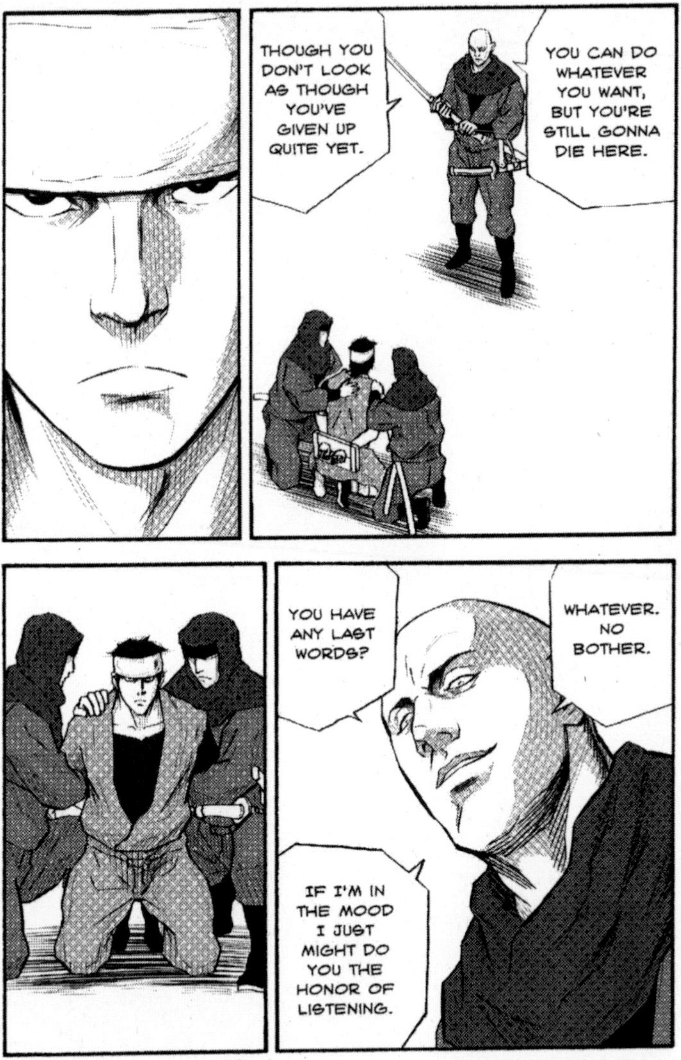
YOU CAN DO WHATEVER YOU WANT, BUT YOU'RE STILL GONNA DIE HERE.
THOUGH YOU DON'T LOOK AS THOUGH YOU'VE GIVEN UP QUITE YET.
WHATEVER. NO BOTHER.
YOU HAVE ANY LAST WORDS?
IF I'M IN THE MOOD I JUST MIGHT DO YOU THE HONOR OF LISTENING.

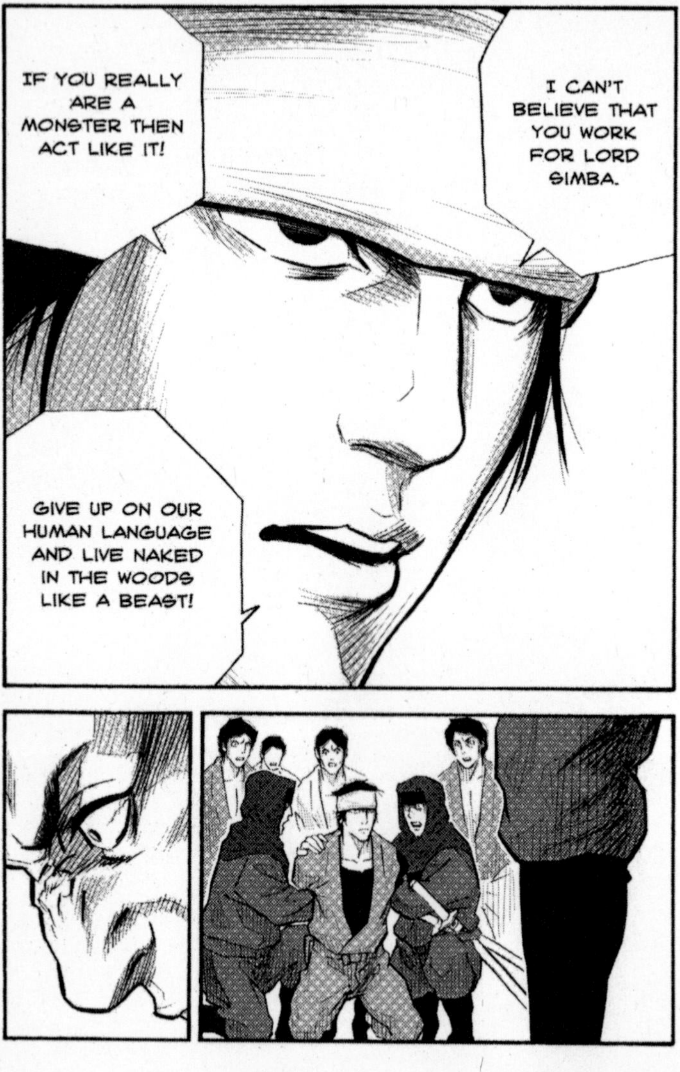
I CAN'T BELIEVE THAT YOU WORK FOR LORD SIMBA.
IF YOU REALLY ARE A MONSTER THEN ACT LIKE IT!
GIVE UP ON OUR HUMAN LANGUAGE AND LIVE NAKED IN THE WOODS LIKE A BEAST!

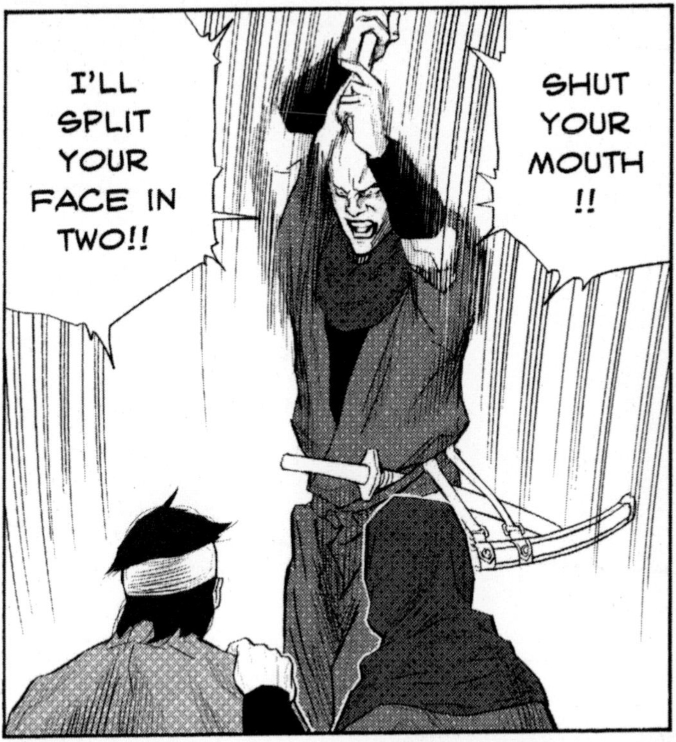
SHUT YOUR MOUTH !!
I'LL SPLIT YOUR FACE IN TWO!!

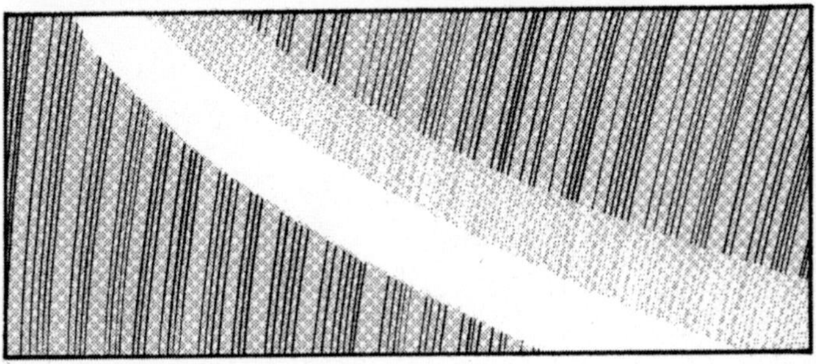

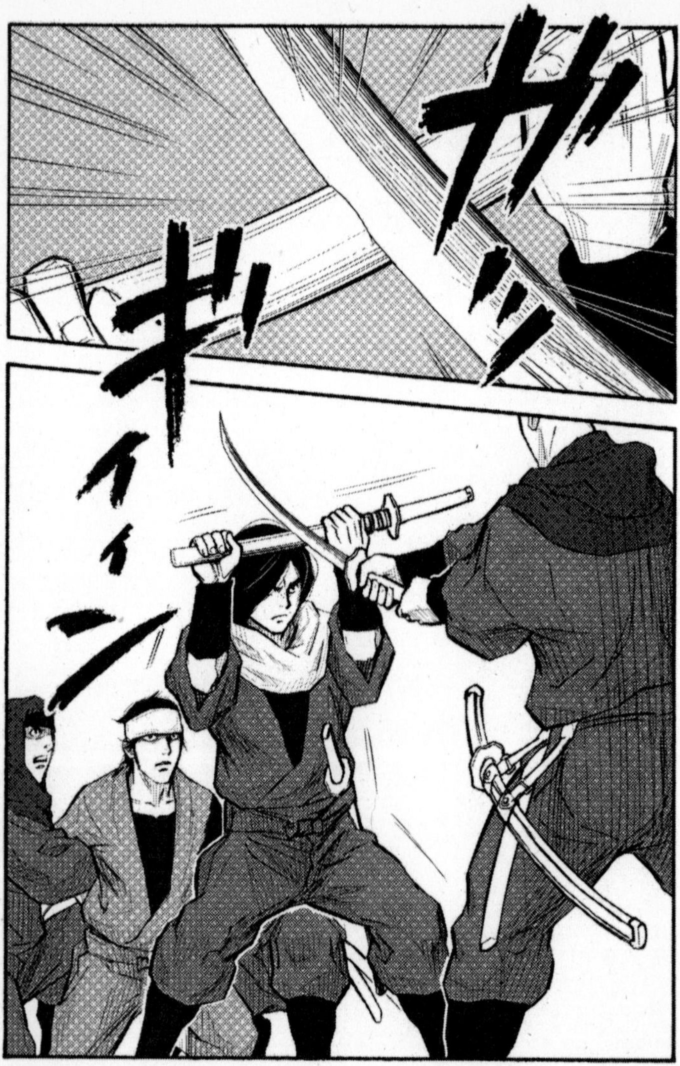
ガッ
ギィィーン

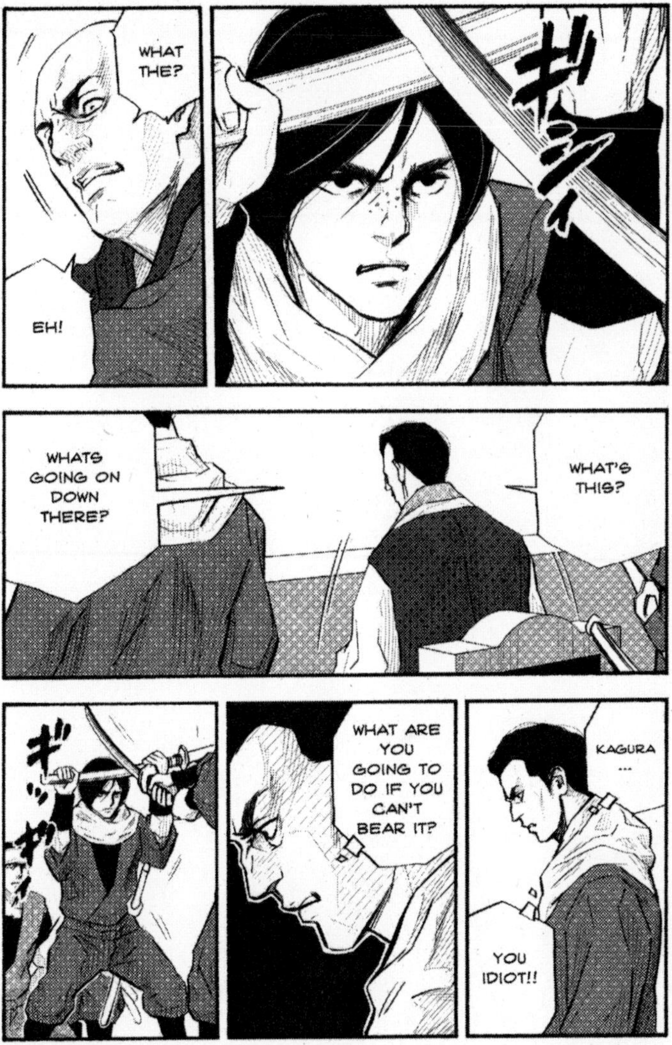
ギシィ
WHAT THE?
EH!
WHAT'S THIS?
WHATS GOING ON DOWN THERE?
KAGURA ...
YOU IDIOT!!
WHAT ARE YOU GOING TO DO IF YOU CAN'T BEAR IT?

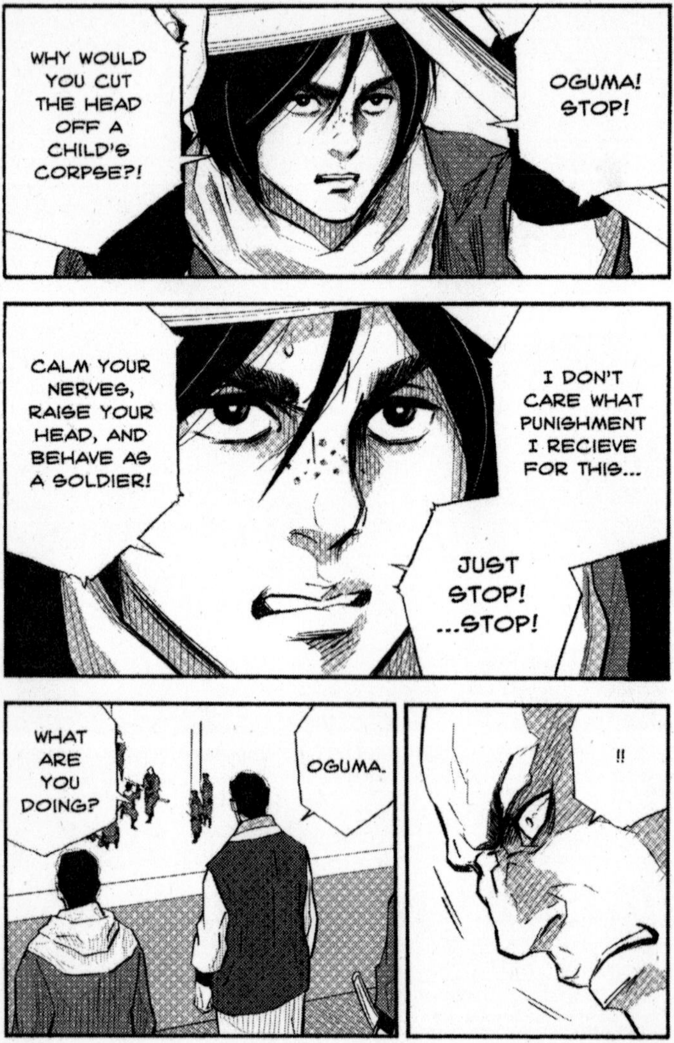
OGUMA! STOP!
WHY WOULD YOU CUT THE HEAD OFF A CHILD'S CORPSE?!
I DON'T CARE WHAT PUNISHMENT I RECIEVE FOR THIS...
CALM YOUR NERVES, RAISE YOUR HEAD, AND BEHAVE AS A SOLDIER!
JUST STOP! ...STOP!
!!
OGUMA.
WHAT ARE YOU DOING?

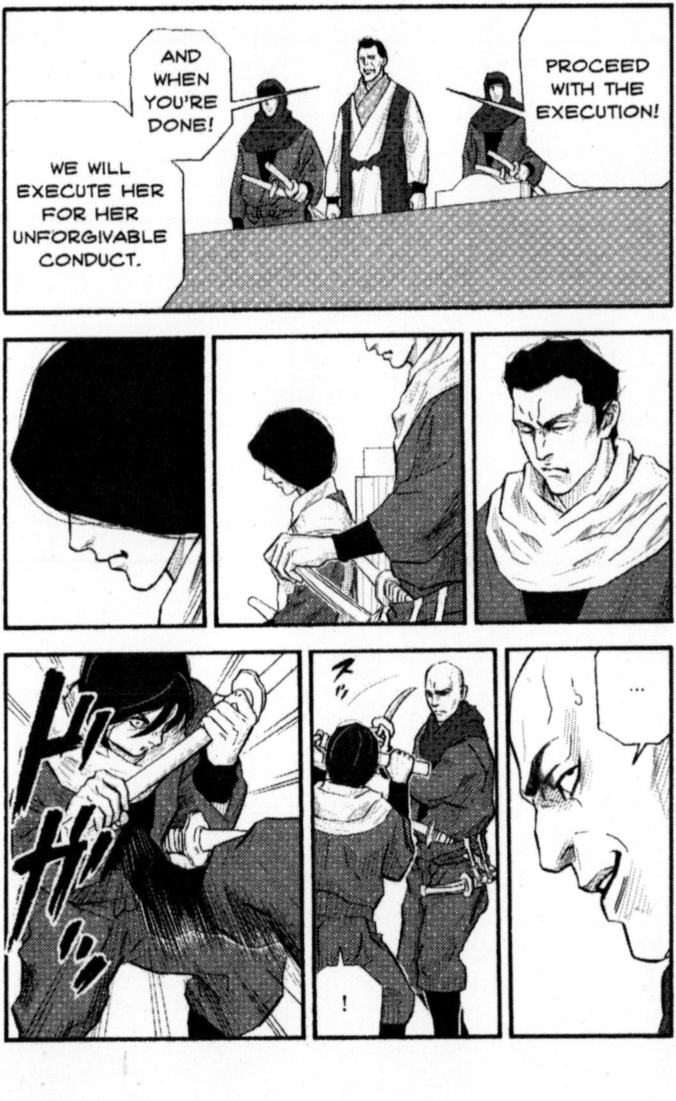
PROCEED WITH THE EXECUTION!
AND WHEN YOU'RE DONE!
WE WILL EXECUTE HER FOR HER UNFORGIVABLE CONDUCT.
...
!

UGH.
OH!!
!
ドッ
ドカッ
ギッ
ガッ
...
ズッ
...

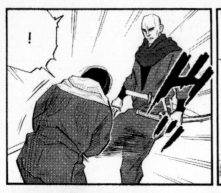

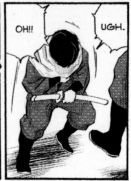

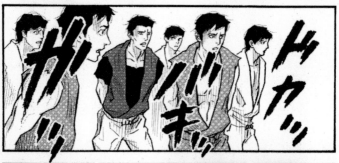

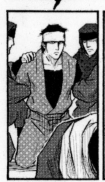

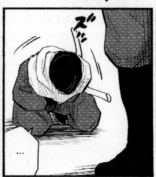

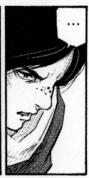

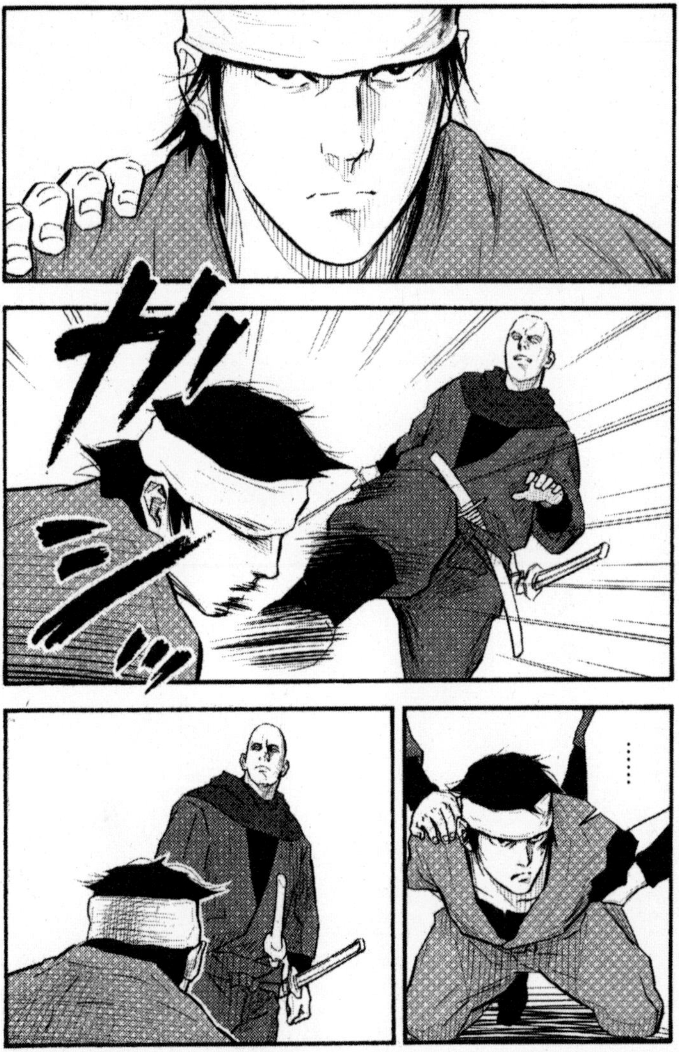
……

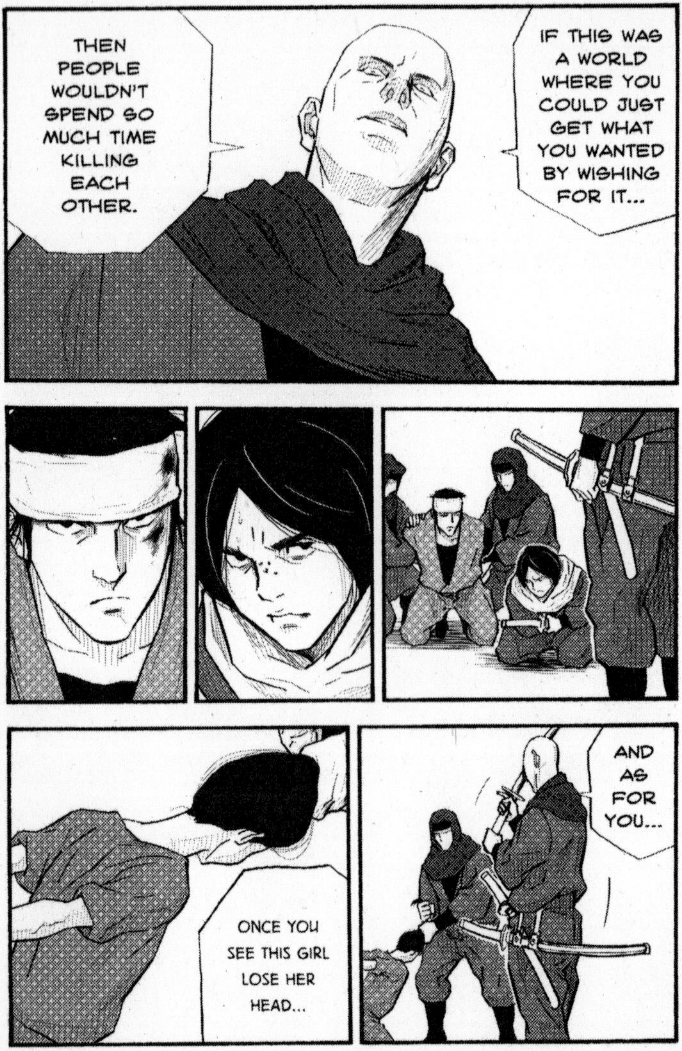
IF THIS WAS A WORLD WHERE YOU COULD JUST GET WHAT YOU WANTED BY WISHING FOR IT...
THEN PEOPLE WOULDN'T SPEND SO MUCH TIME KILLING EACH OTHER.
AND AS FOR YOU...
ONCE YOU SEE THIS GIRL LOSE HER HEAD...

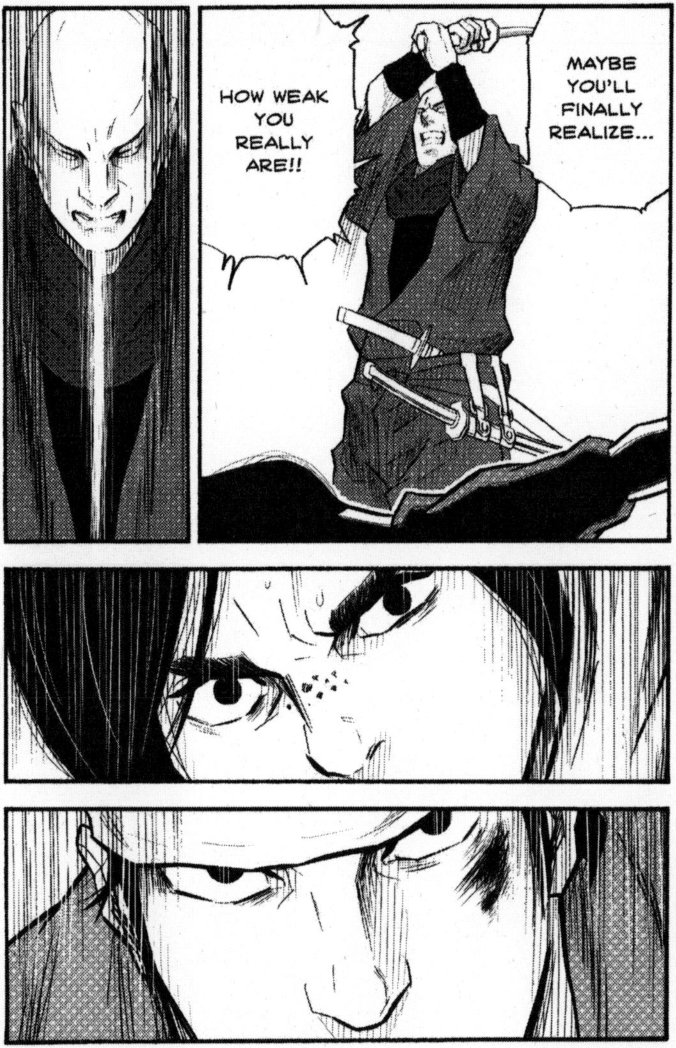
MAYBE YOU'LL FINALLY REALIZE...
HOW WEAK YOU REALLY ARE!!

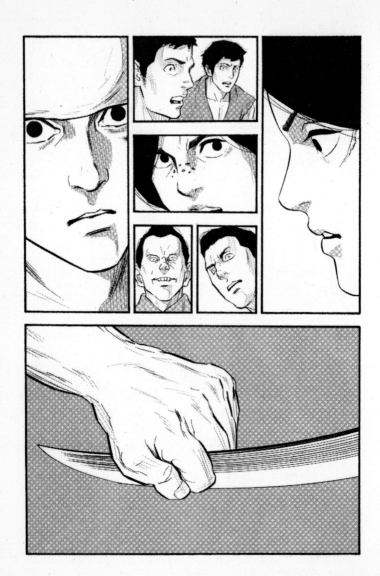

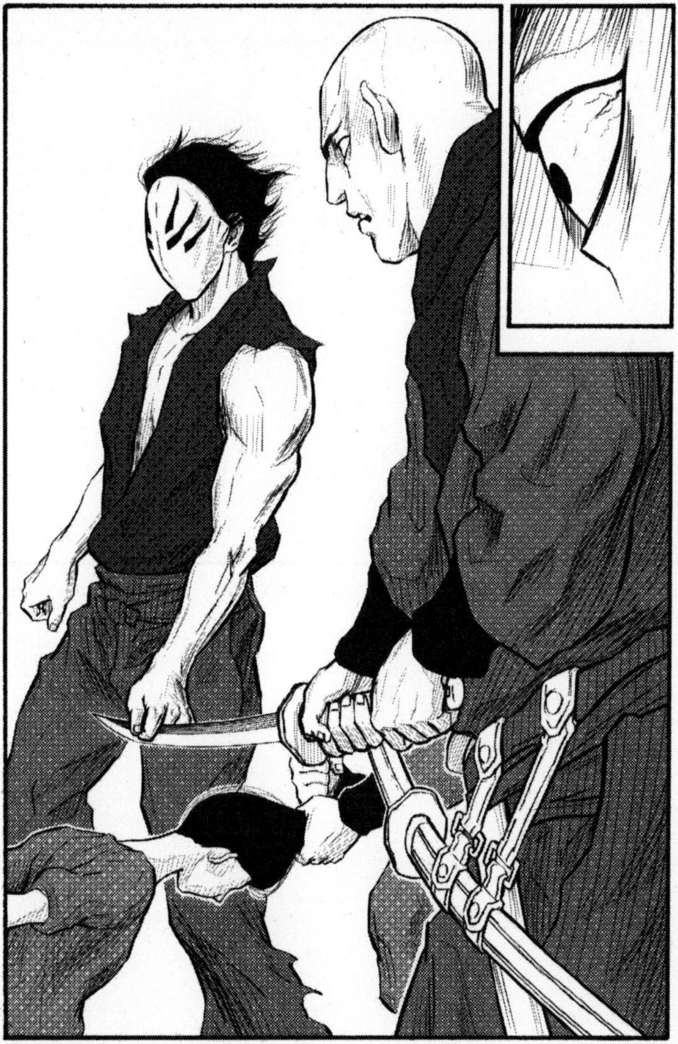

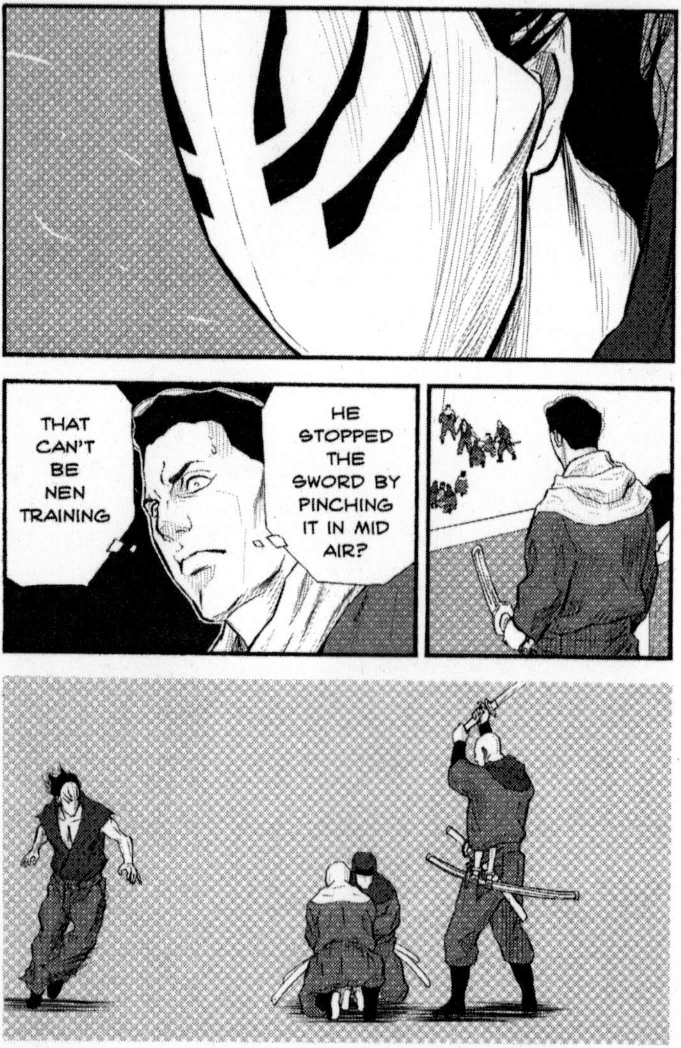
HE STOPPED THE SWORD BY PINCHING IT IN MID AIR?
THAT CAN'T BE NEN TRAINING

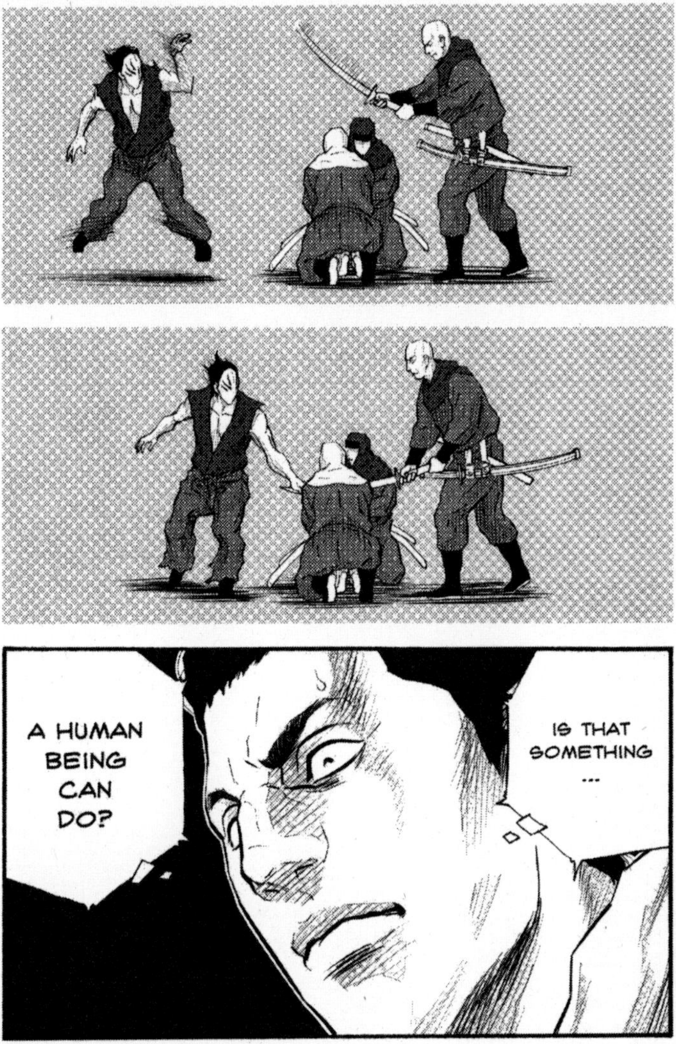
IS THAT SOMETHING ...
A HUMAN BEING CAN DO?

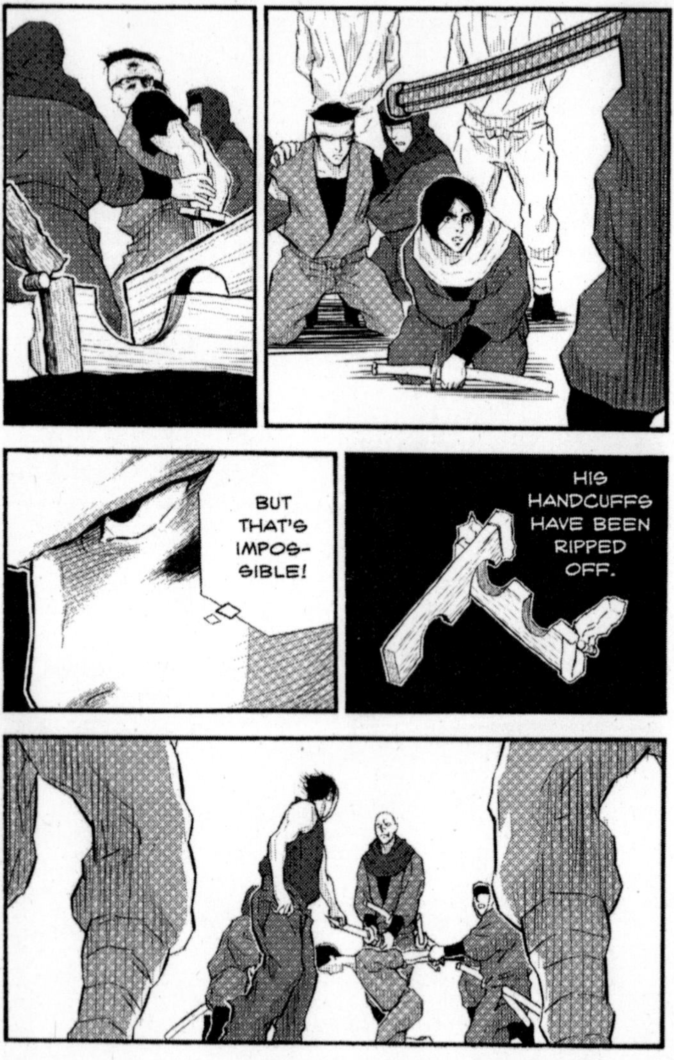
HIS HANDCUFFS HAVE BEEN RIPPED OFF.
BUT THAT'S IMPOSSIBLE!

UGH ...
ギッ
ギッ
AHHH!
ミシッ
フッ
!
ザッ

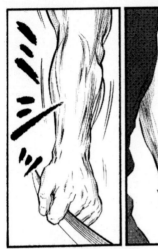

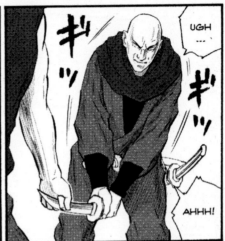

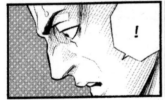

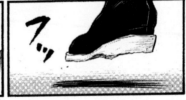

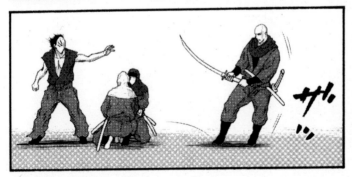

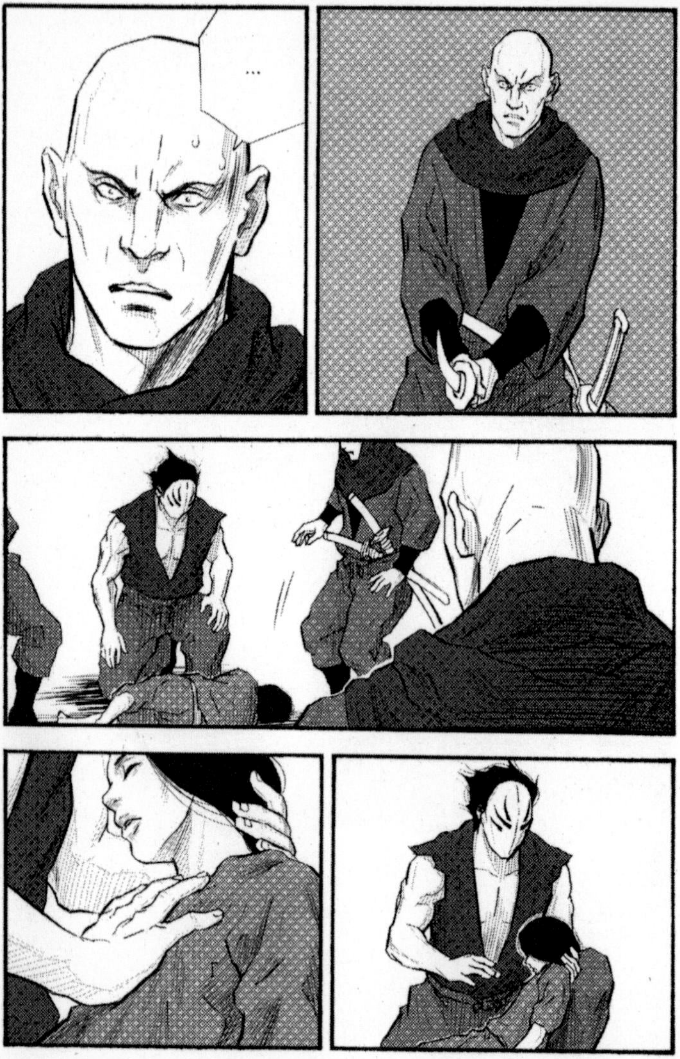
...

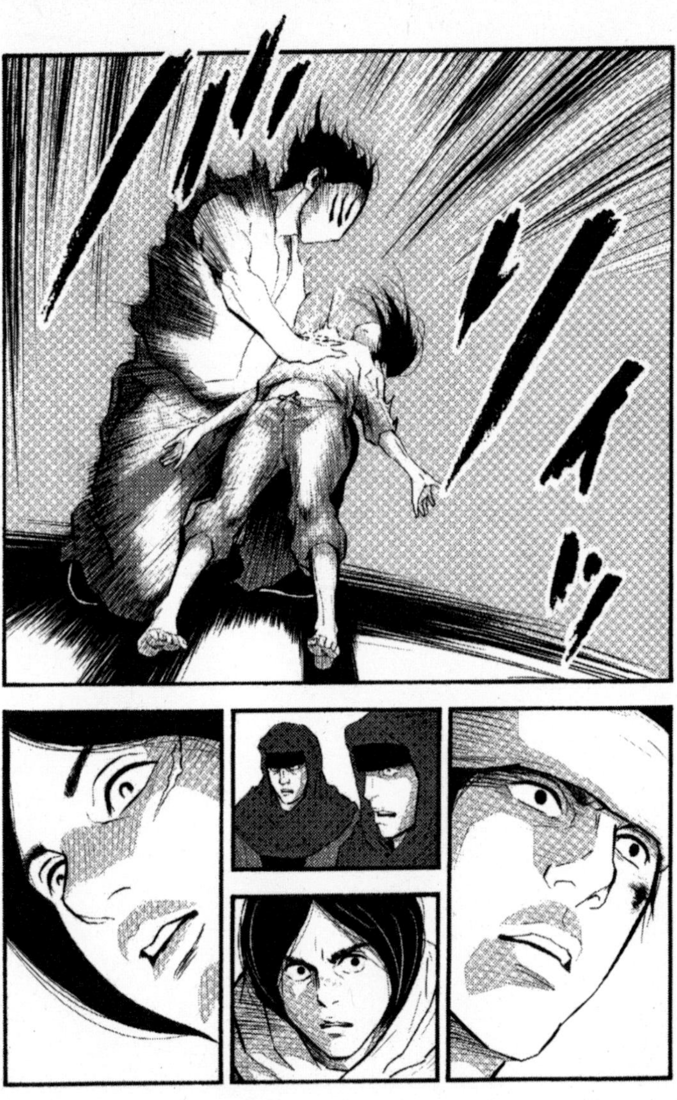

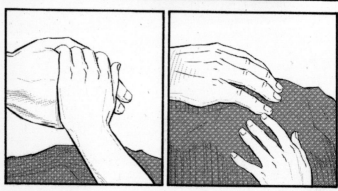

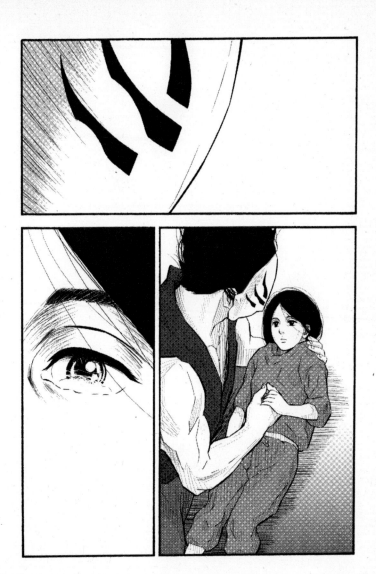

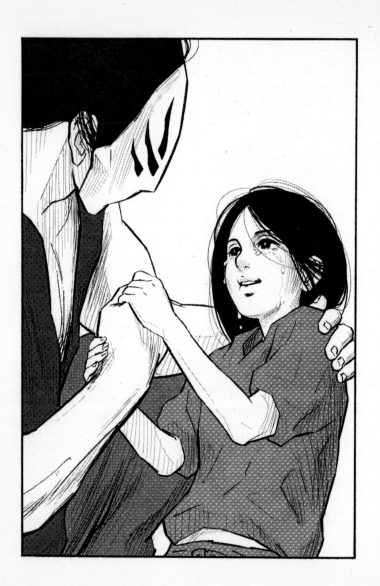

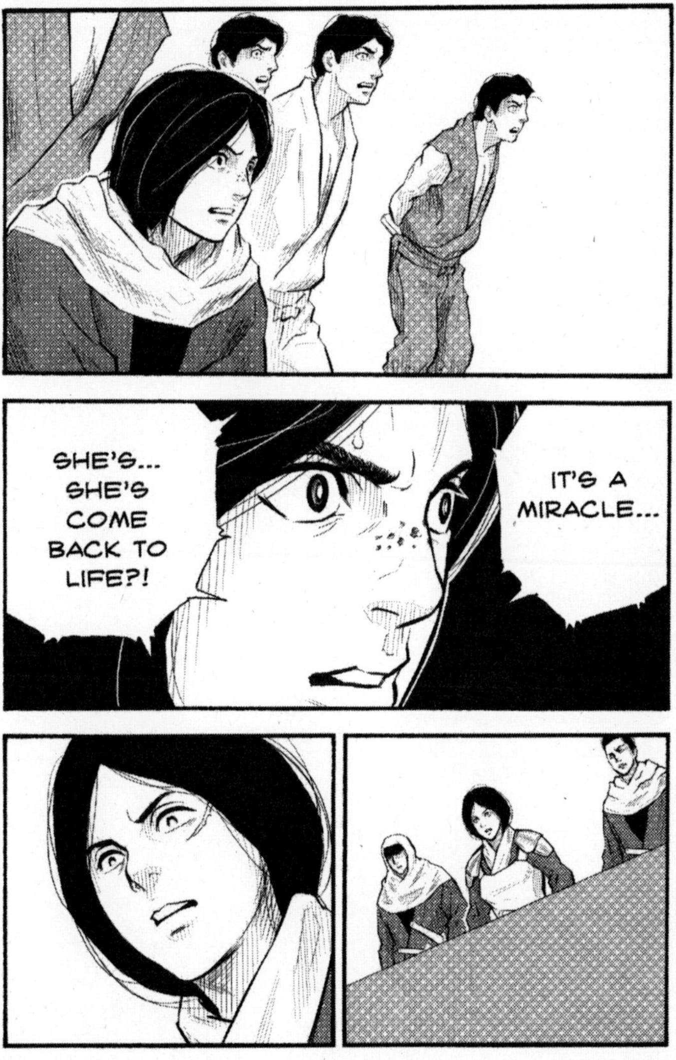
IT'S A MIRACLE...
SHE'S... SHE'S COME BACK TO LIFE?!

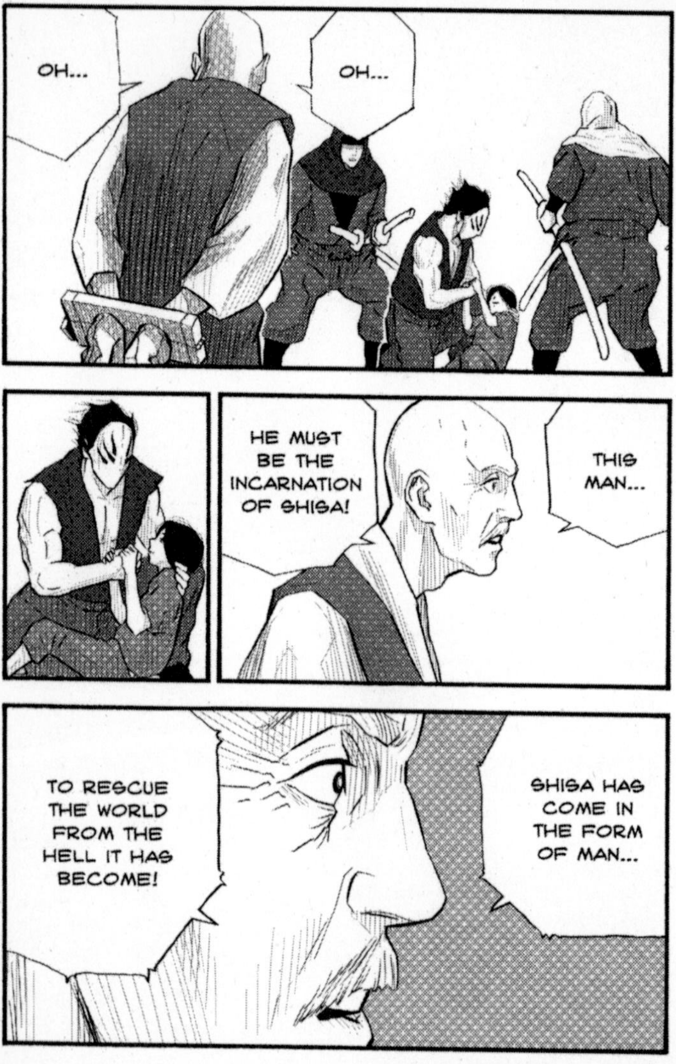
OH...
OH...
THIS MAN...
HE MUST BE THE INCARNATION OF SHISA!
SHISA HAS COME IN THE FORM OF MAN...
TO RESCUE THE WORLD FROM THE HELL IT HAS BECOME!

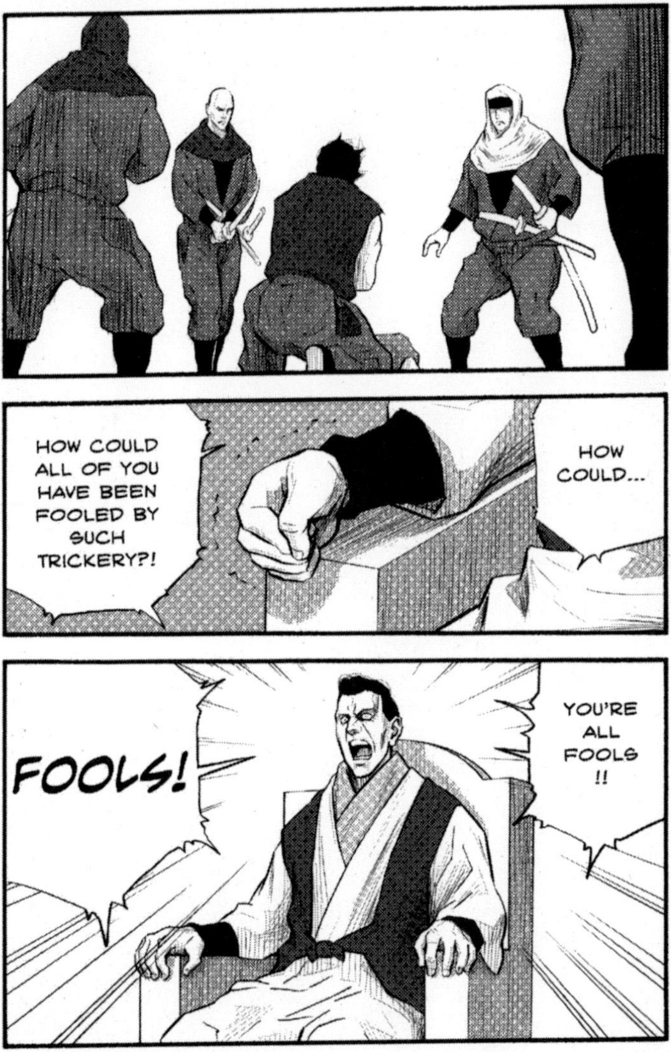
HOW COULD...
HOW COULD ALL OF YOU HAVE BEEN FOOLED BY SUCH TRICKERY?!
YOU'RE ALL FOOLS !!
FOOLS!

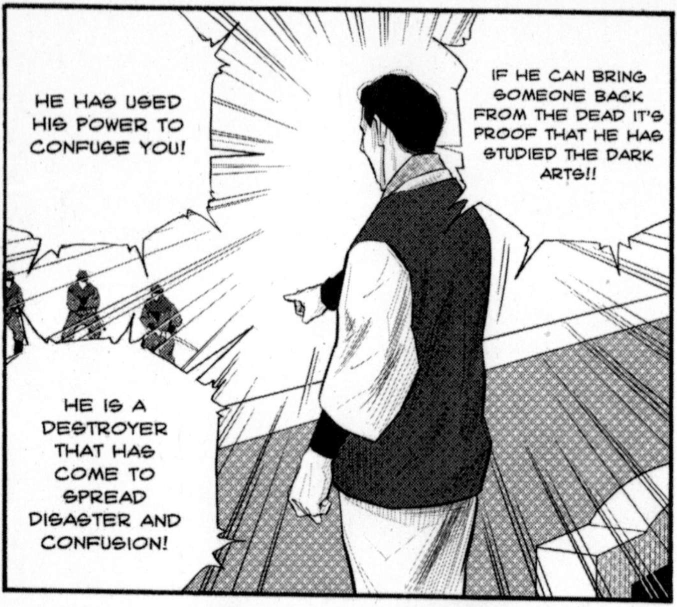
IF HE CAN BRING SOMEONE BACK FROM THE DEAD IT'S PROOF THAT HE HAS STUDIED THE DARK ARTS!!
HE HAS USED HIS POWER TO CONFUSE YOU!
HE IS A DESTROYER THAT HAS COME TO SPREAD DISASTER AND CONFUSION!
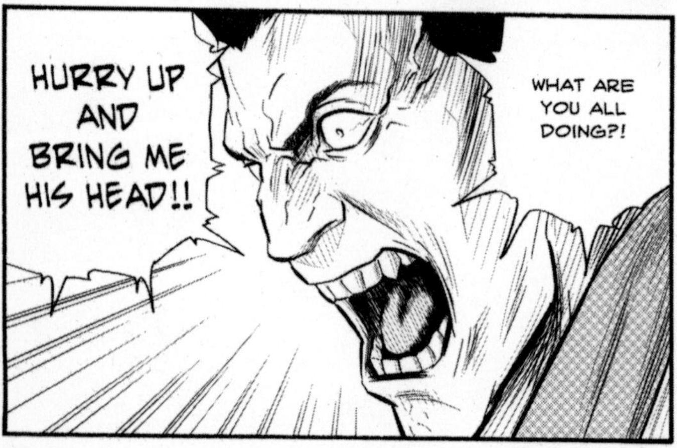
WHAT ARE YOU ALL DOING?!
HURRY UP AND BRING ME HIS HEAD!!

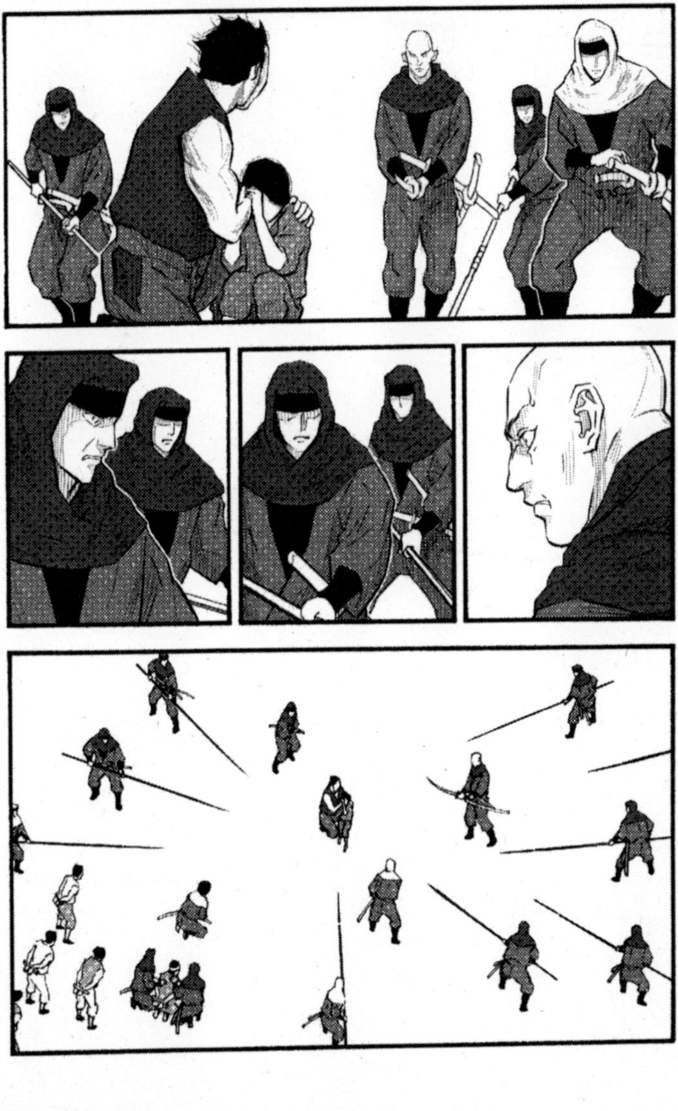

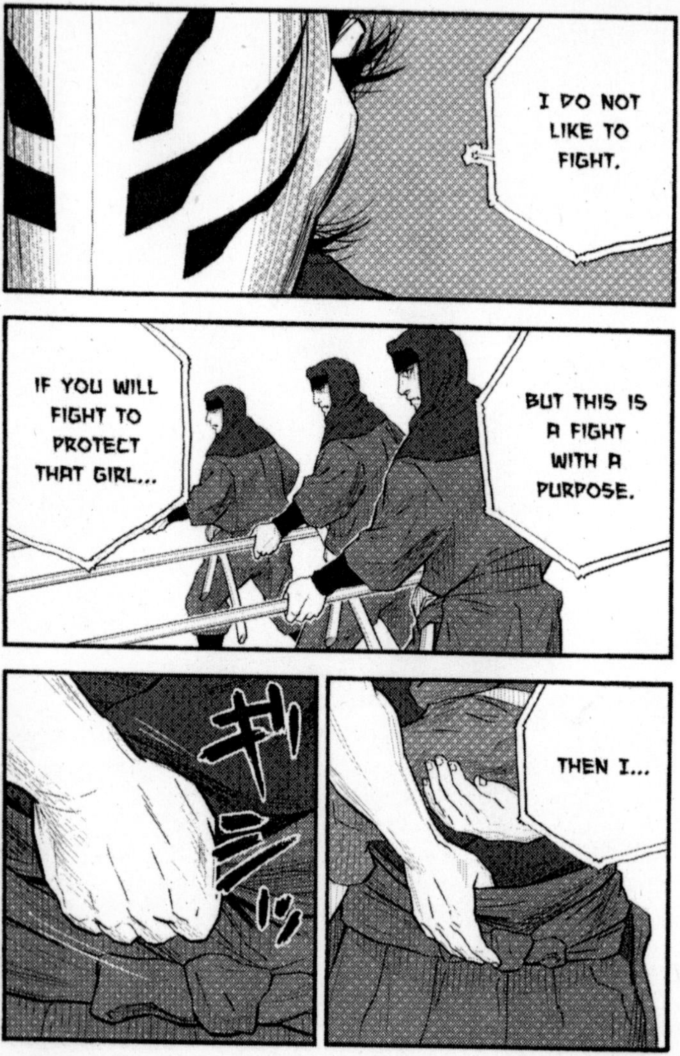
I DO NOT LIKE TO FIGHT.
BUT THIS IS A FIGHT WITH A PURPOSE.
IF YOU WILL FIGHT TO PROTECT THAT GIRL...
THEN I...

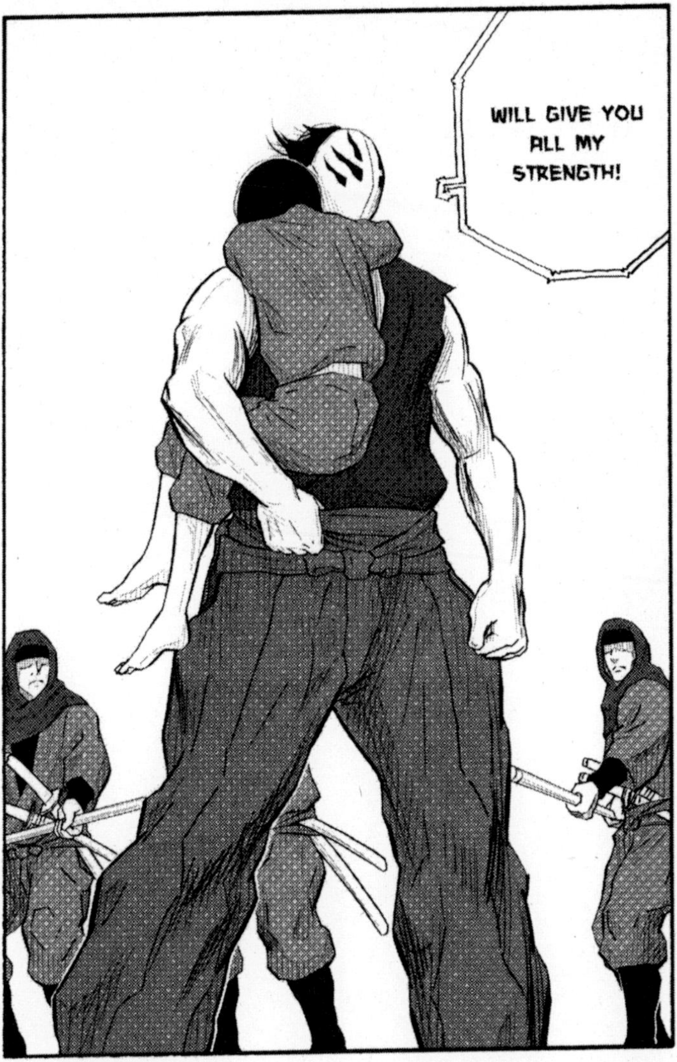
WILL GIVE YOU ALL MY STRENGTH!

NO MATTER HOW MUCH POWER YOU MAY HAVE...
IF YOU ARE STABBED WITH ONE OF THOSE SPEARS, YOU WILL DIE.
THE ENEMIES WILL COME AT YOU FROM ALL SIDES...
IF YOU WANT TO SURVIVE THEN YOU NEED TO FOCUS ON ONE AT A TIME.
AND TAKE THEM ALL OUT WITH ONE HIT!
THE MAN IN FRONT OF YOU...
AND HIS MEN THAT SURROUND YOU... I KNOW THEIR STRENGTH...
THE PROBLEM IS THE ARCHERS UP THERE.

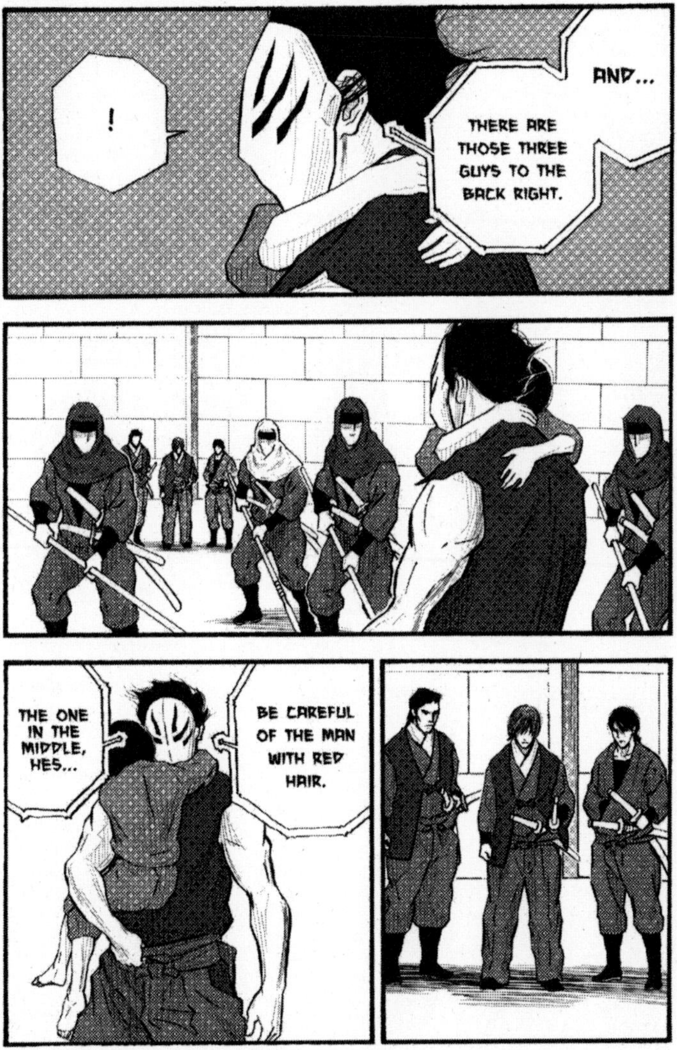
AND...
THERE ARE THOSE THREE GUYS TO THE BACK RIGHT.
!
BE CAREFUL OF THE MAN WITH RED HAIR.
THE ONE IN THE MIDDLE, HES...

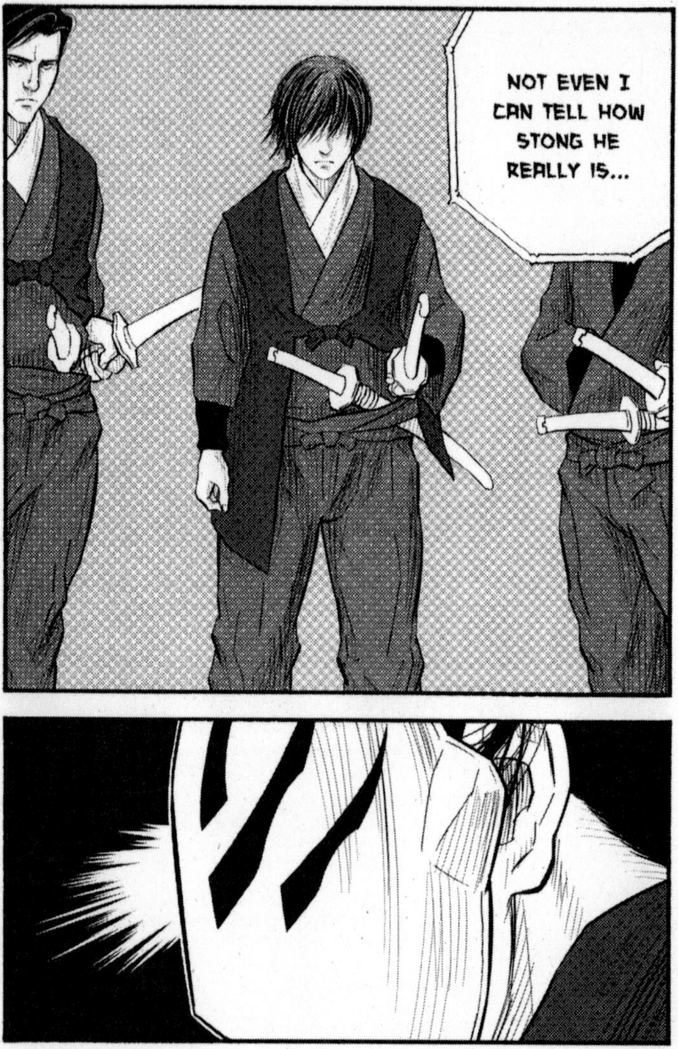
NOT EVEN I CAN TELL HOW STONG HE REALLY IS...

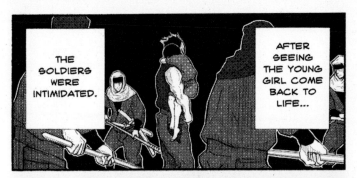

AFTER SEEING THE YOUNG GIRL COME BACK TO LIFE...
THE SOLDIERS WERE INTIMIDATED.
HOWEVER ...
THEY HAD A LOT OF EXPERIENCE IN BATTLE.
AND THEY KNEW THAT ONE MAN SURROUNDED BY ENEMIES...
WOULD NEVER BE ABLE TO FEND THEM OFF AND SURVIVE...

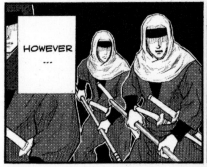

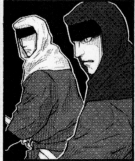

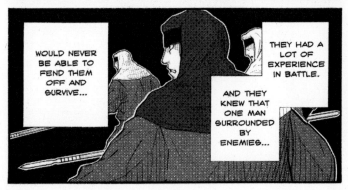

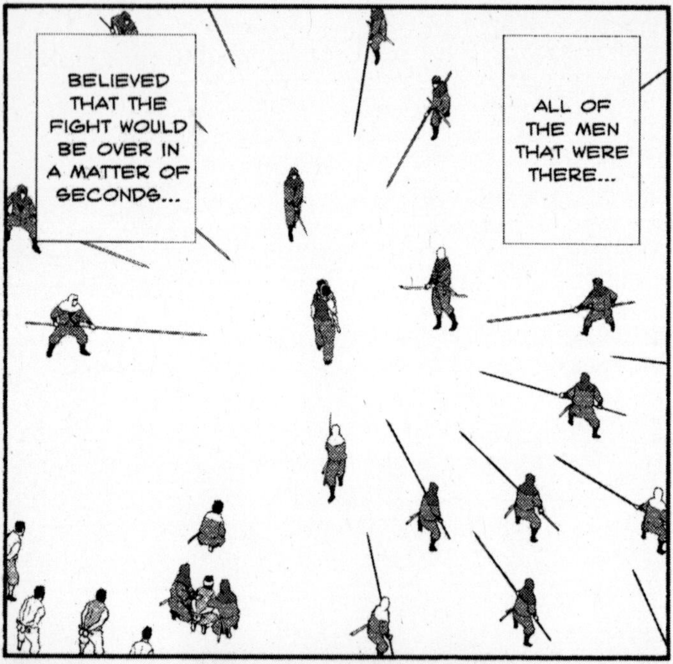
ALL OF THE MEN THAT WERE THERE...
BELIEVED THAT THE FIGHT WOULD BE OVER IN A MATTER OF SECONDS...

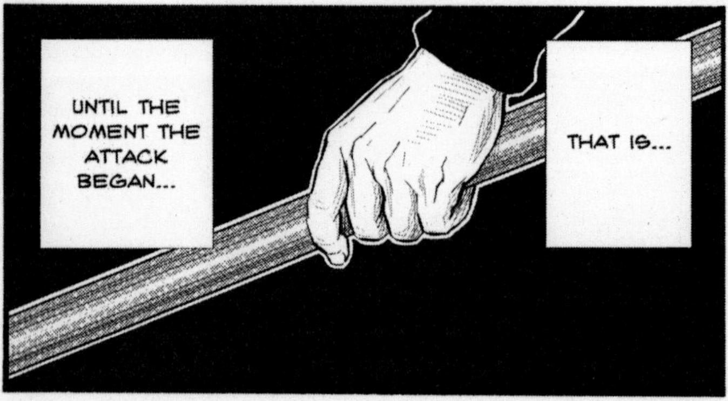
THAT IS...
UNTIL THE MOMENT THE ATTACK BEGAN...

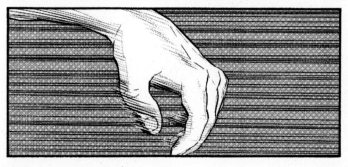

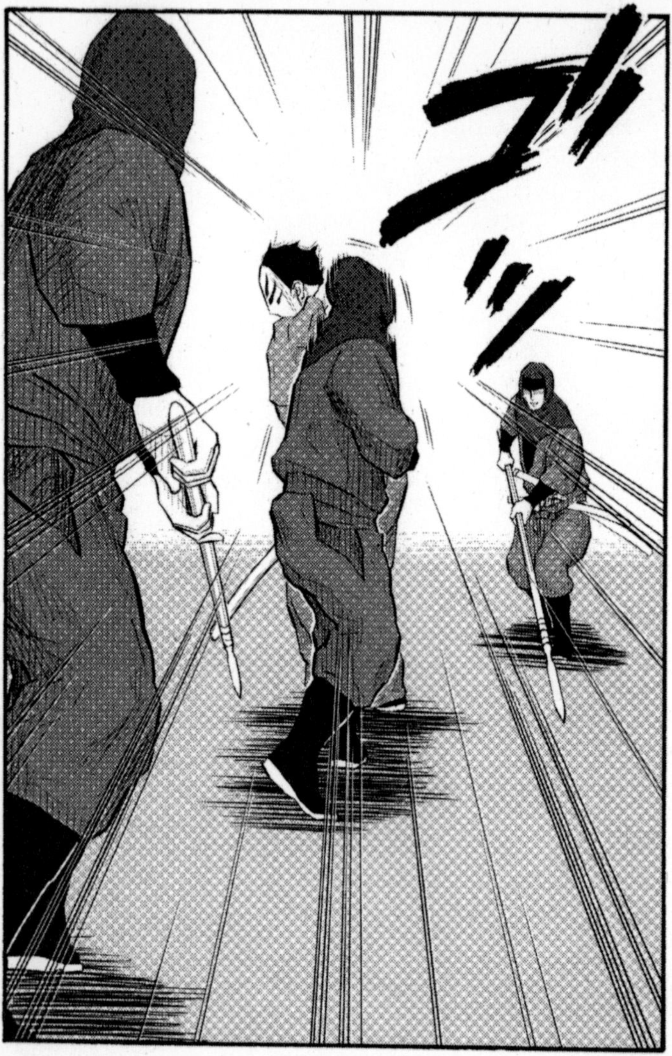
ブッ

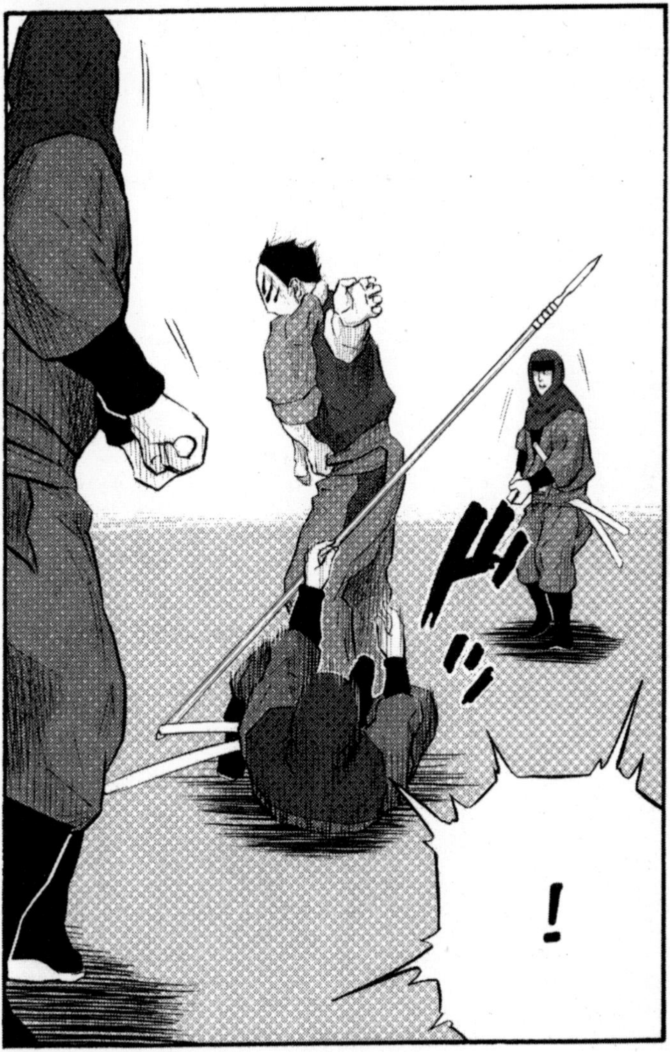
!

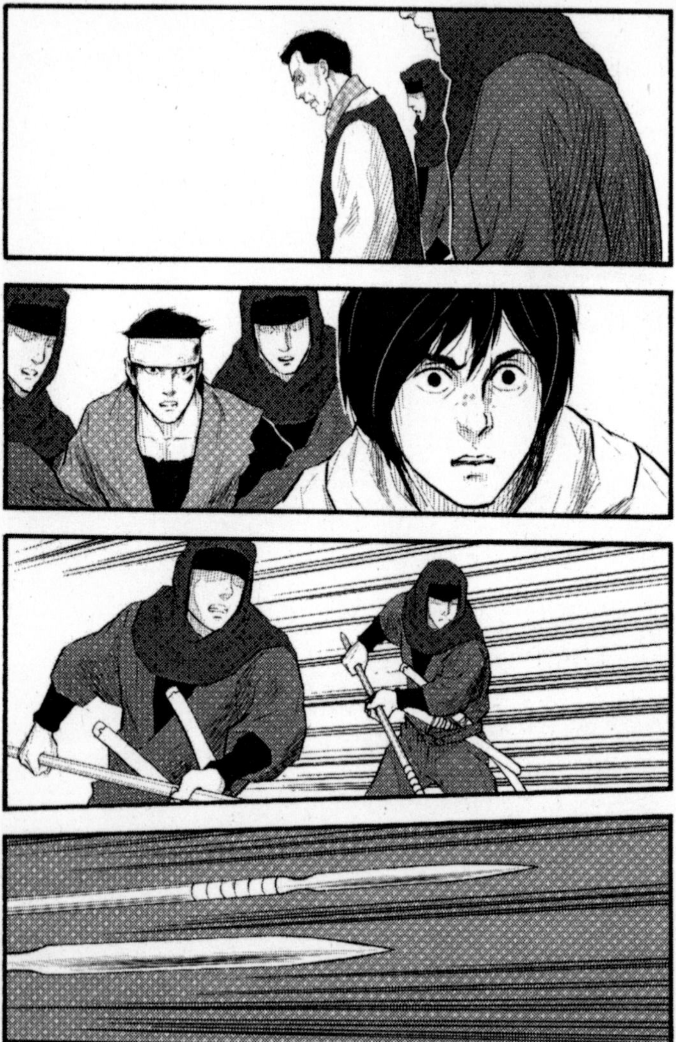

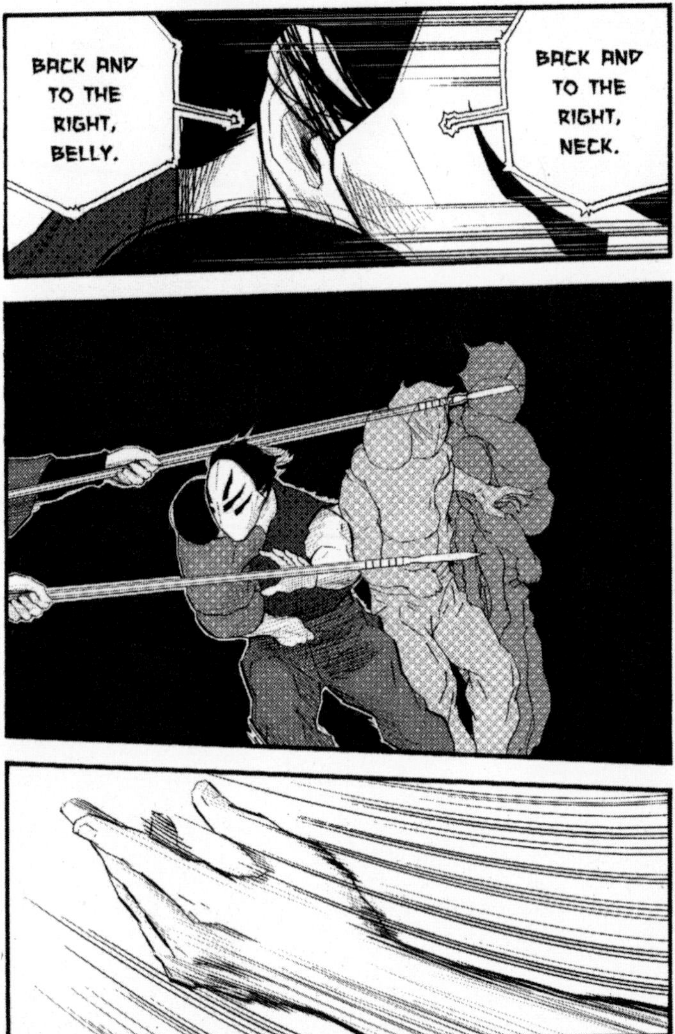
BACK AND TO THE RIGHT, NECK.
BACK AND TO THE RIGHT, BELLY.

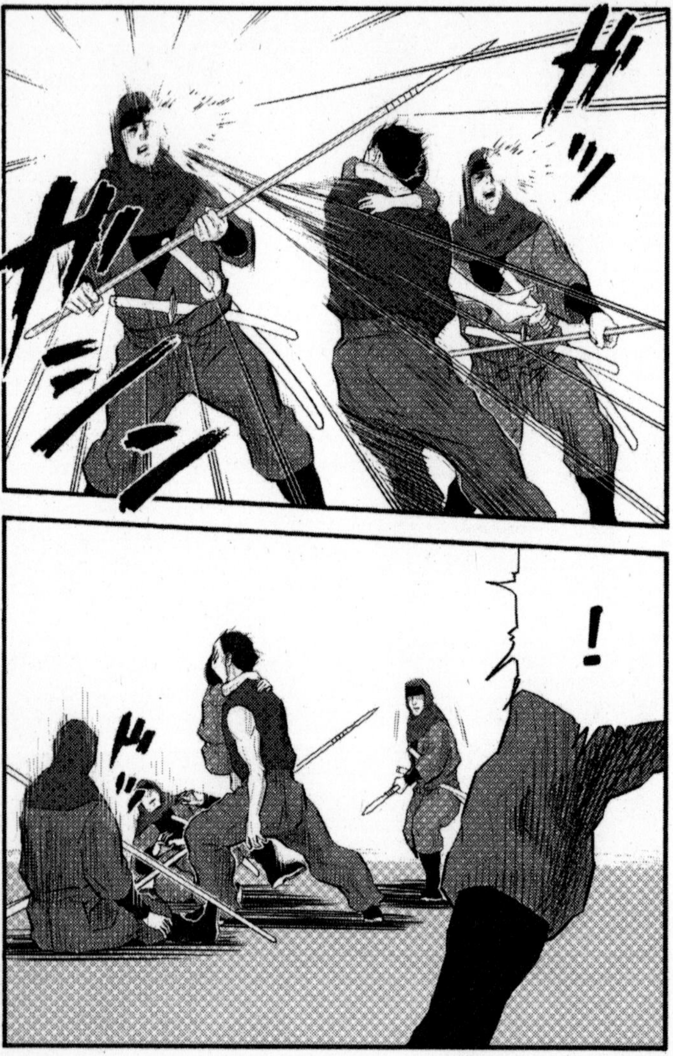
ザッ
!

BACK RIGHT, HEAD.

TO THE LEFT, BELLY SHOT.

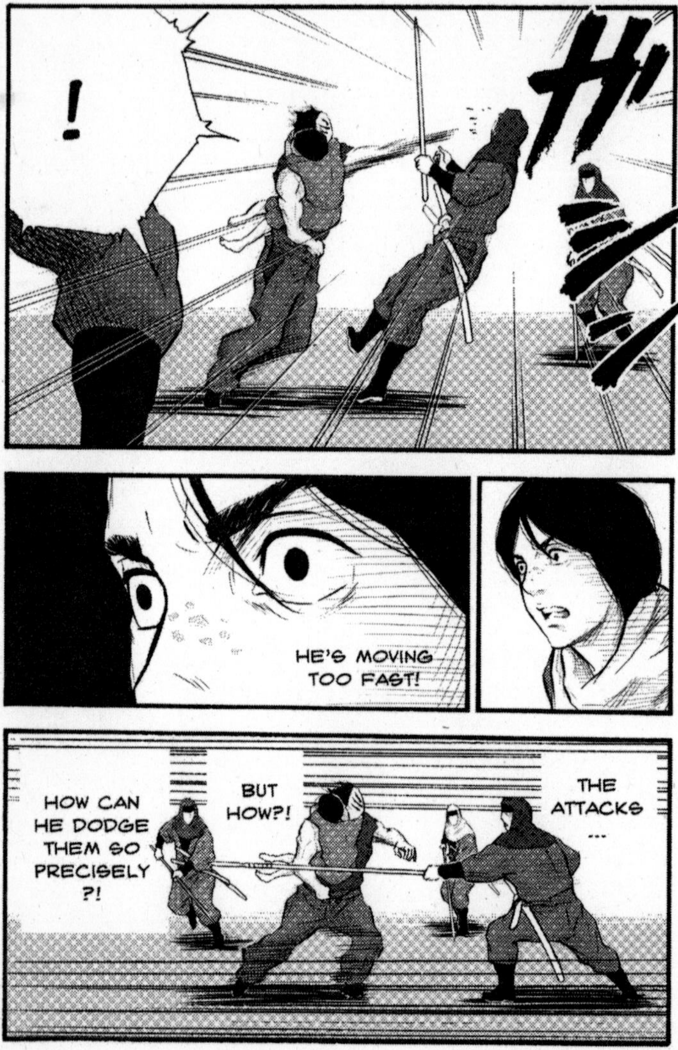
!
HE'S MOVING TOO FAST!
THE ATTACKS ...
BUT HOW?!
HOW CAN HE DODGE THEM SO PRECISELY ?!

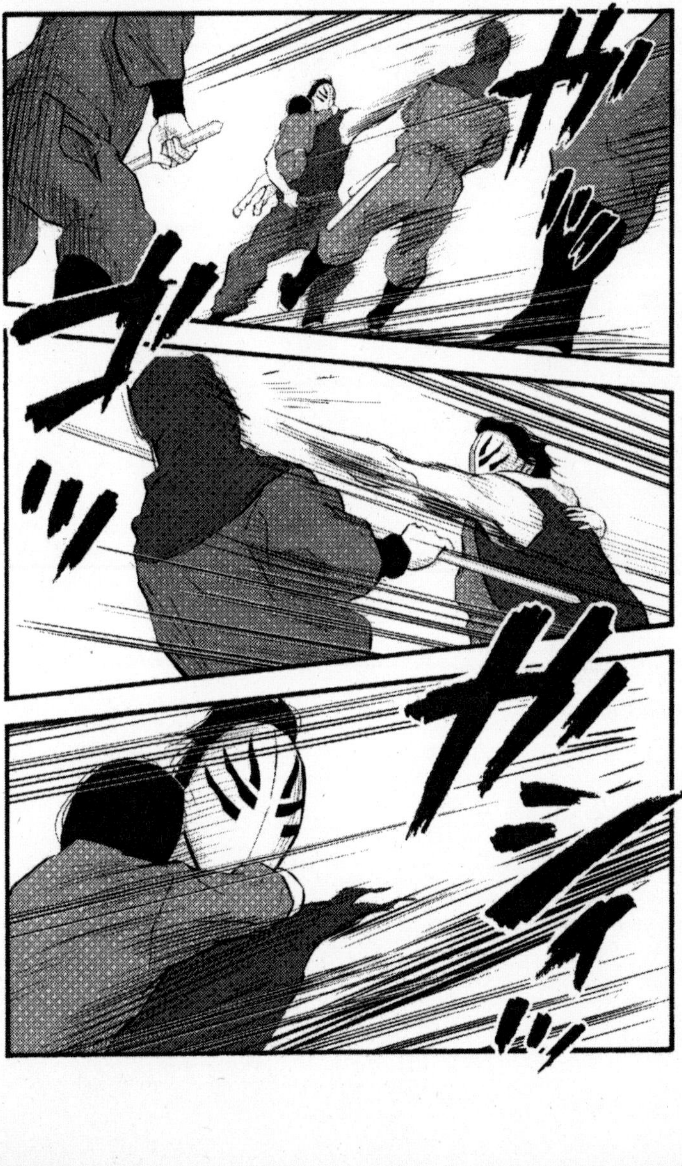
ザッ
ザッ
ザシィッ

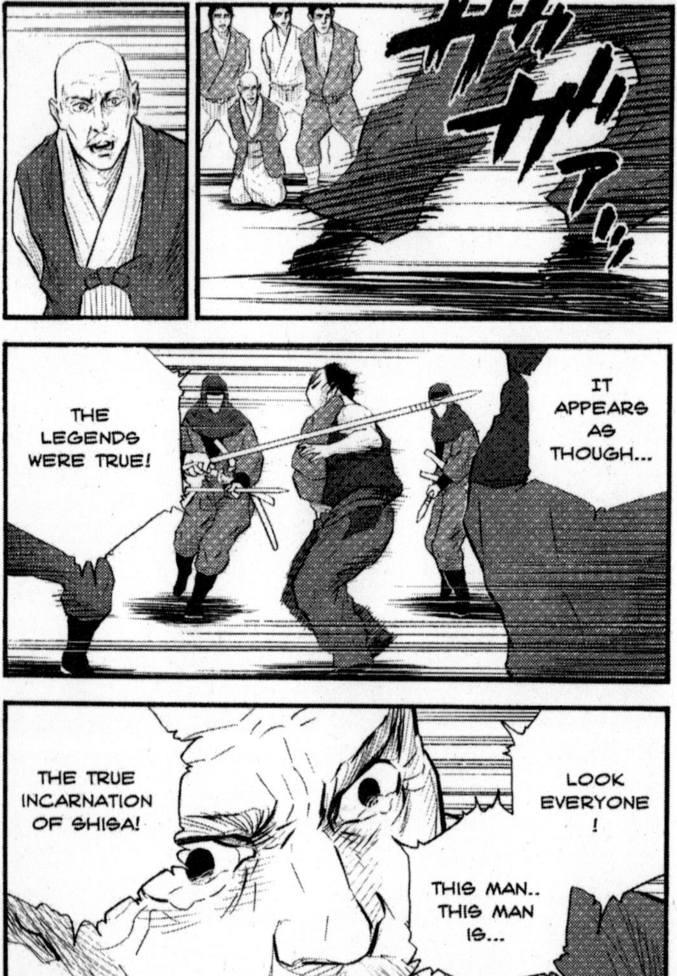
ザザァッ
IT APPEARS AS THOUGH...
THE LEGENDS WERE TRUE!
LOOK EVERYONE !
THIS MAN.. THIS MAN IS...
THE TRUE INCARNATION OF SHISA!

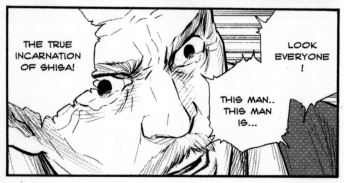

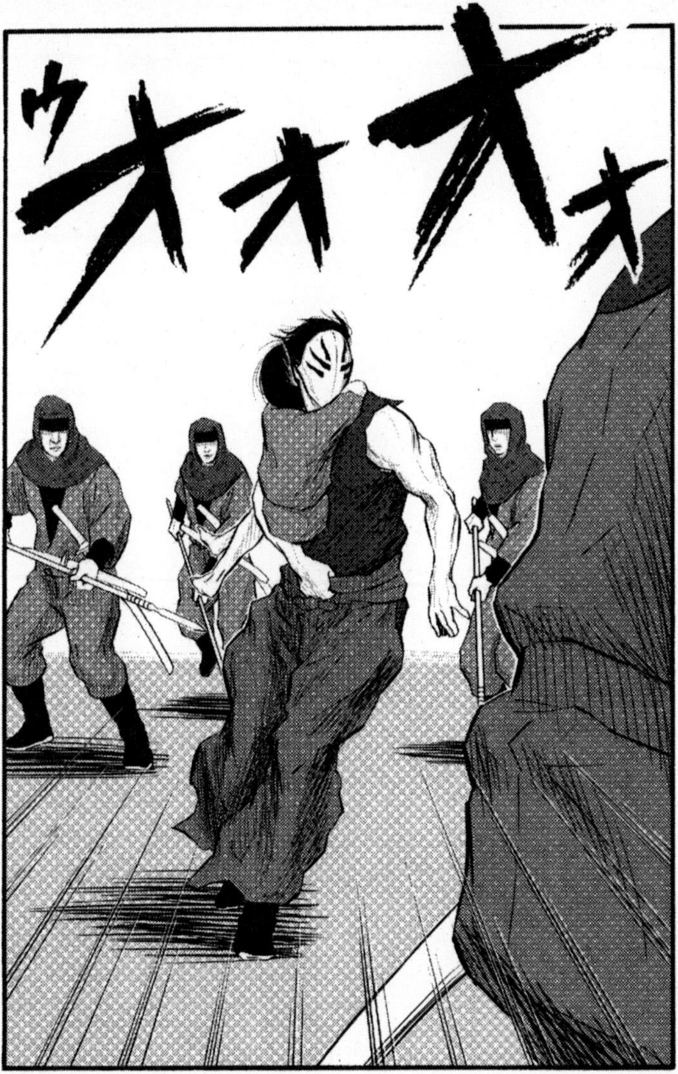
ウオオオォ

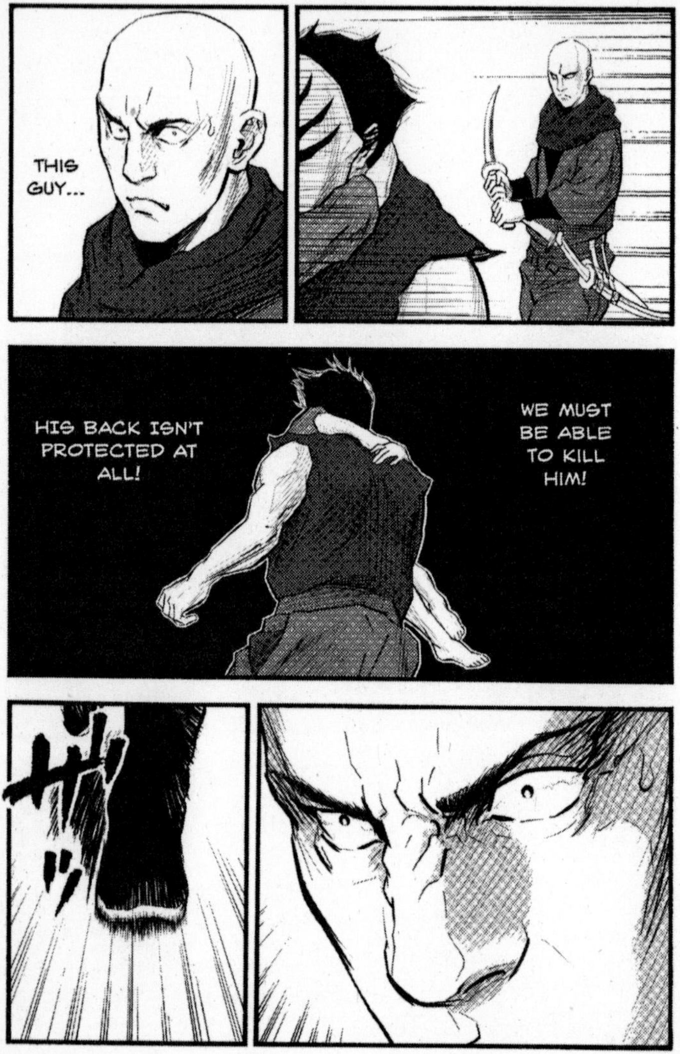
THIS GUY...
WE MUST BE ABLE TO KILL HIM!
HIS BACK ISN'T PROTECTED AT ALL!
ザッ

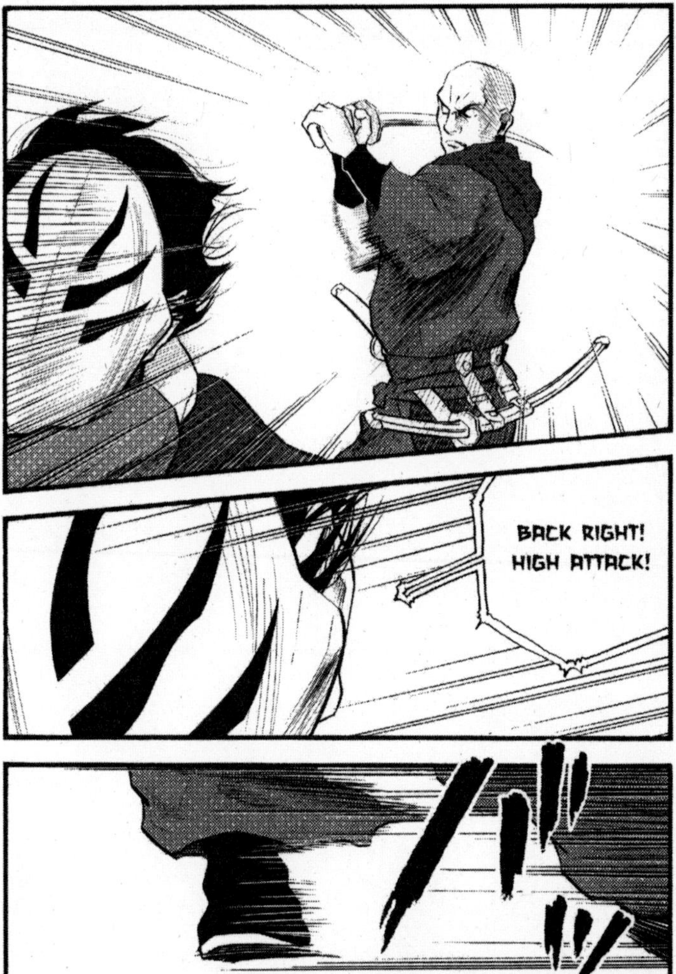
BACK RIGHT!
HIGH ATTACK!

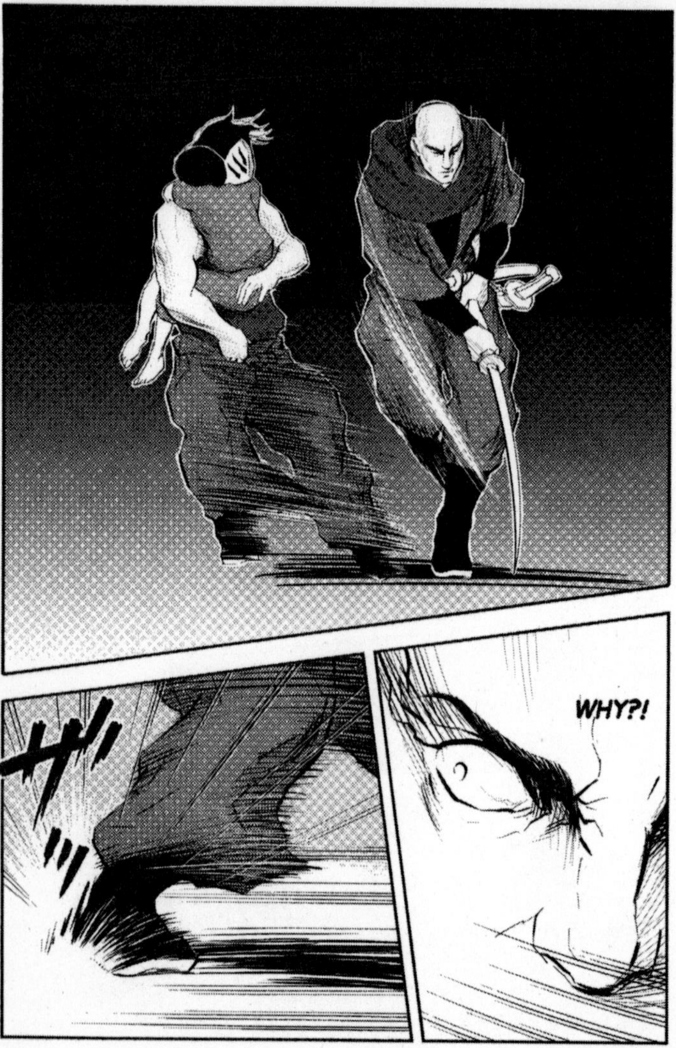
WHY?!

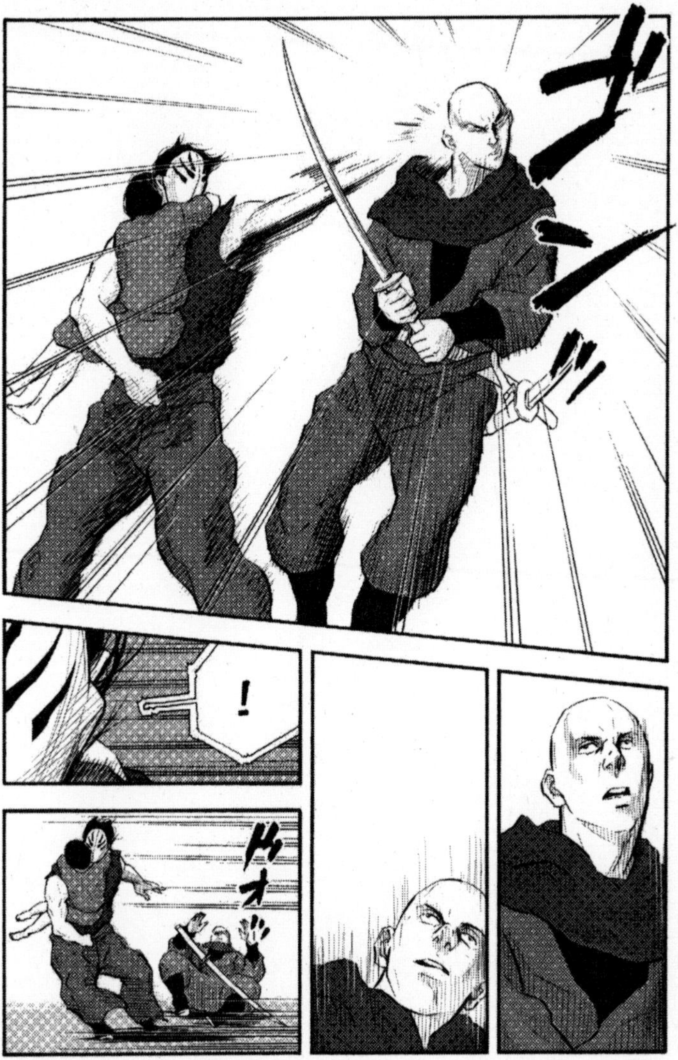
!

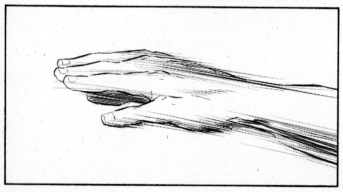

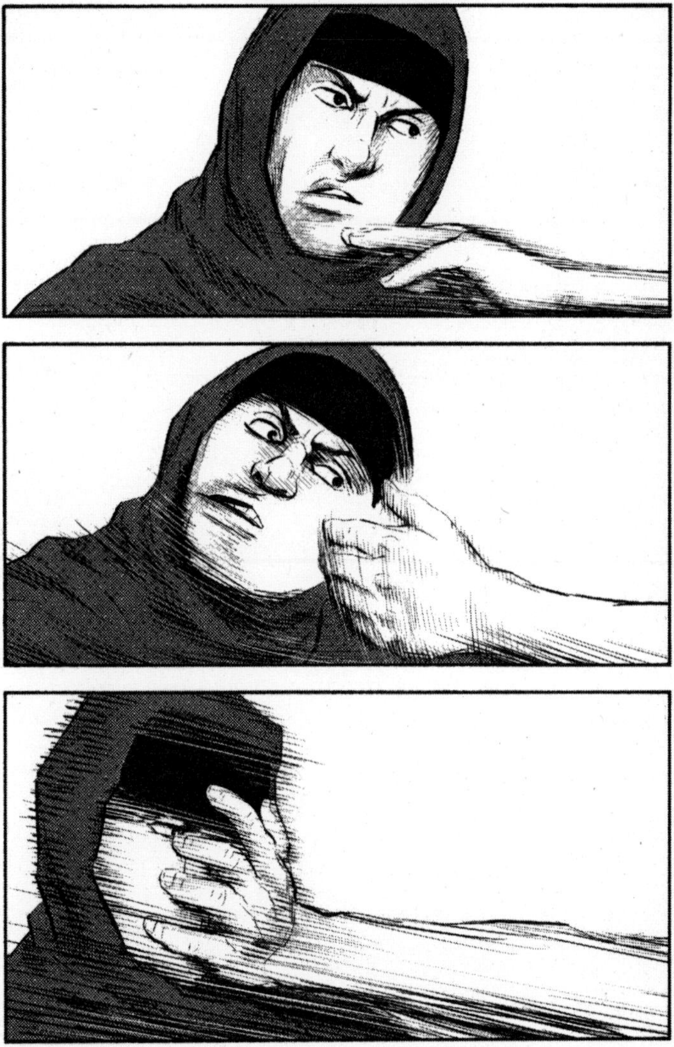

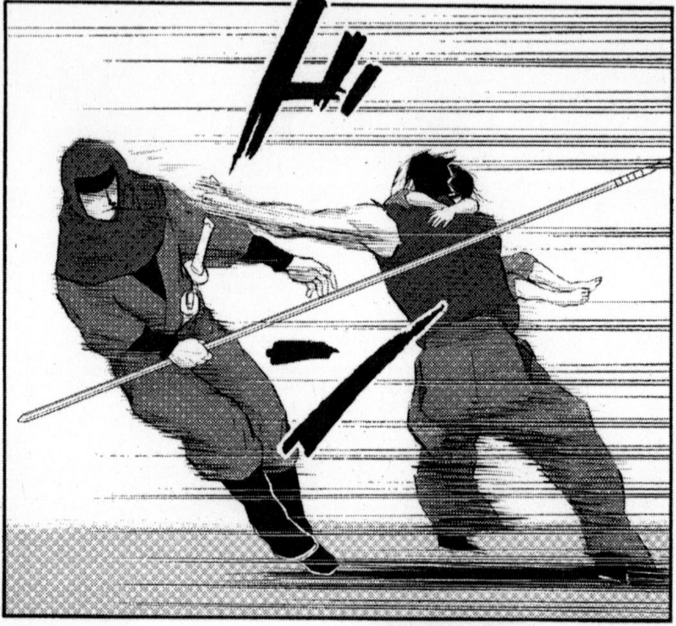
ドン

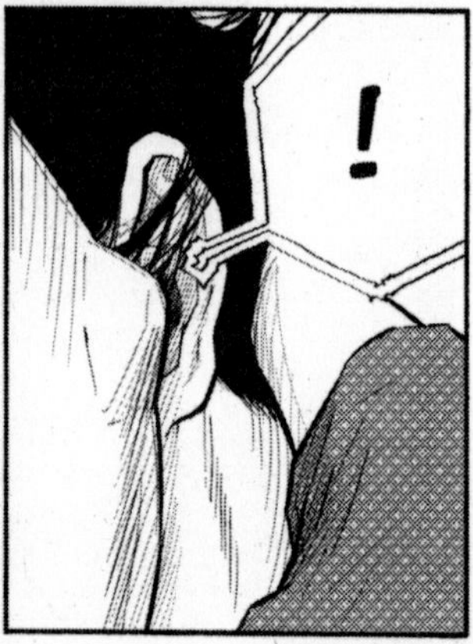
!

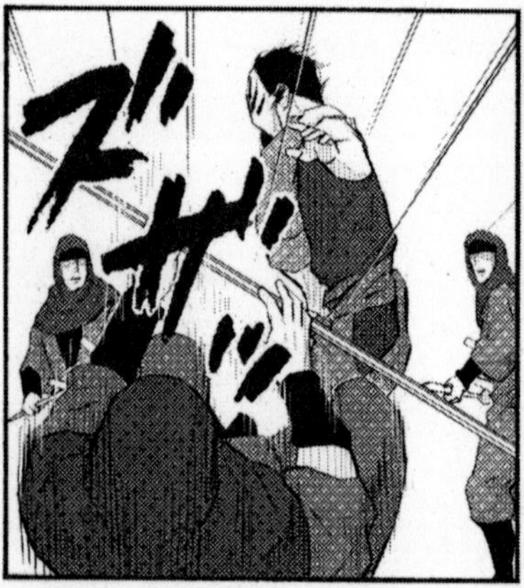
ズザッ

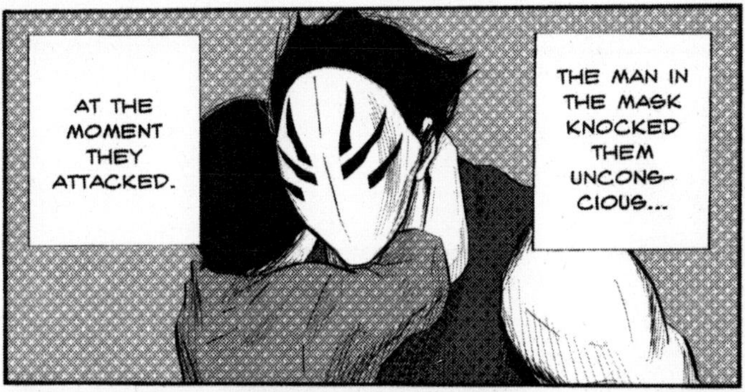
THE MAN IN THE MASK KNOCKED THEM UNCONSCIOUS...
AT THE MOMENT THEY ATTACKED.

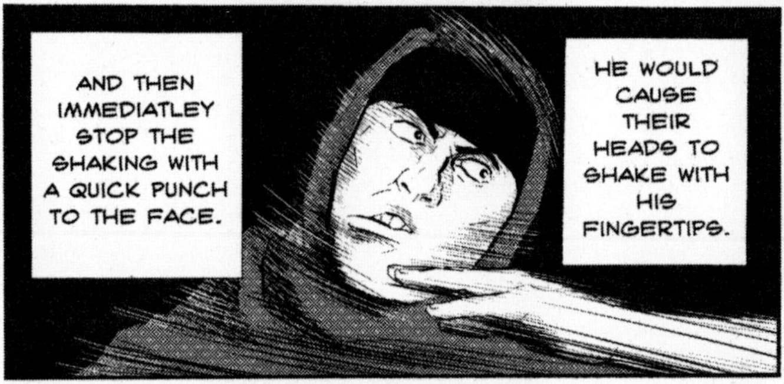
HE WOULD CAUSE THEIR HEADS TO SHAKE WITH HIS FINGERTIPS.
AND THEN IMMEDIATLEY STOP THE SHAKING WITH A QUICK PUNCH TO THE FACE.

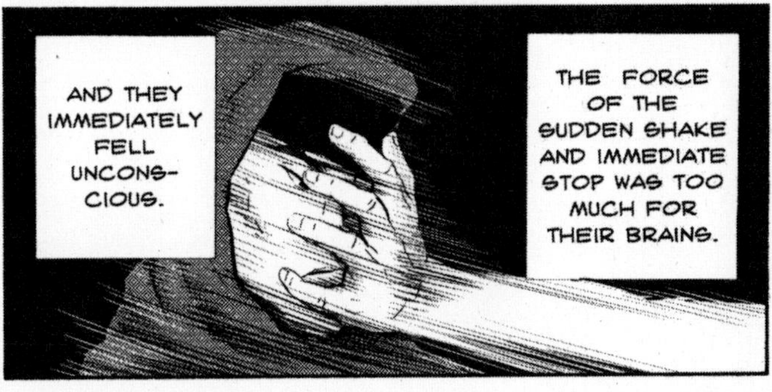
THE FORCE OF THE SUDDEN SHAKE AND IMMEDIATE STOP WAS TOO MUCH FOR THEIR BRAINS.
AND THEY IMMEDIATELY FELL UNCONSCIOUS.

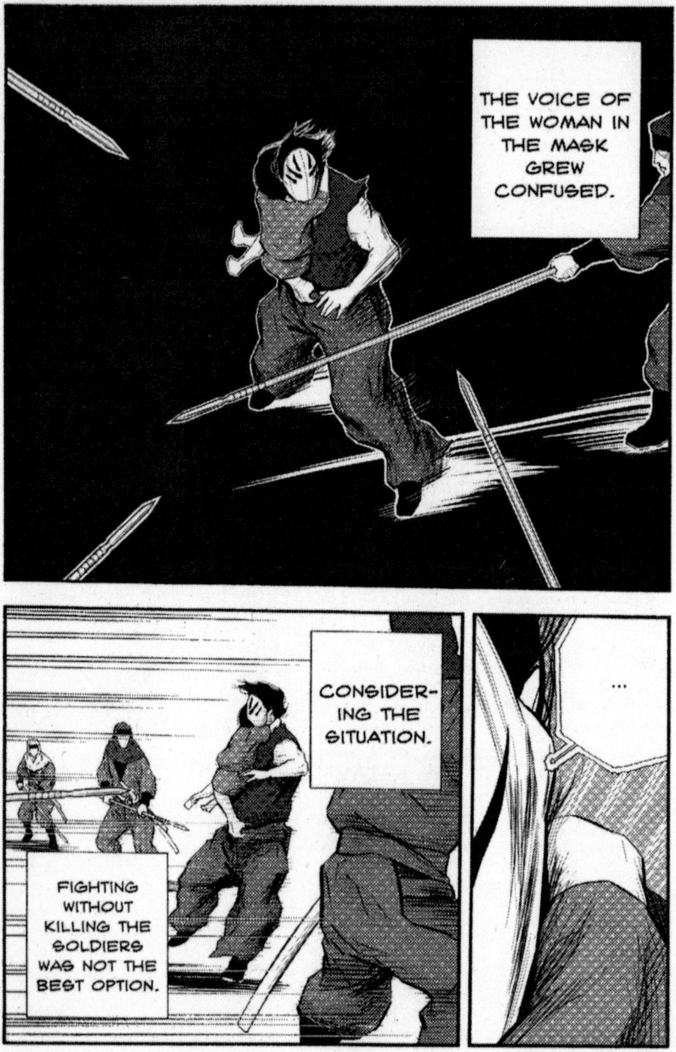
THE VOICE OF THE WOMAN IN THE MASK GREW CONFUSED.
...
CONSIDERING THE SITUATION.
FIGHTING WITHOUT KILLING THE SOLDIERS WAS NOT THE BEST OPTION.

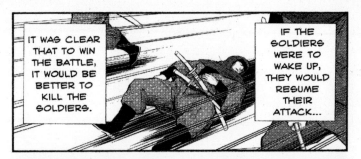

IF THE SOLDIERS WERE TO WAKE UP, THEY WOULD RESUME THEIR ATTACK...
IT WAS CLEAR THAT TO WIN THE BATTLE, IT WOULD BE BETTER TO KILL THE SOLDIERS.
WITH THE ABILITIES OF THE MASKED MAN...
HE COULD HAVE SHATTERED THE SKULLS OF THE SOLDIERS WITH HIS BARE HANDS.
SO WHY DIDN'T HE?

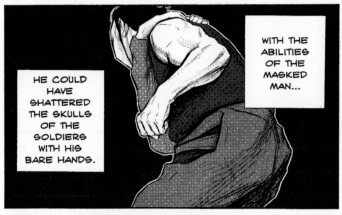

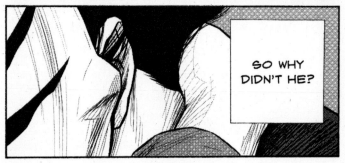

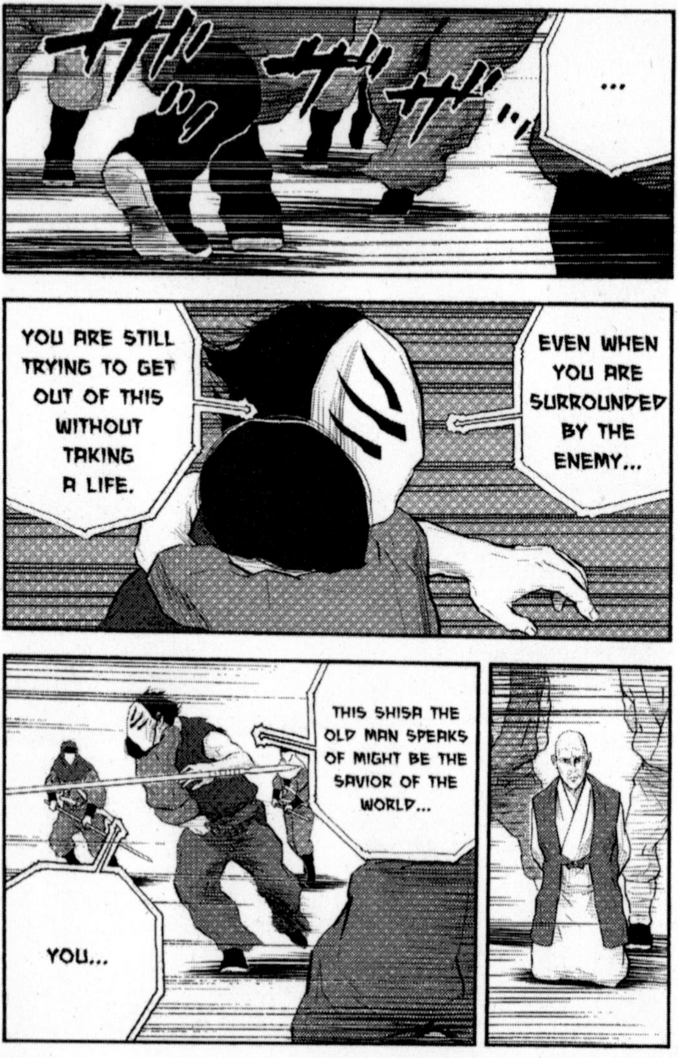
...
EVEN WHEN YOU ARE SURROUNDED BY THE ENEMY...
YOU ARE STILL TRYING TO GET OUT OF THIS WITHOUT TAKING A LIFE.
THIS SHISA THE OLD MAN SPEAKS OF MIGHT BE THE SAVIOR OF THE WORLD...
YOU...

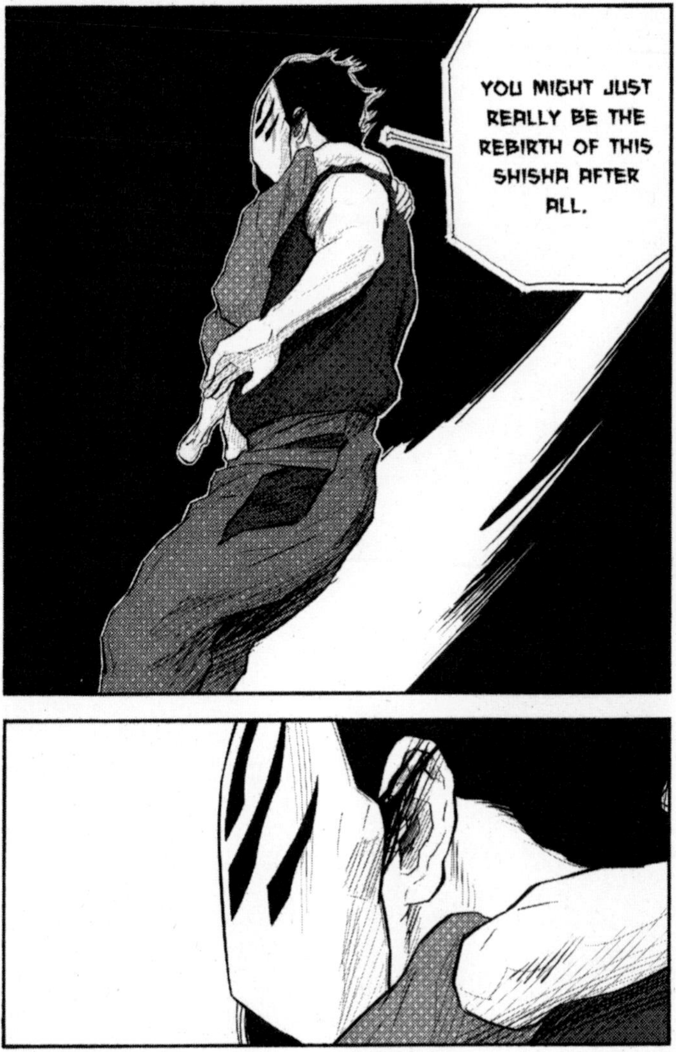
YOU MIGHT JUST REALLY BE THE REBIRTH OF THIS SHISHA AFTER ALL.

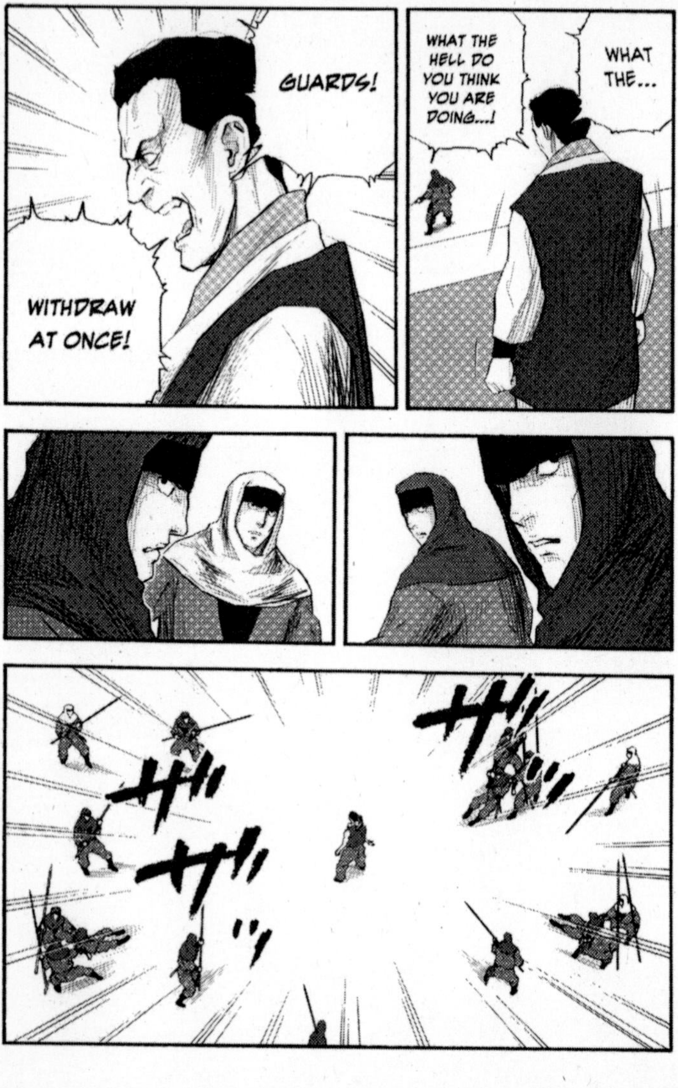
WHAT THE...
WHAT THE HELL DO YOU THINK YOU ARE DOING...!
GUARDS!
WITHDRAW AT ONCE!

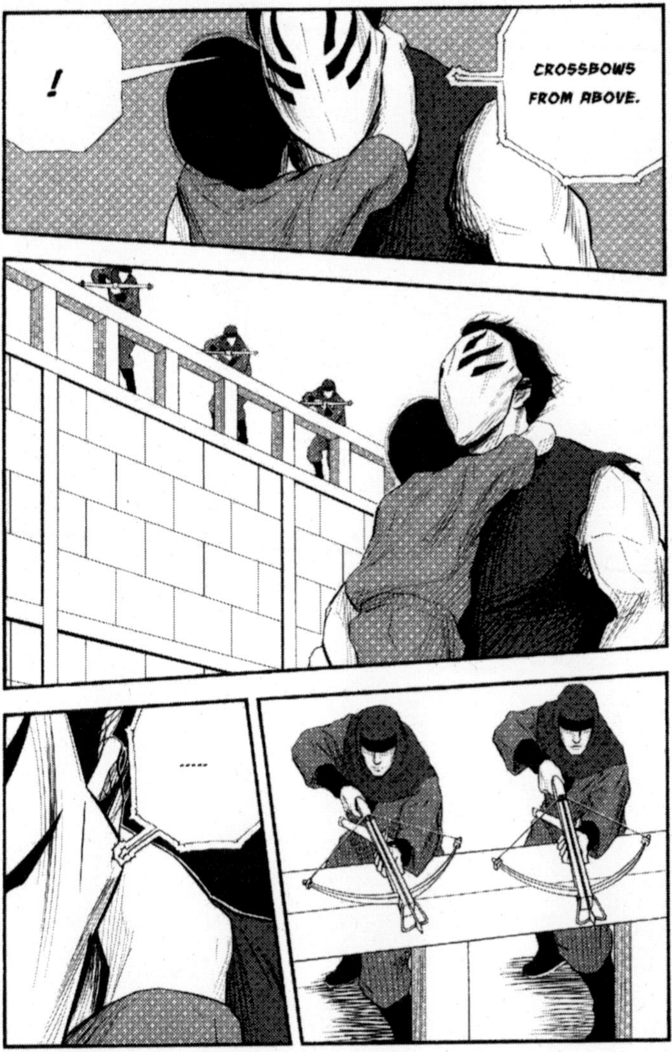
CROSSBOWS FROM ABOVE.
!
.....

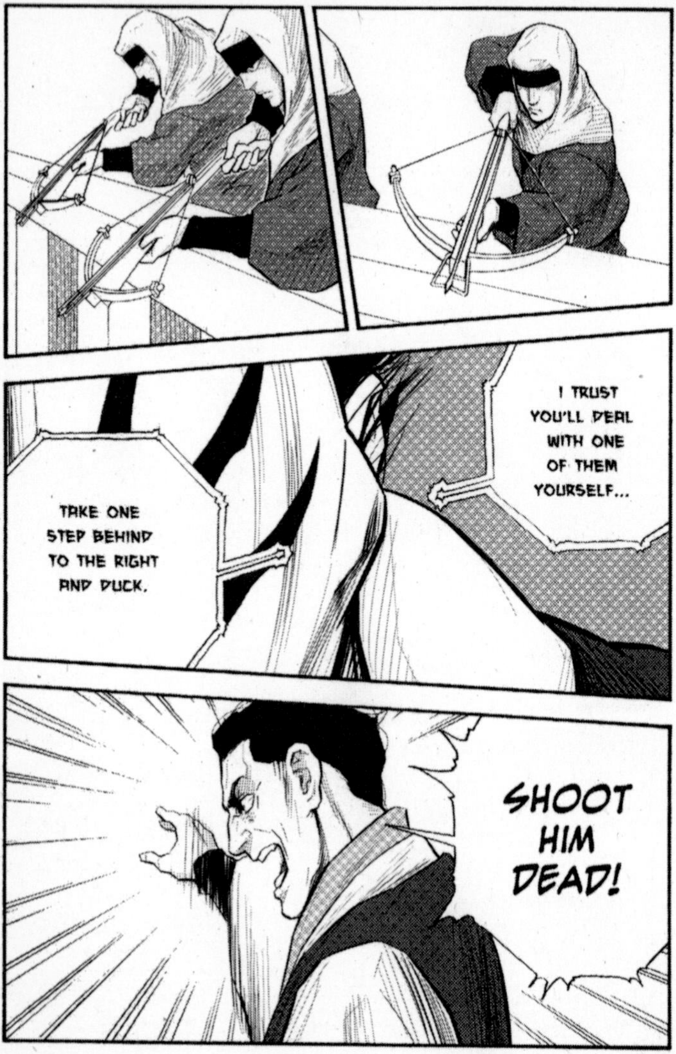
I TRUST YOU'LL DEAL WITH ONE OF THEM YOURSELF...
TAKE ONE STEP BEHIND TO THE RIGHT AND DUCK.
SHOOT HIM DEAD!

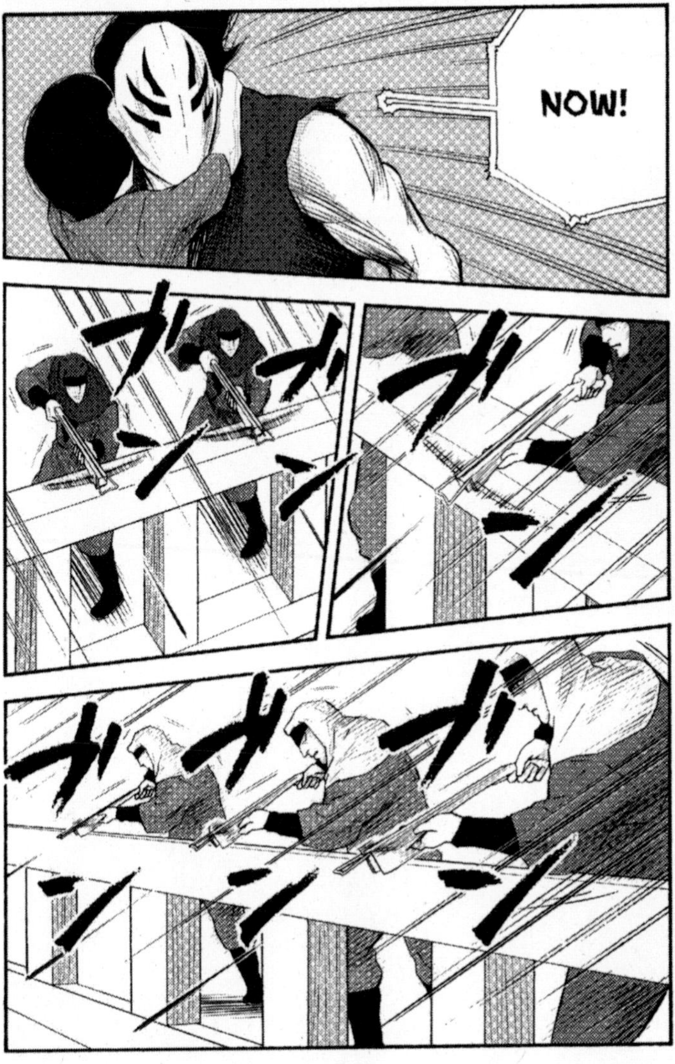
NOW!

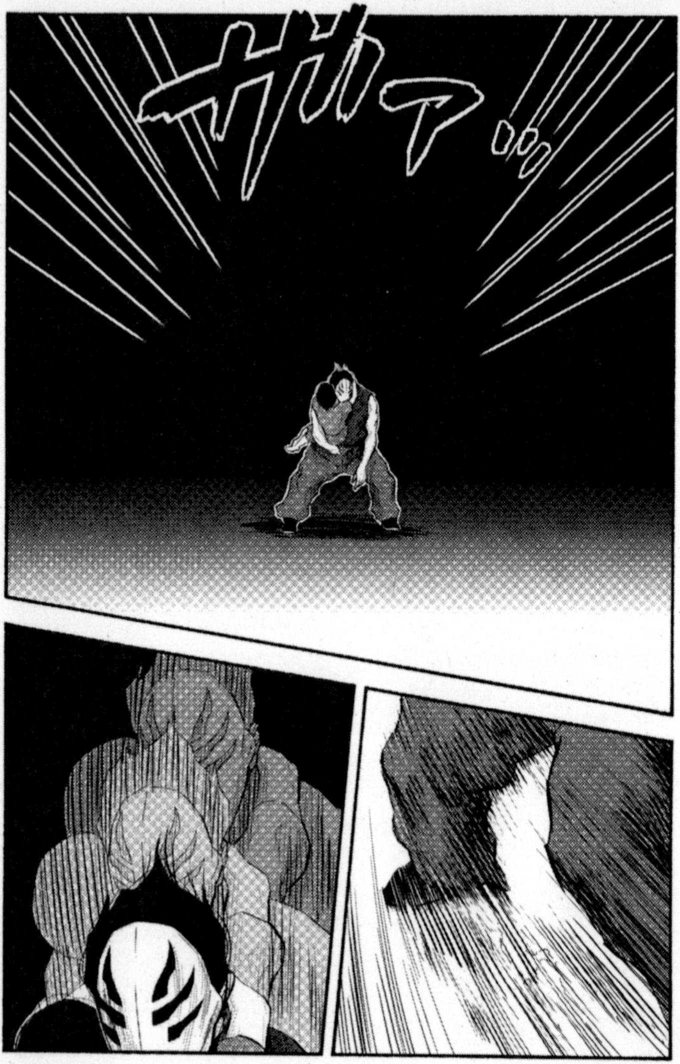
ガバァ...

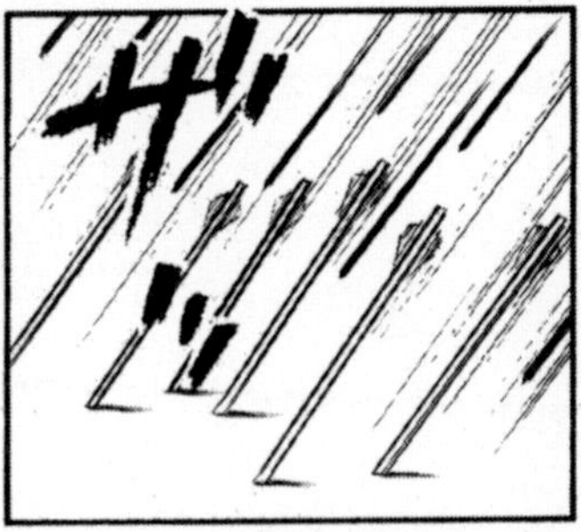
ザッ
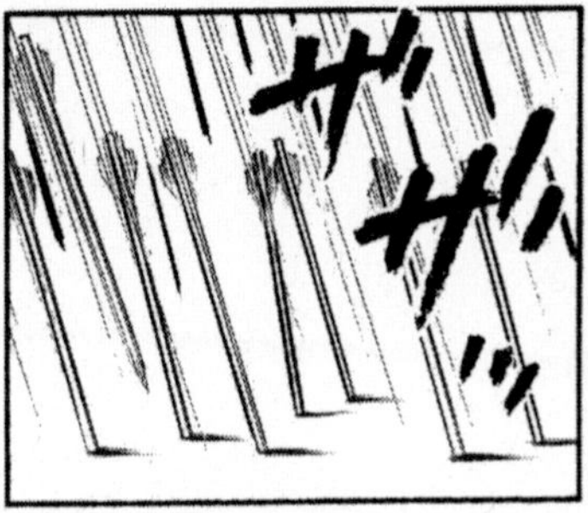
ザザッ
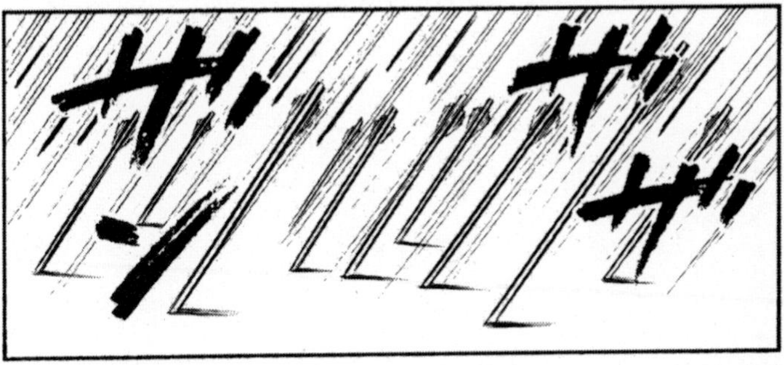
ザッ
ザザ
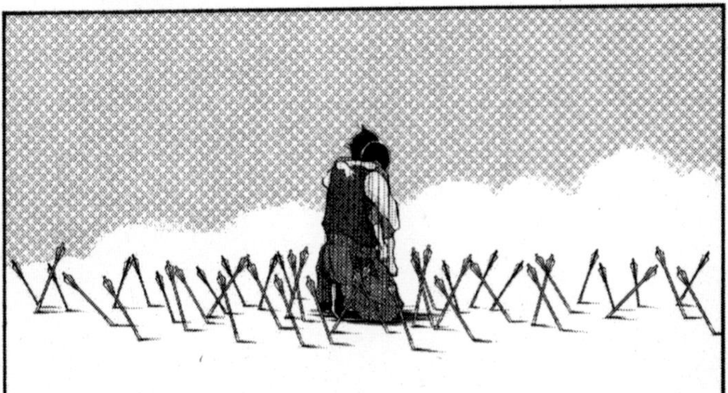

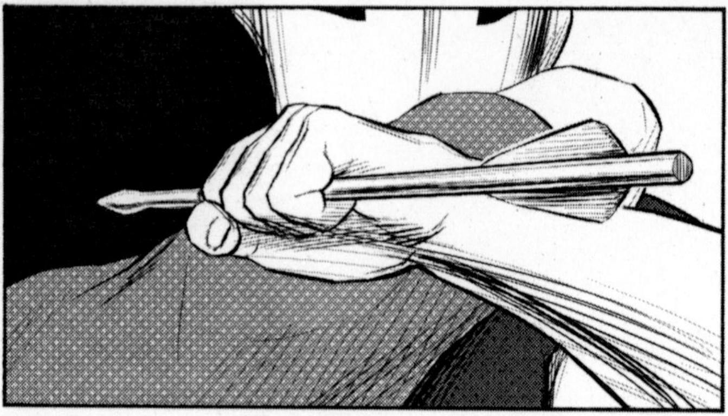
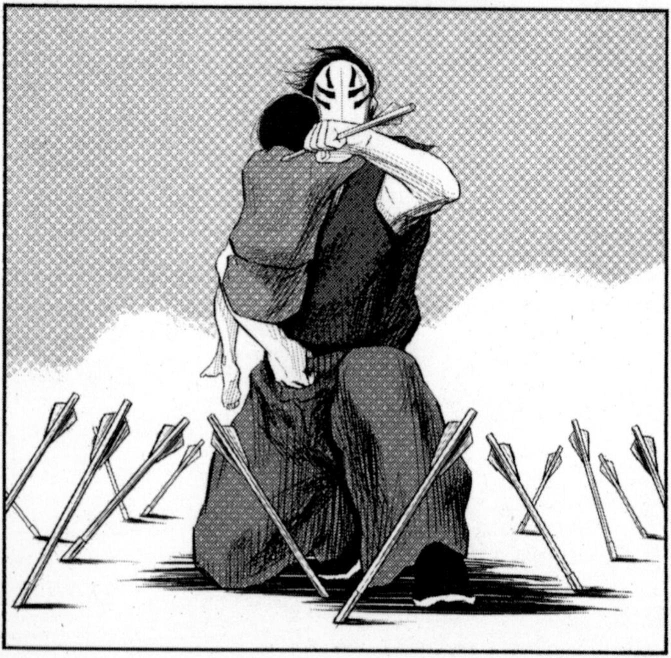

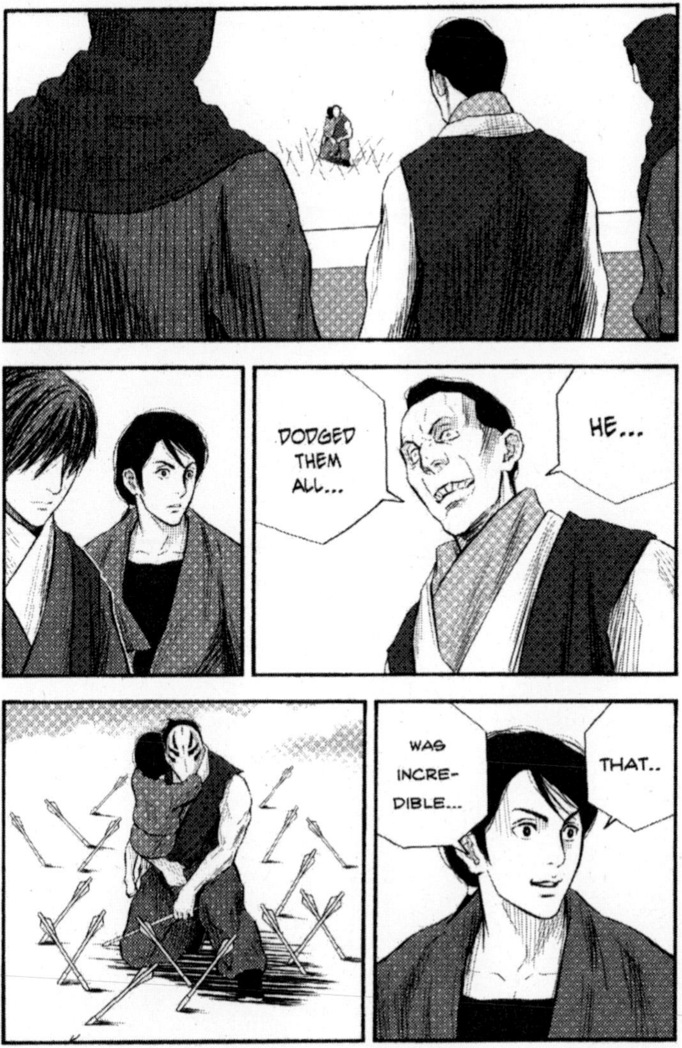
HE...
DODGED THEM ALL...
THAT..
WAS INCREDIBLE...

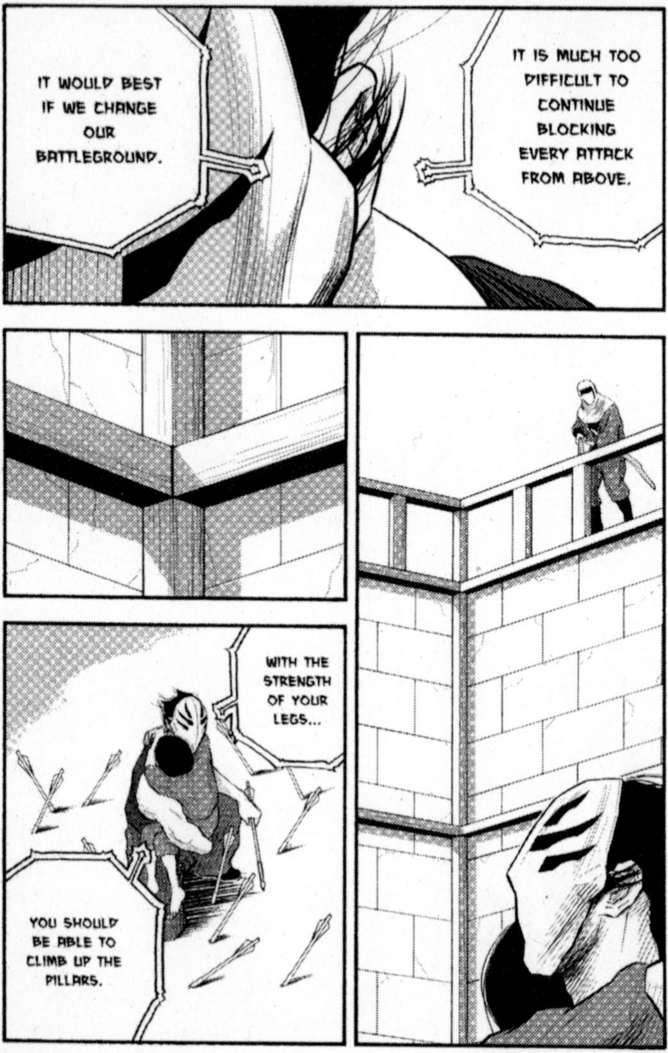
IT IS MUCH TOO DIFFICULT TO CONTINUE BLOCKING EVERY ATTACK FROM ABOVE.
IT WOULD BEST IF WE CHANGE OUR BATTLEGROUND.
WITH THE STRENGTH OF YOUR LEGS...
YOU SHOULD BE ABLE TO CLIMB UP THE PILLARS.

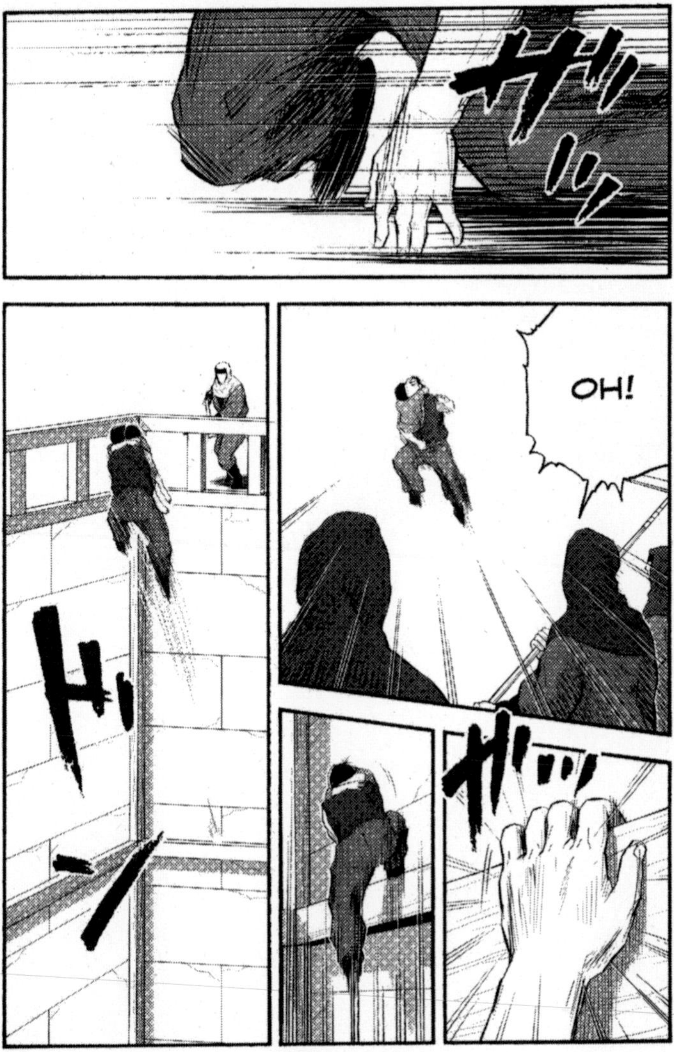
ザッ
OH!
ガッ
トッ

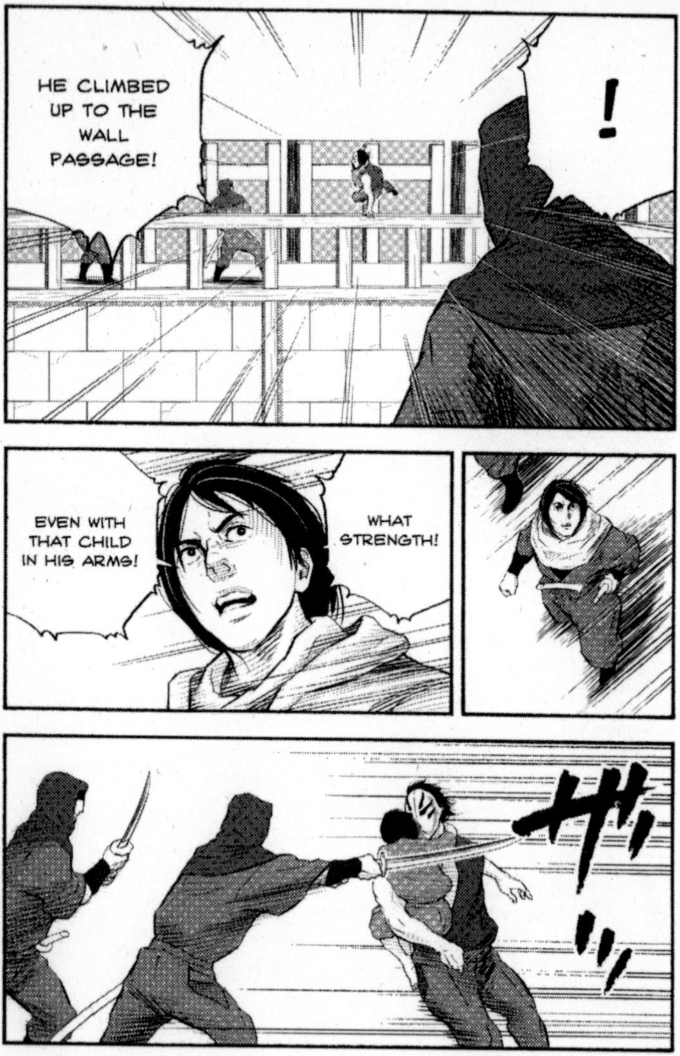
!
HE CLIMBED UP TO THE WALL PASSAGE!
WHAT STRENGTH!
EVEN WITH THAT CHILD IN HIS ARMS!
ザッ

HE'S HEADED THIS WAY!

HE'S...

AIM FOR THE TWO IN THE CHAIRS.

IF THEY LOSE THEIR HEADS THE OTHERS WILL SCATTER.

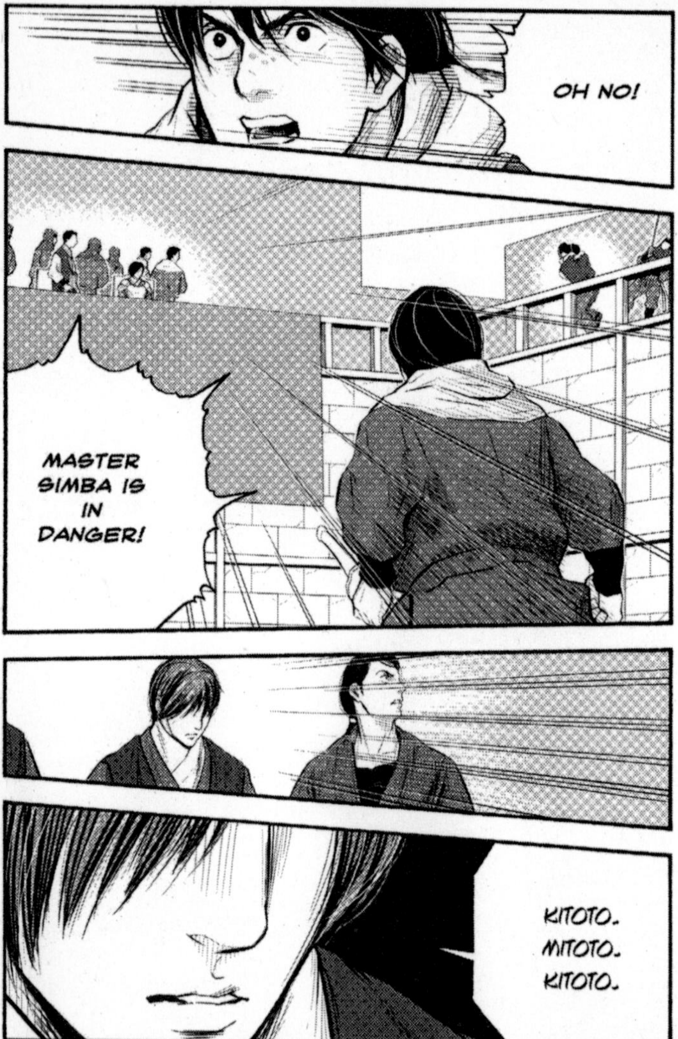
OH NO!
MASTER SIMBA IS IN DANGER!
KITOTO. MITOTO. KITOTO.

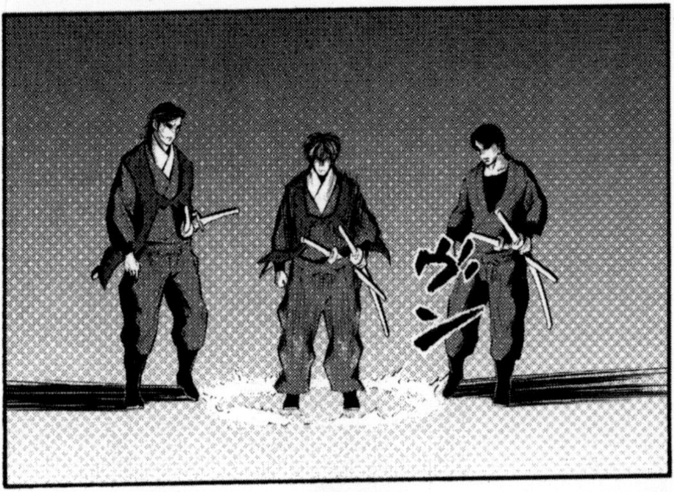
ヴン
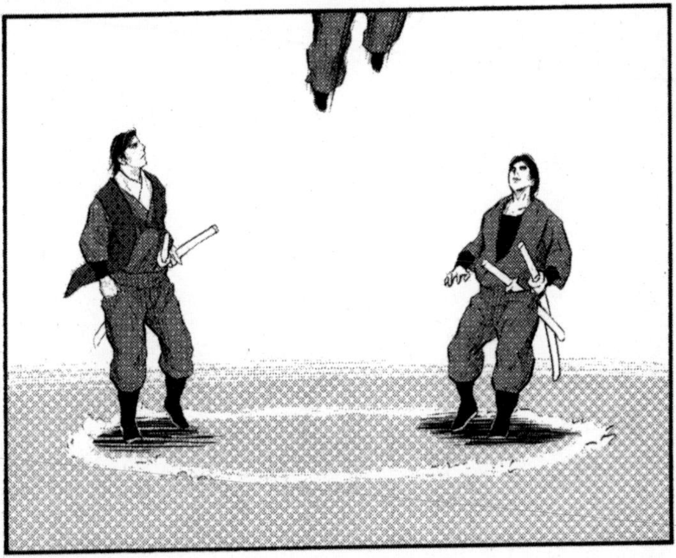

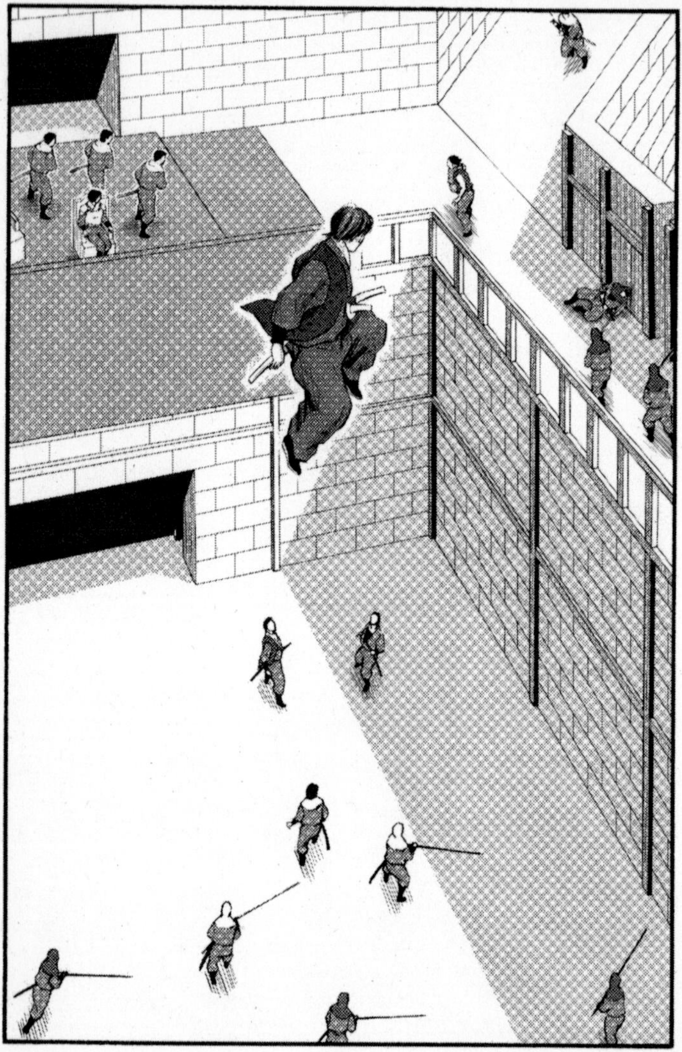

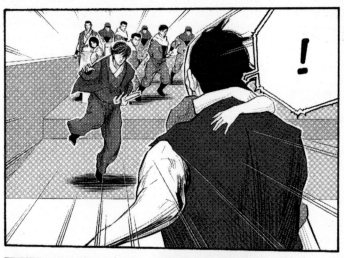

!
HE FLEW THROUGH THE AIR.
THE AURA THAT SURROUNDS THIS MAN IS UNLIKE THOSE OF OTHER HUMAN BEINGS.

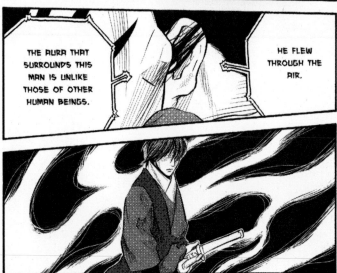

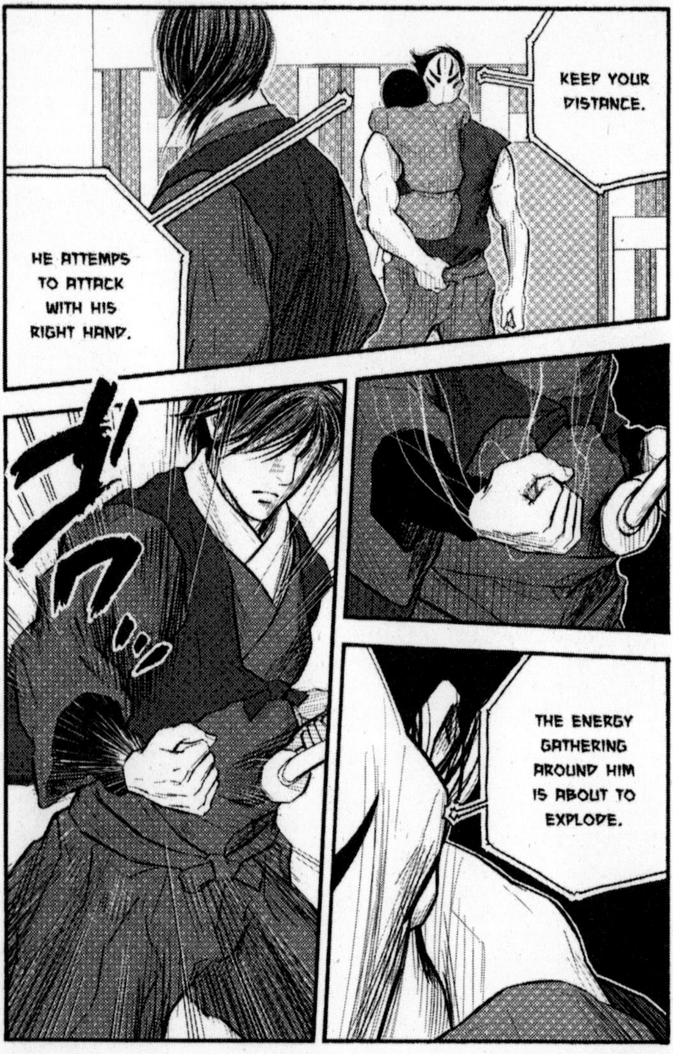
KEEP YOUR DISTANCE.
HE ATTEMPS TO ATTACK WITH HIS RIGHT HAND.
THE ENERGY GATHERING AROUND HIM IS ABOUT TO EXPLODE.

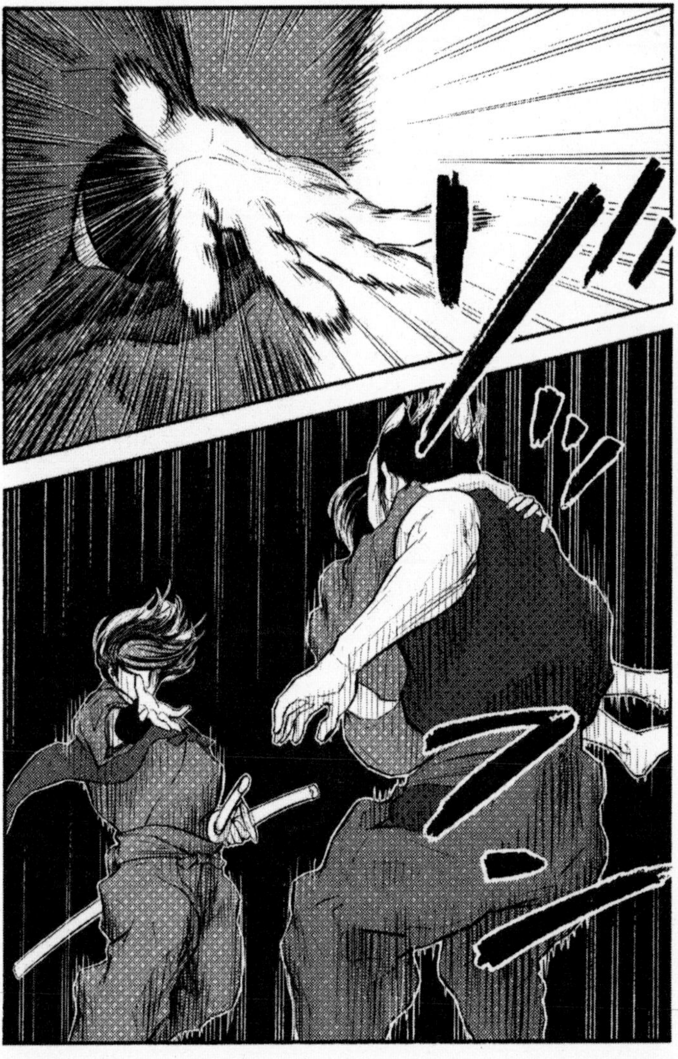

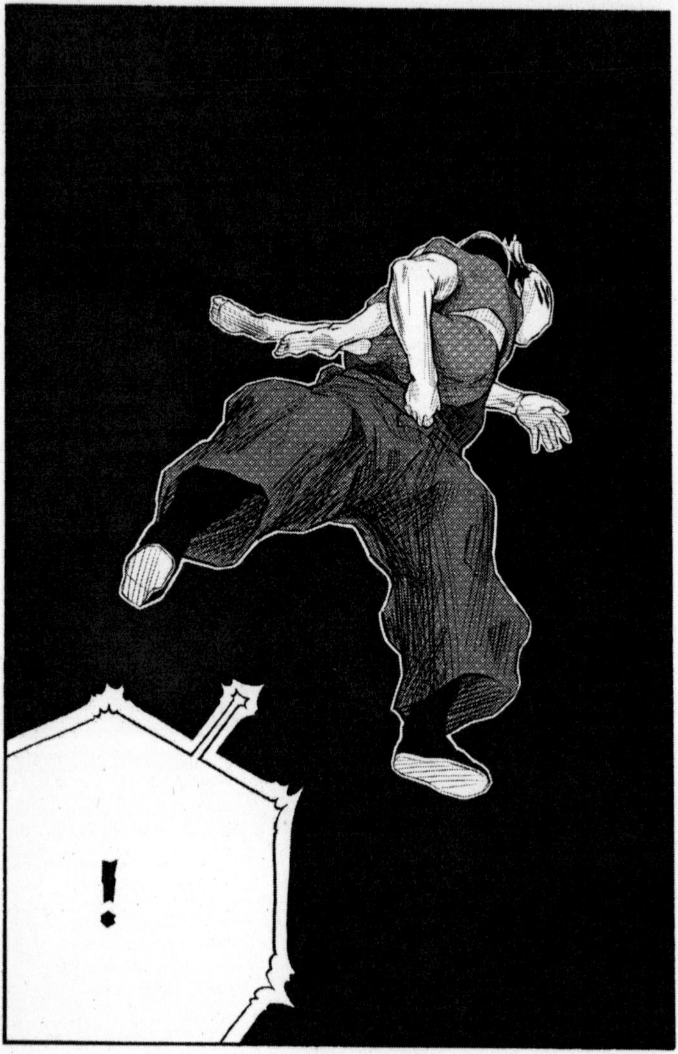
!

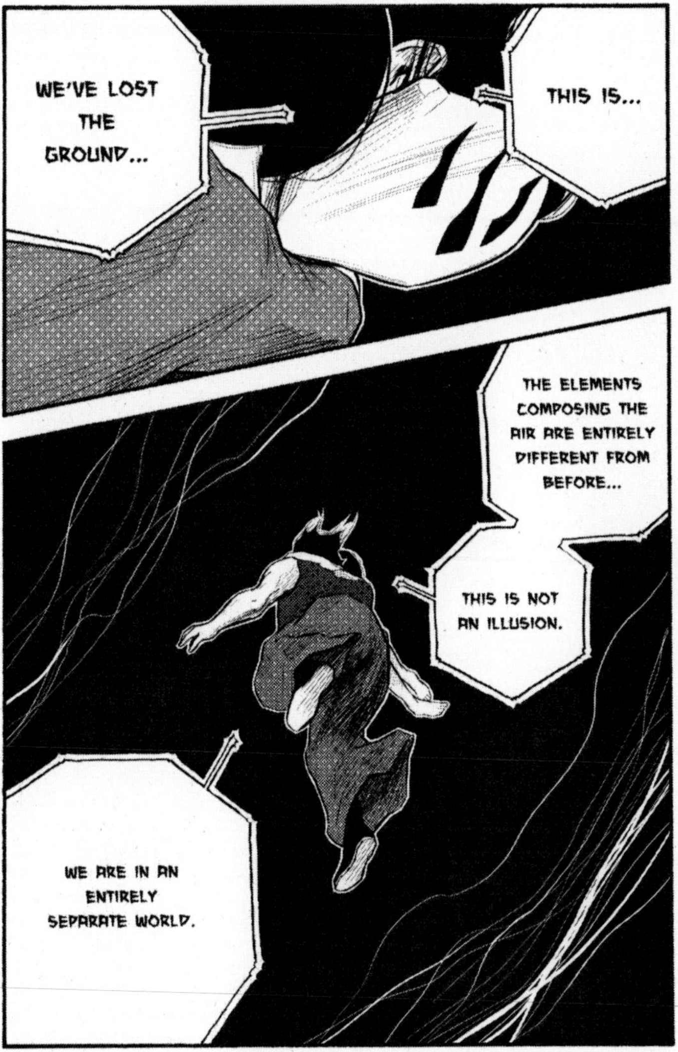
THIS IS...
WE'VE LOST THE GROUND...
THE ELEMENTS COMPOSING THE AIR ARE ENTIRELY DIFFERENT FROM BEFORE...
THIS IS NOT AN ILLUSION.
WE ARE IN AN ENTIRELY SEPARATE WORLD.

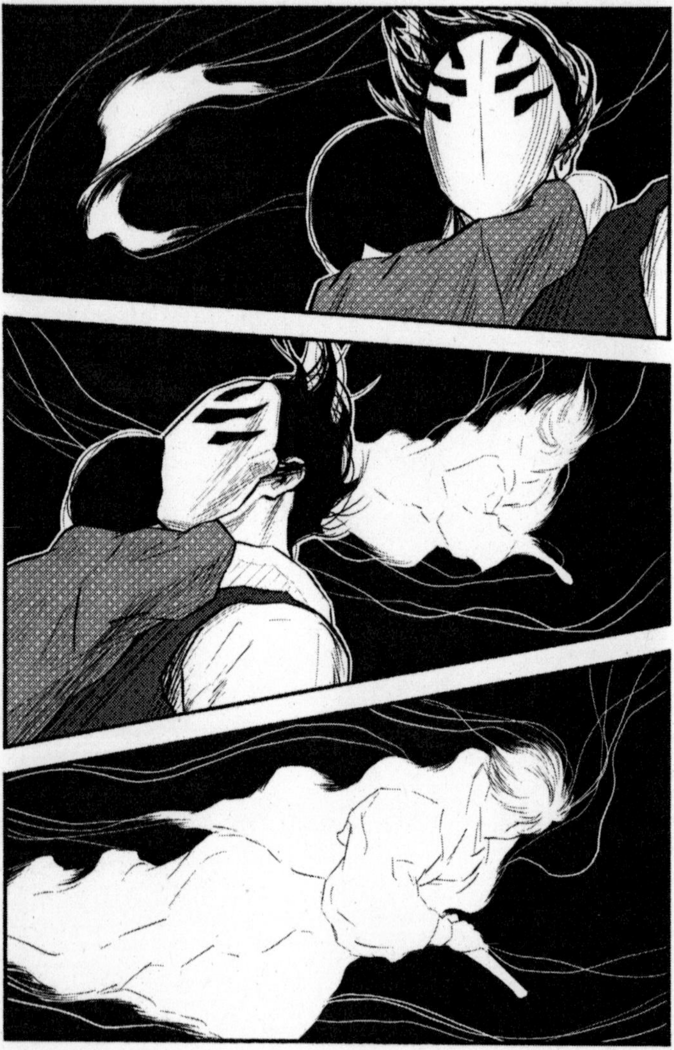

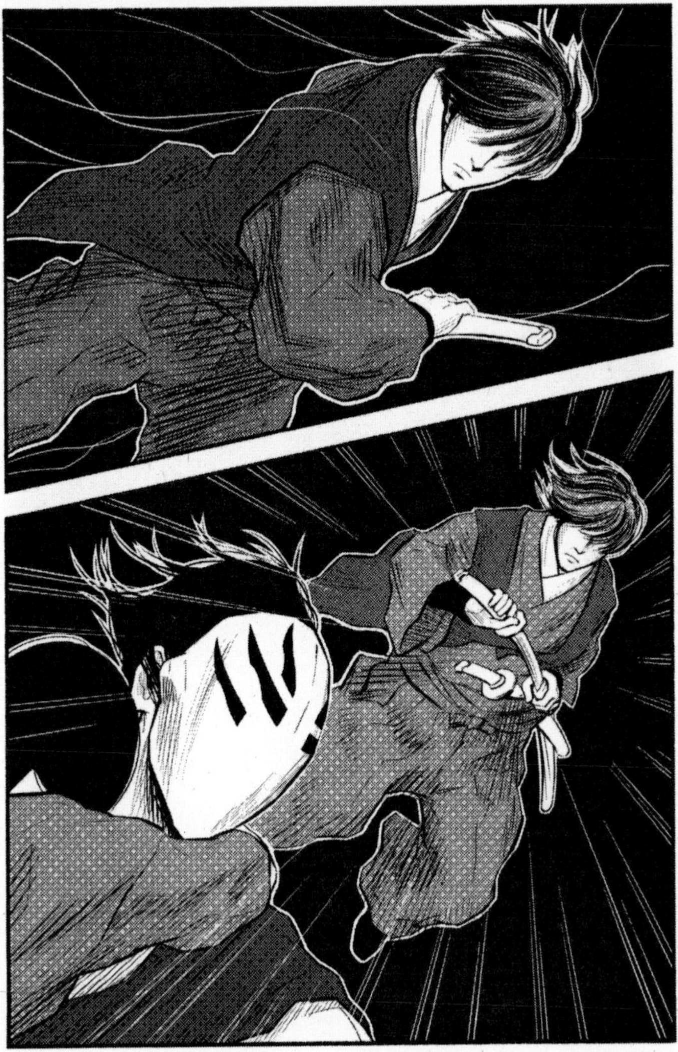

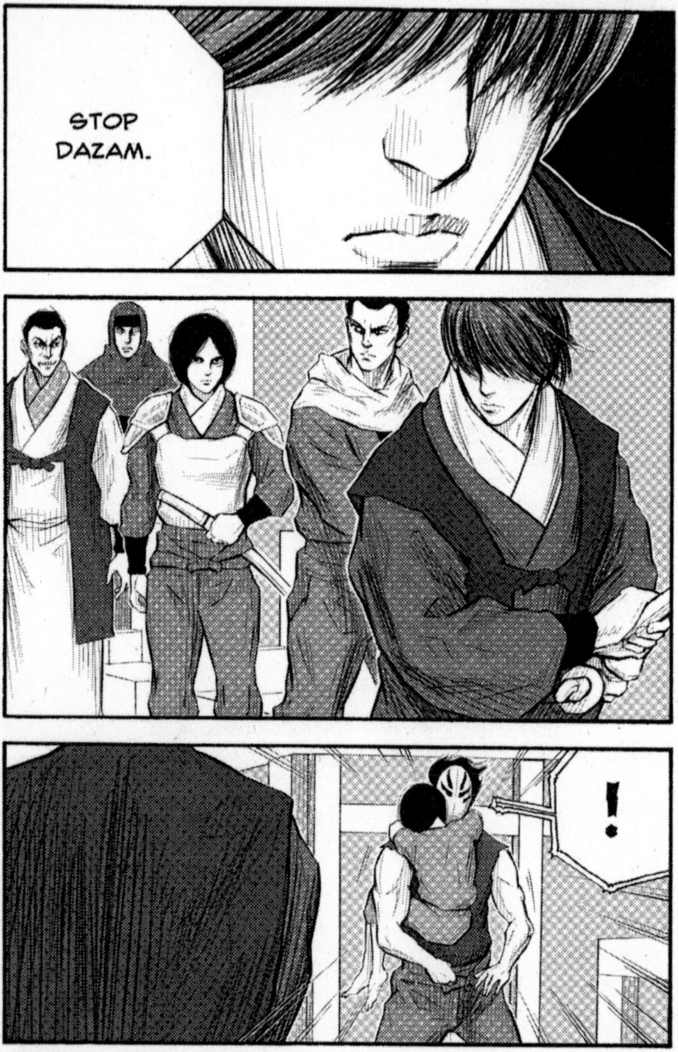
STOP
DAZAM.
!

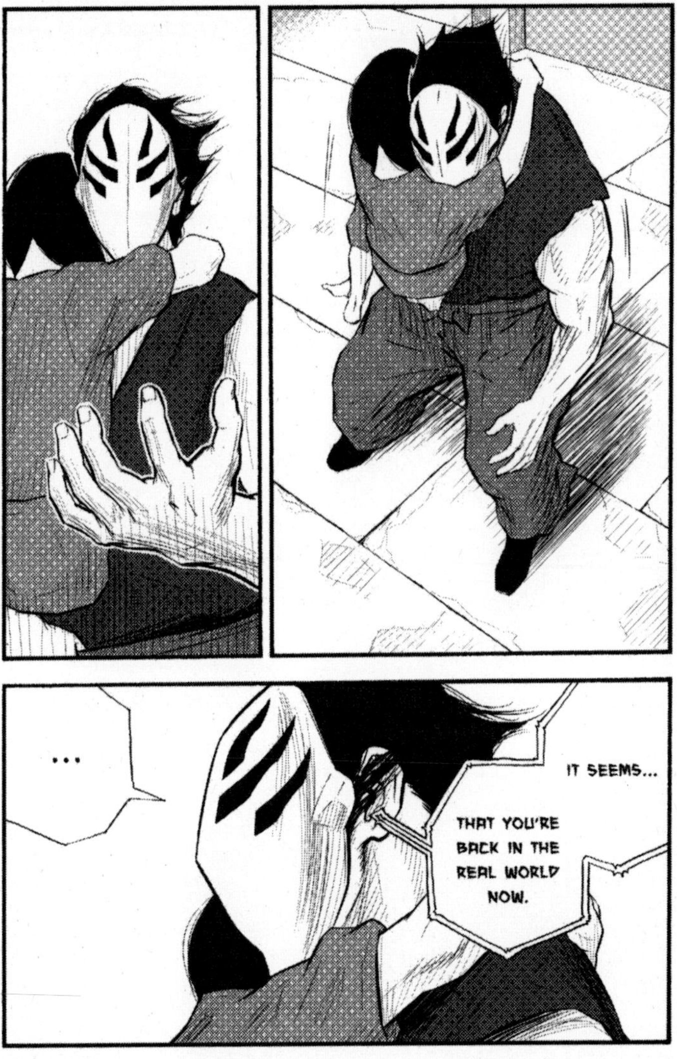
IT SEEMS...
THAT YOU'RE BACK IN THE REAL WORLD NOW.
...

WHAT DO YOU WANT, MASKED MAN?

FREEDOM?

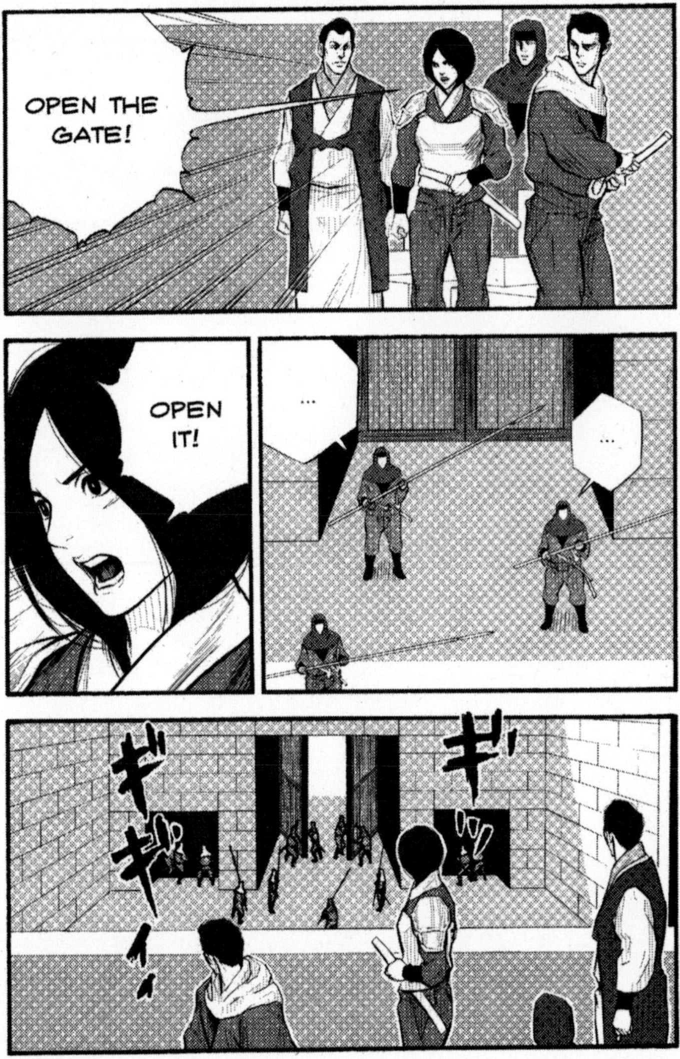
OPEN THE GATE!
...
...
OPEN IT!

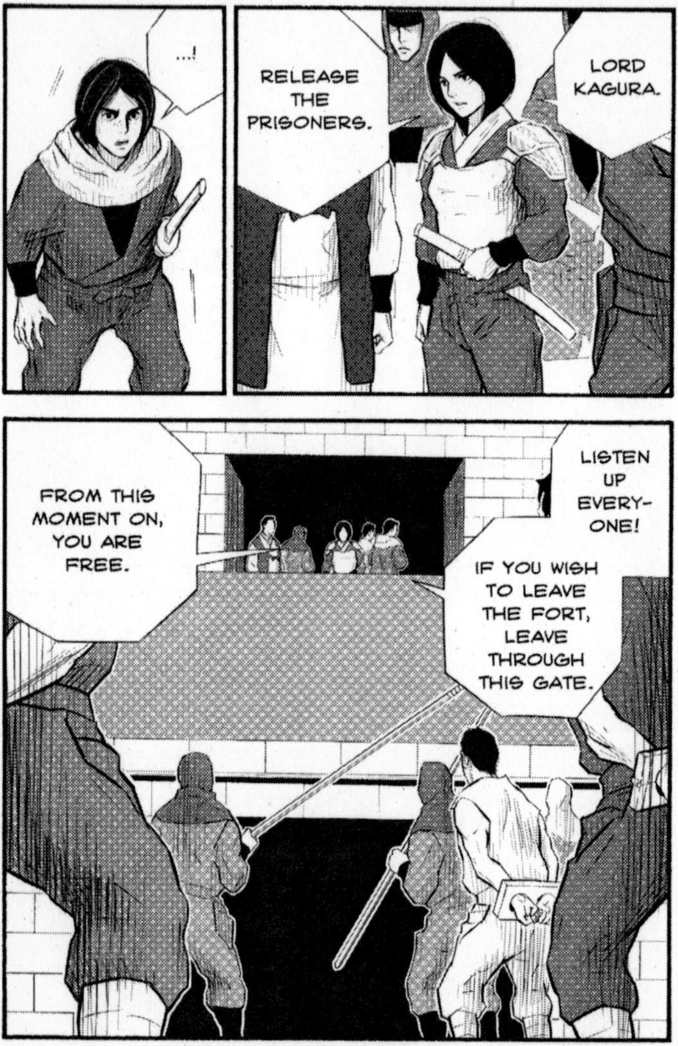
LORD KAGURA.
RELEASE THE PRISONERS.
...!
LISTEN UP EVERY-ONE!
IF YOU WISH TO LEAVE THE FORT, LEAVE THROUGH THIS GATE.
FROM THIS MOMENT ON, YOU ARE FREE.

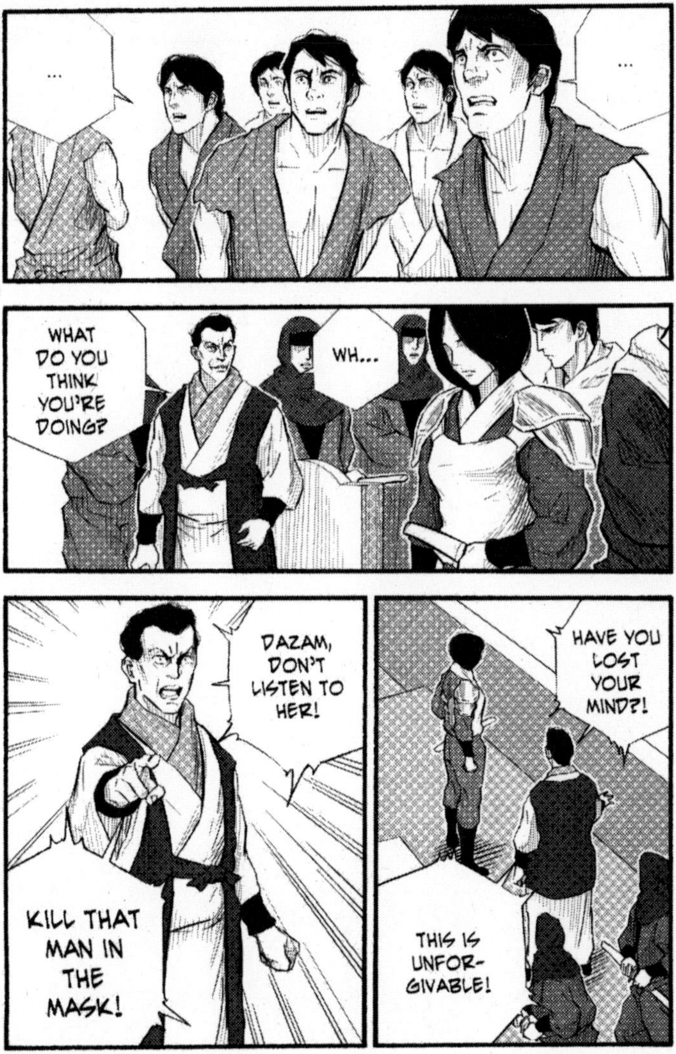
...
...
WH...
WHAT DO YOU THINK YOU'RE DOING?
HAVE YOU LOST YOUR MIND?!
THIS IS UNFORGIVABLE!
DAZAM, DON'T LISTEN TO HER!
KILL THAT MAN IN THE MASK!

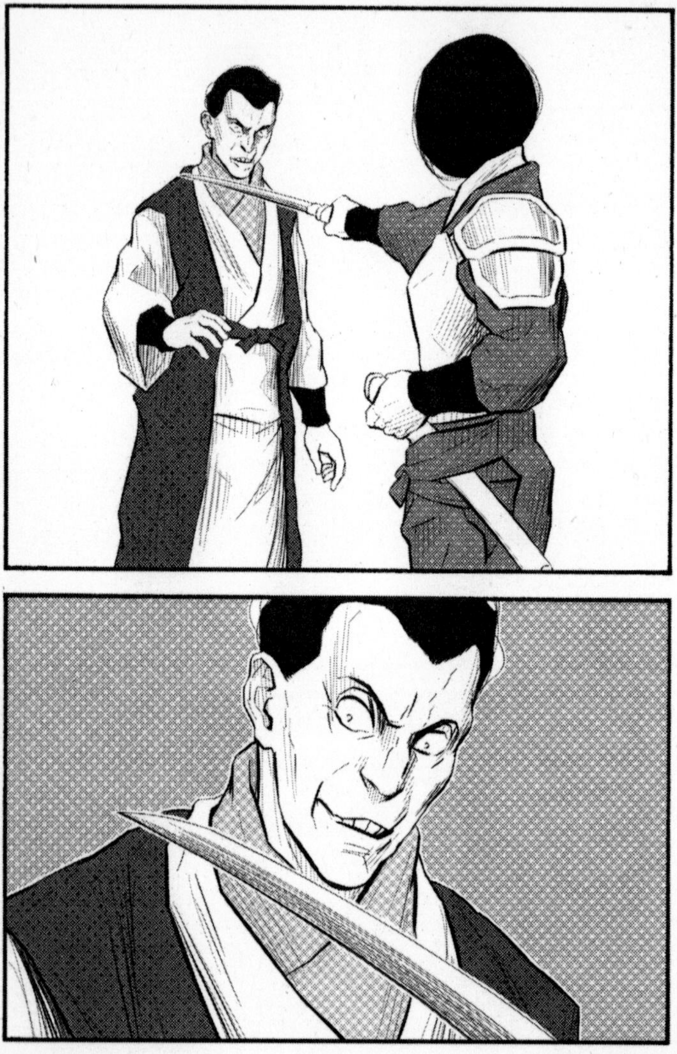

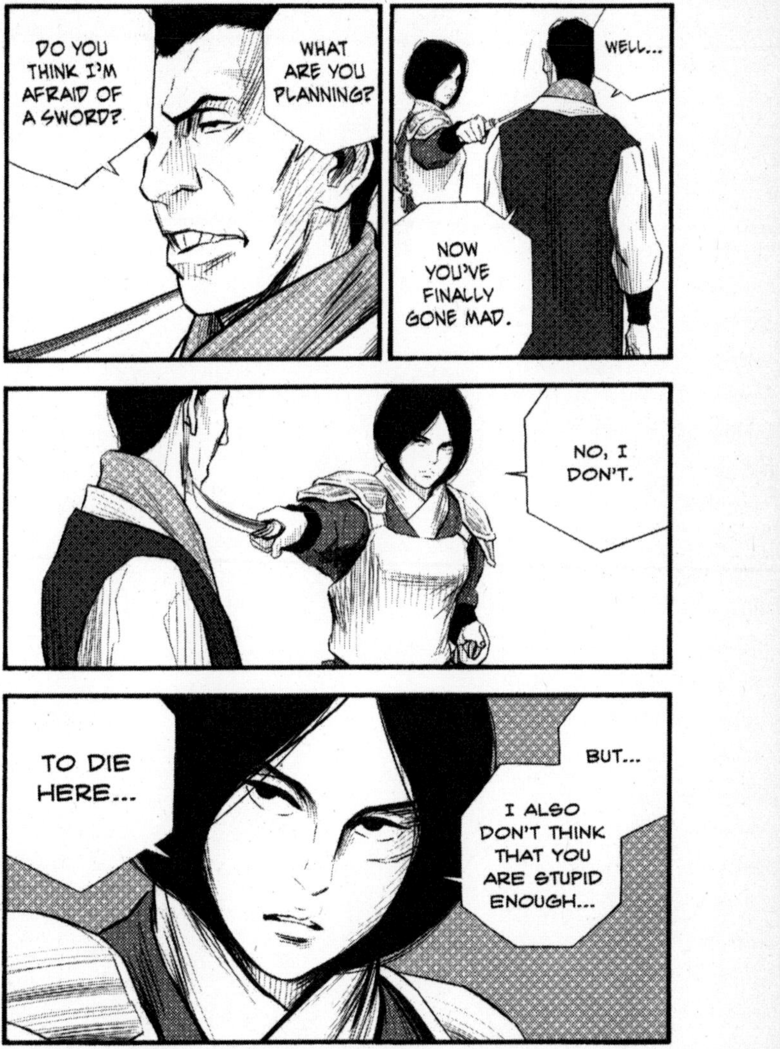
WELL...
NOW YOU'VE FINALLY GONE MAD.
WHAT ARE YOU PLANNING?
DO YOU THINK I'M AFRAID OF A SWORD?
NO, I DON'T.
BUT...
I ALSO DON'T THINK THAT YOU ARE STUPID ENOUGH...
TO DIE HERE...

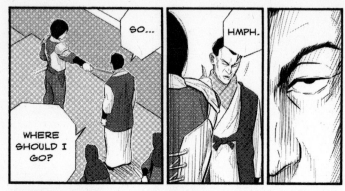

HMPH.
SO...
WHERE SHOULD I GO?
LORD NANASE.
TAKE THE WEAPONS FROM THE SOLDIERS AND MY UNCLE.
AND BRING THEM TO THE MEETING.
...
SIMBA...

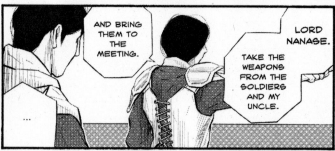

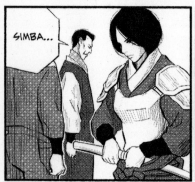

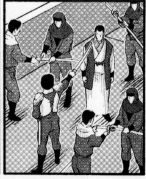

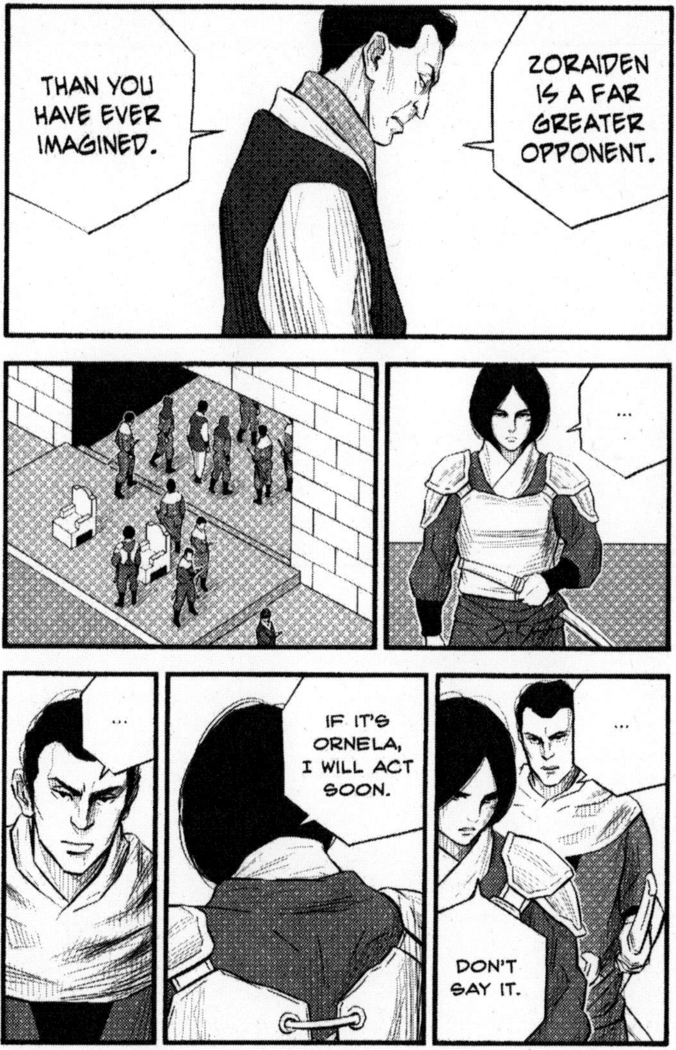
ZORAIDEN IS A FAR GREATER OPPONENT.
THAN YOU HAVE EVER IMAGINED.
...
...
DON'T SAY IT.
IF IT'S ORNELA, I WILL ACT SOON.
...

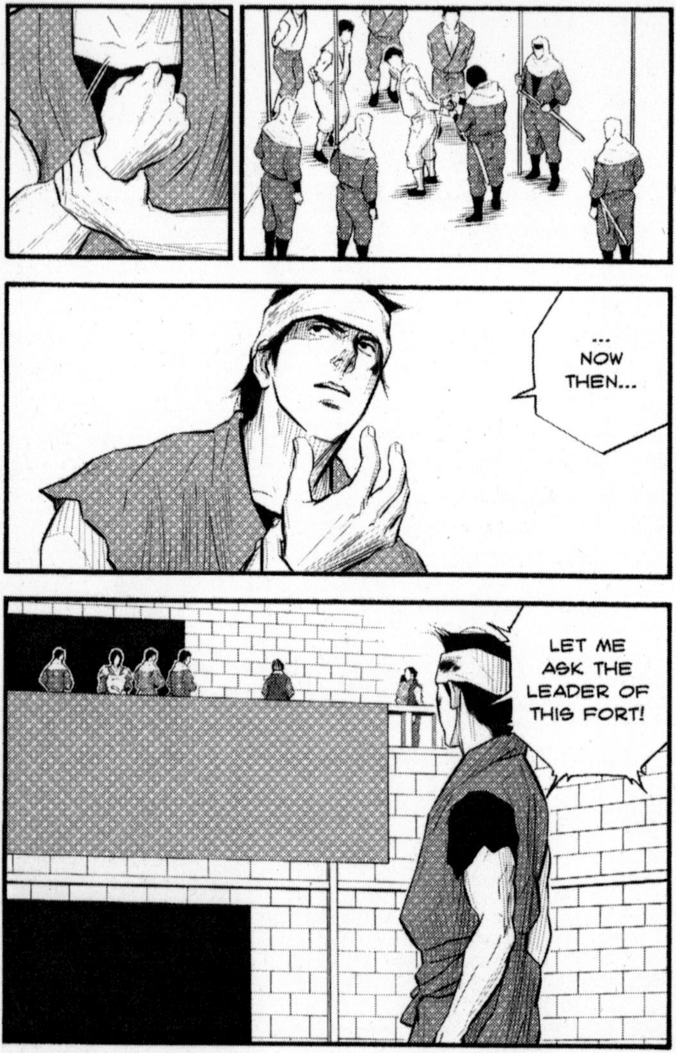
...
NOW
THEN...
LET ME
ASK THE
LEADER OF
THIS FORT!

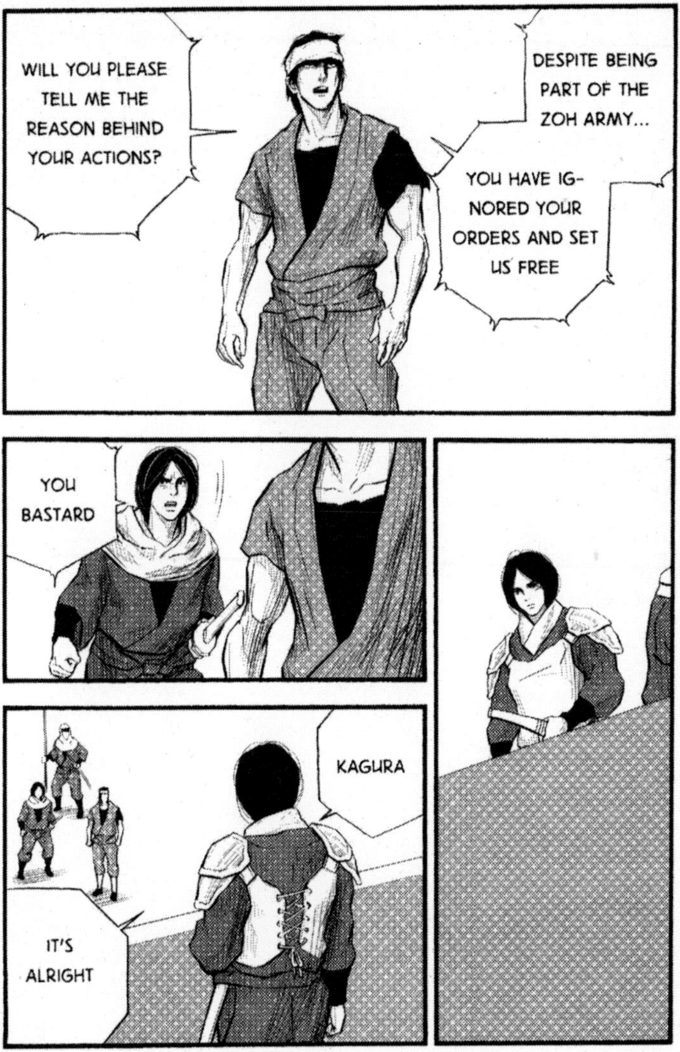
DESPITE BEING PART OF THE ZOH ARMY...
YOU HAVE IG-NORED YOUR ORDERS AND SET US FREE
WILL YOU PLEASE TELL ME THE REASON BEHIND YOUR ACTIONS?
YOU BASTARD
KAGURA
IT'S ALRIGHT

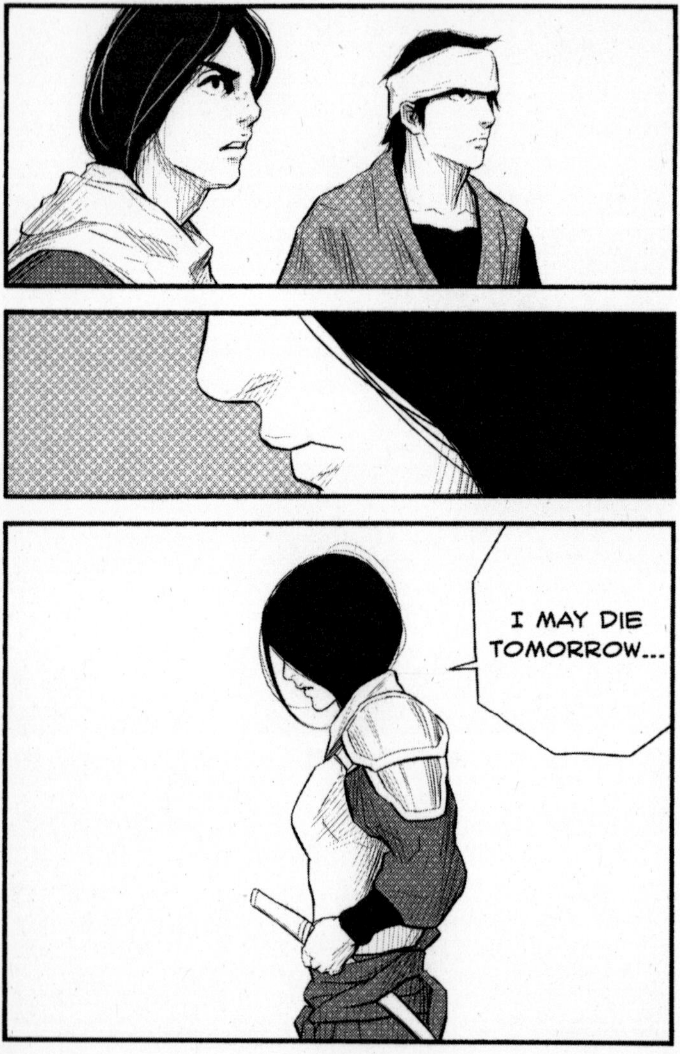
I MAY DIE
TOMORROW...

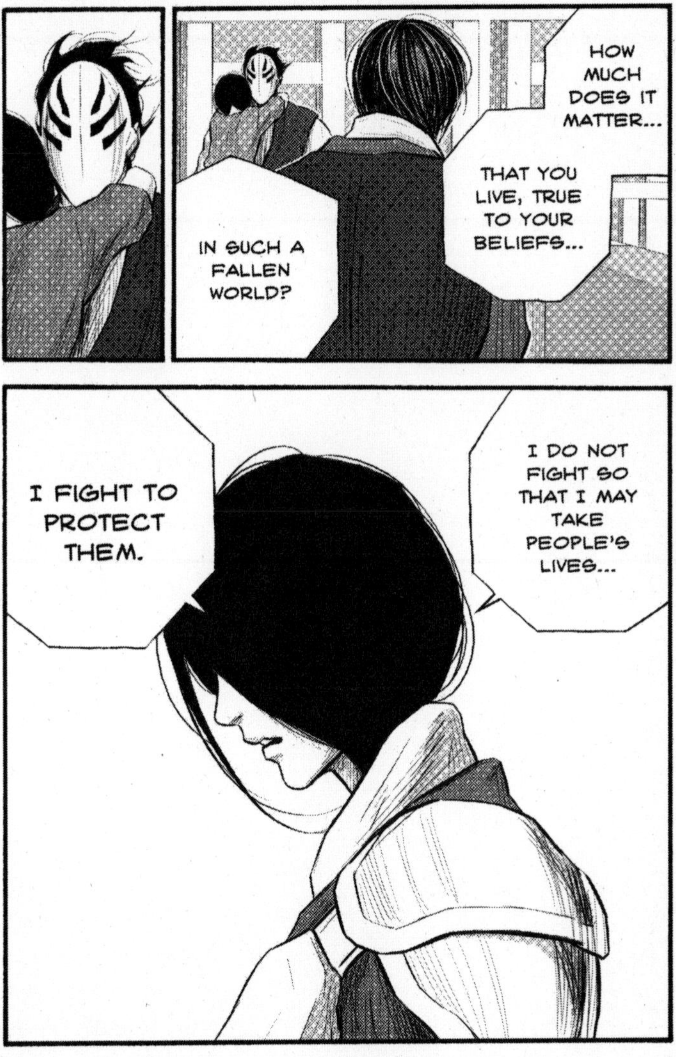
HOW MUCH DOES IT MATTER...
THAT YOU LIVE, TRUE TO YOUR BELIEFS...
IN SUCH A FALLEN WORLD?
I DO NOT FIGHT SO THAT I MAY TAKE PEOPLE'S LIVES...
I FIGHT TO PROTECT THEM.

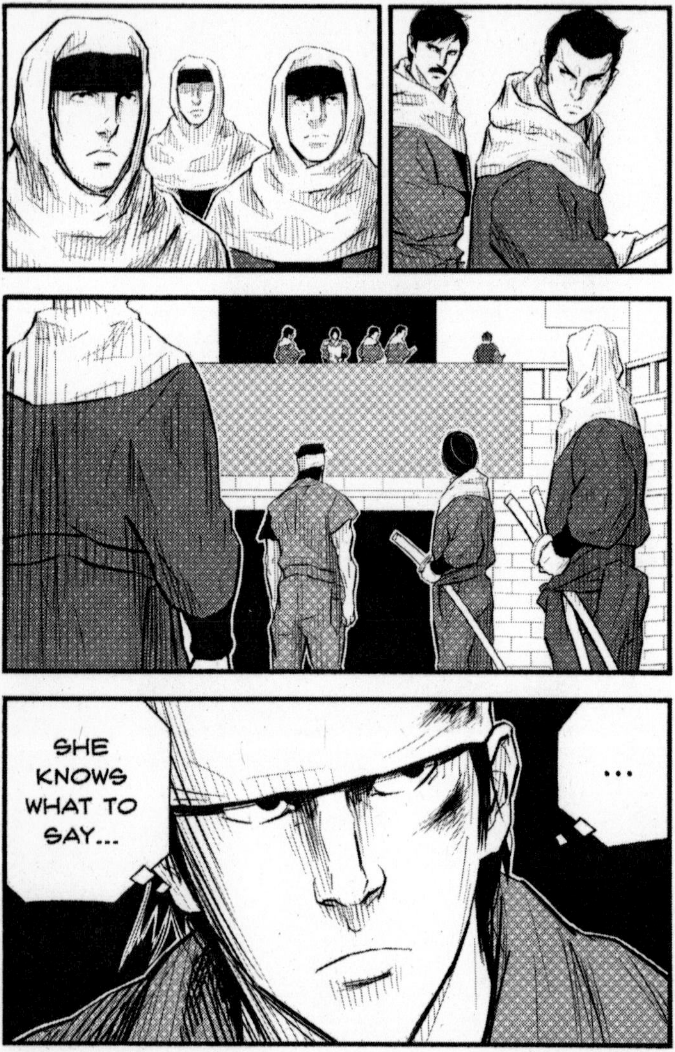
...
SHE KNOWS WHAT TO SAY...

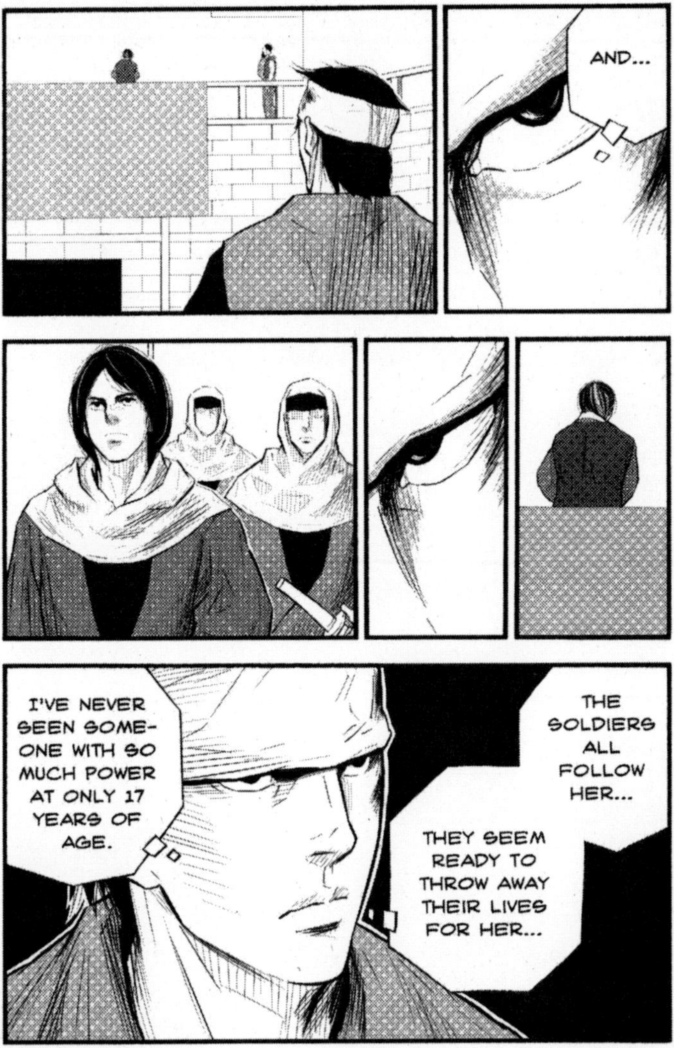
AND...
THE SOLDIERS ALL FOLLOW HER...
THEY SEEM READY TO THROW AWAY THEIR LIVES FOR HER...
I'VE NEVER SEEN SOME-ONE WITH SO MUCH POWER AT ONLY 17 YEARS OF AGE.

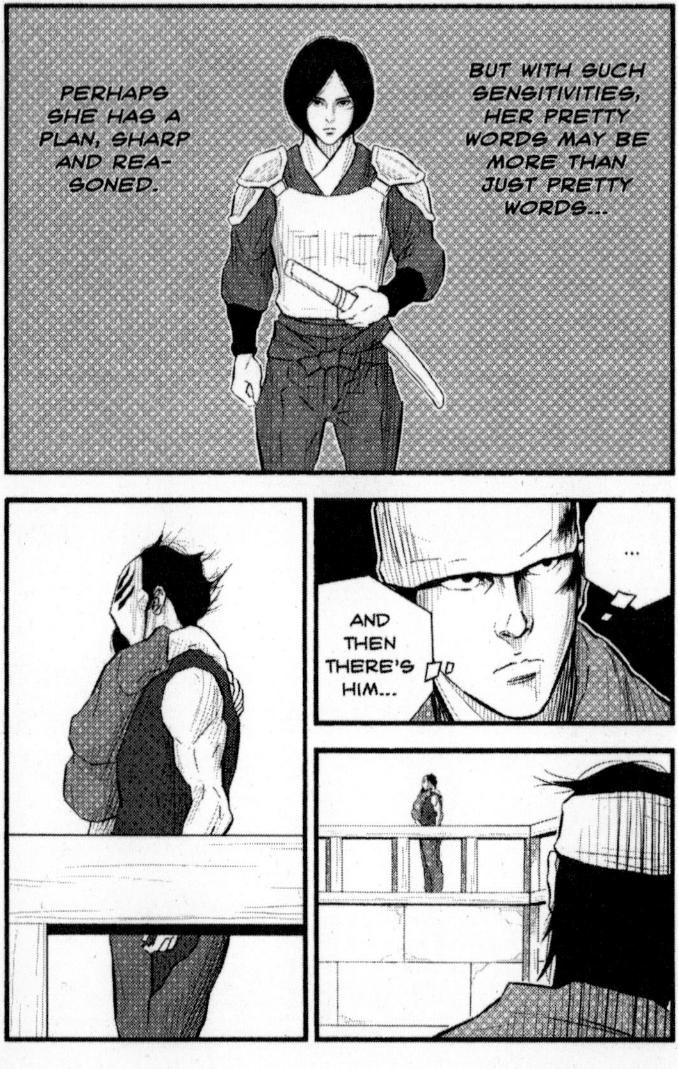
BUT WITH SUCH SENSITIVITIES, HER PRETTY WORDS MAY BE MORE THAN JUST PRETTY WORDS...
PERHAPS SHE HAS A PLAN, SHARP AND REA-SONED.
...
AND THEN THERE'S HIM...

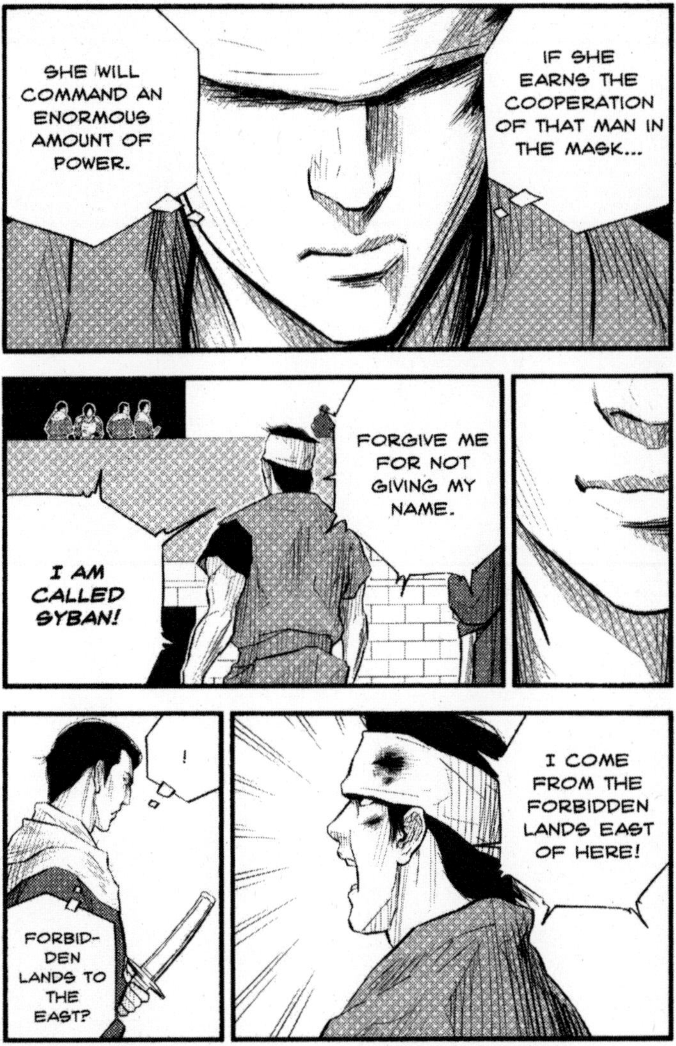
IF SHE EARNS THE COOPERATION OF THAT MAN IN THE MASK...
SHE WILL COMMAND AN ENORMOUS AMOUNT OF POWER.
FORGIVE ME FOR NOT GIVING MY NAME.
I AM CALLED SYBAN!
I COME FROM THE FORBIDDEN LANDS EAST OF HERE!
!
FORBID-DEN LANDS TO THE EAST?

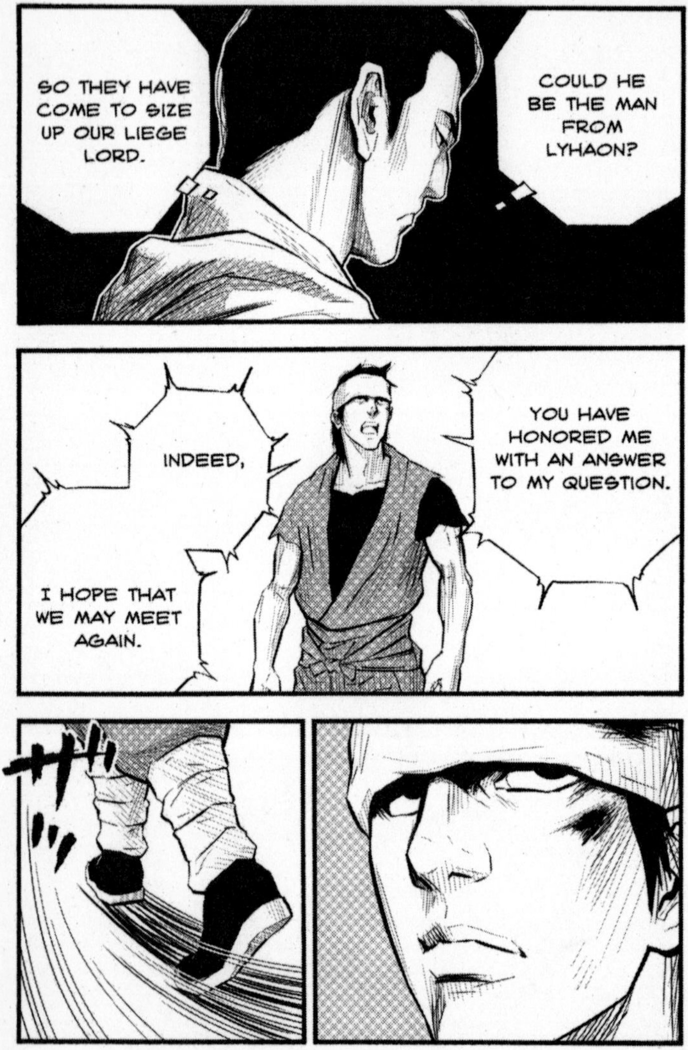
COULD HE BE THE MAN FROM LYHAON?
SO THEY HAVE COME TO SIZE UP OUR LIEGE LORD.
YOU HAVE HONORED ME WITH AN ANSWER TO MY QUESTION.
INDEED,
I HOPE THAT WE MAY MEET AGAIN.

NOW
...

MASKED
MAN...

WHAT WILL
YOU DO?

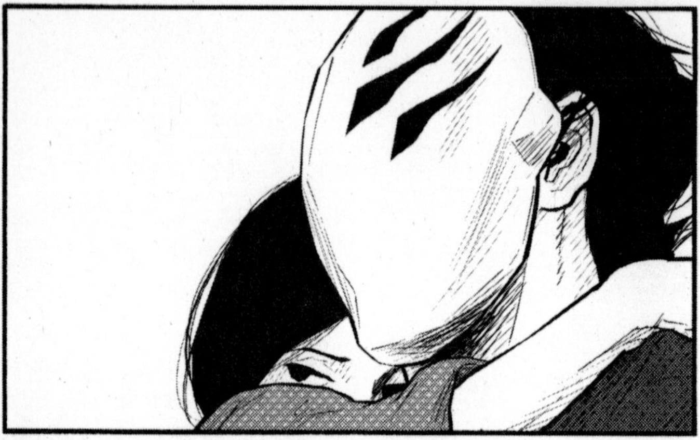

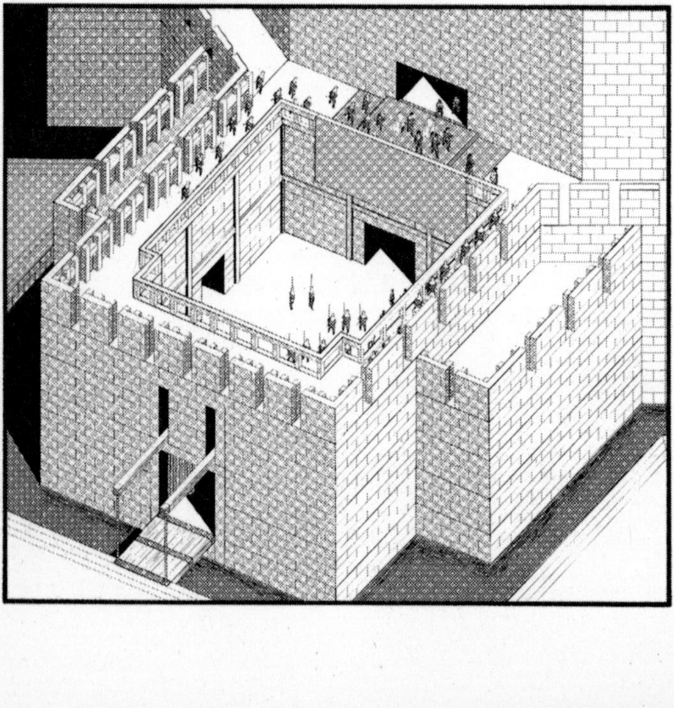

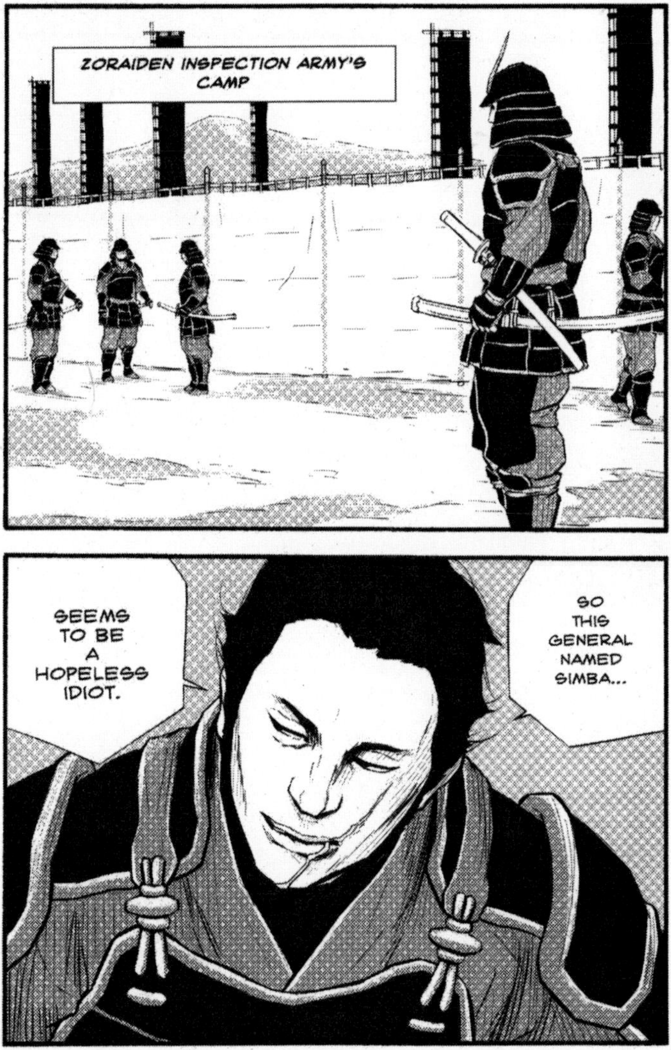
ZORAIDEN INSPECTION ARMY'S CAMP
SO THIS GENERAL NAMED SIMBA...
SEEMS TO BE A HOPELESS IDIOT.

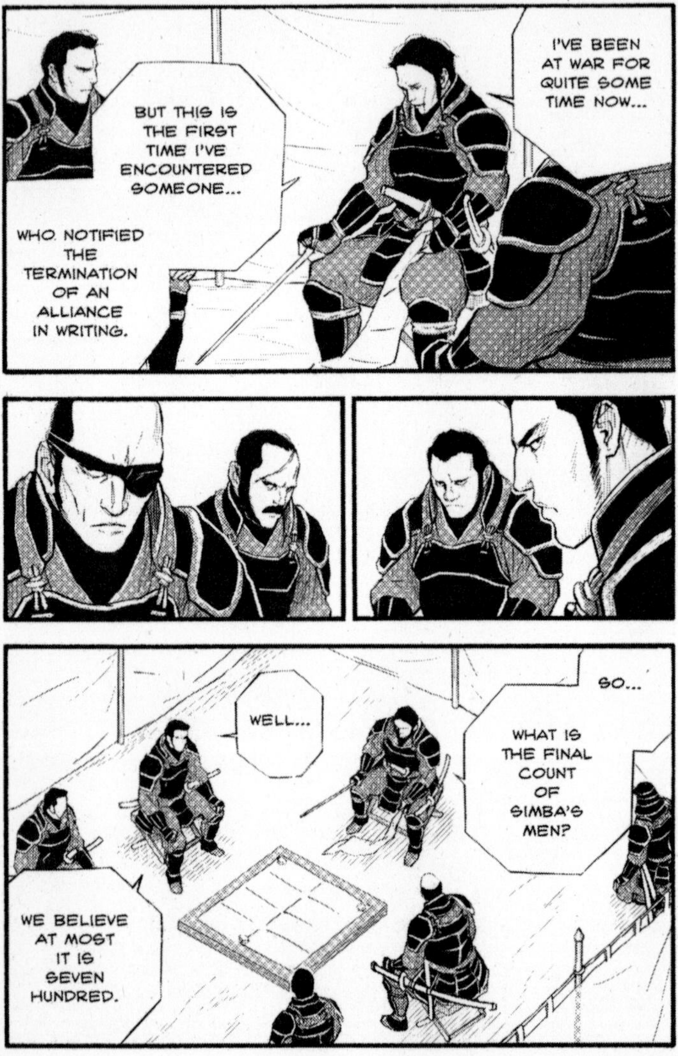
I'VE BEEN AT WAR FOR QUITE SOME TIME NOW...
BUT THIS IS THE FIRST TIME I'VE ENCOUNTERED SOMEONE...
WHO NOTIFIED THE TERMINATION OF AN ALLIANCE IN WRITING.
SO...
WHAT IS THE FINAL COUNT OF SIMBA'S MEN?
WELL...
WE BELIEVE AT MOST IT IS SEVEN HUNDRED.

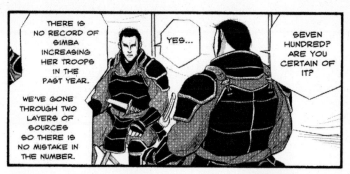

SEVEN HUNDRED? ARE YOU CERTAIN OF IT?
YES...
THERE IS NO RECORD OF SIMBA INCREASING HER TROOPS IN THE PAST YEAR.
WE'VE GONE THROUGH TWO LAYERS OF SOURCES SO THERE IS NO MISTAKE IN THE NUMBER.
...
ギッ
TELL KANOMA TO SEND A THOUSAND MORE MEN.
A... THOUSAND?
BUT DUE TO THE CASE IN QUESTION OUR PROVISIONS HAVE...

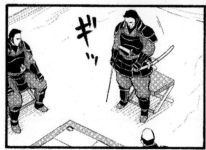

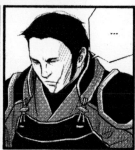

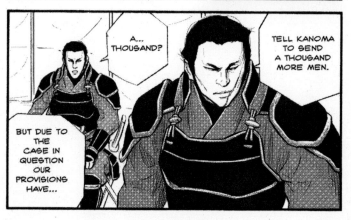

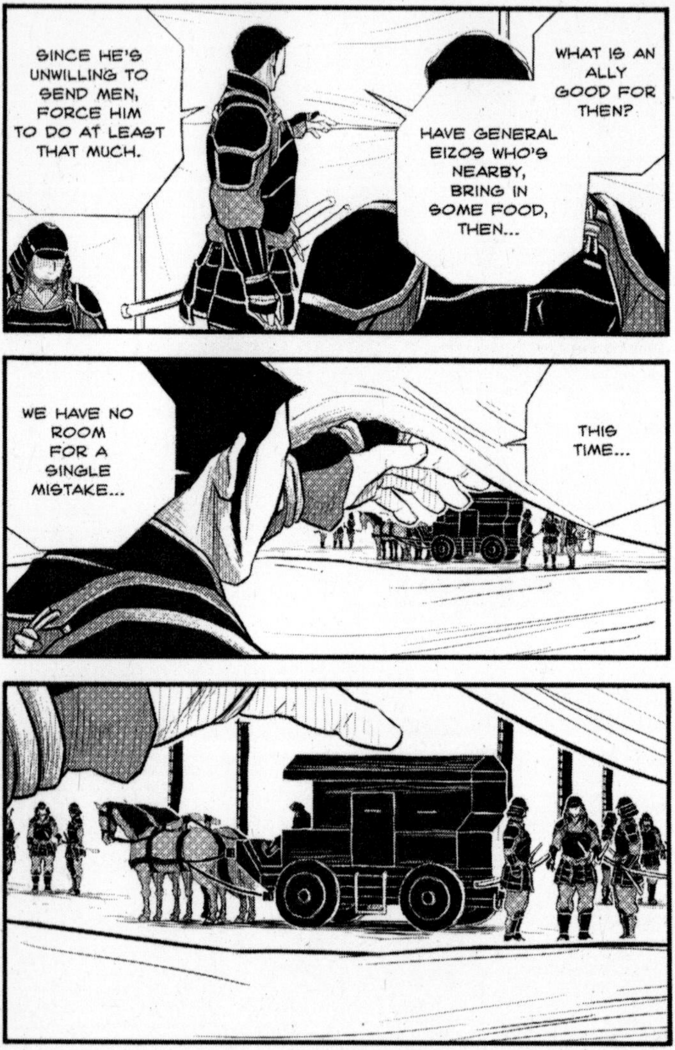
WHAT IS AN ALLY GOOD FOR THEN?
HAVE GENERAL EIZOS WHO'S NEARBY, BRING IN SOME FOOD, THEN...
SINCE HE'S UNWILLING TO SEND MEN, FORCE HIM TO DO AT LEAST THAT MUCH.
THIS TIME...
WE HAVE NO ROOM FOR A SINGLE MISTAKE...

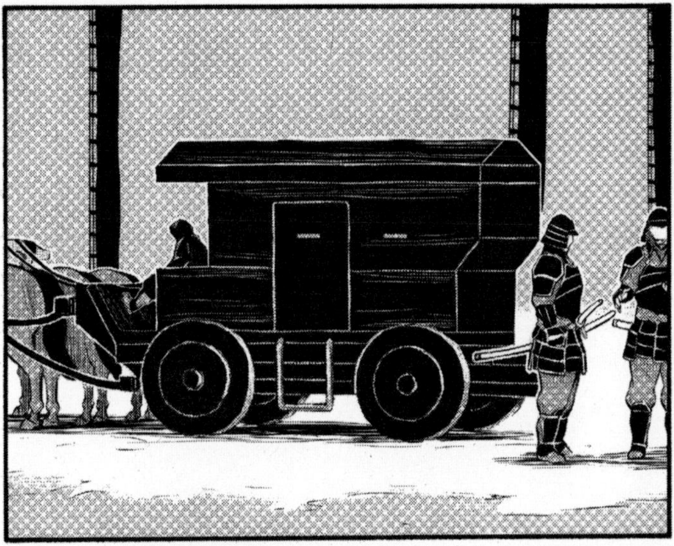

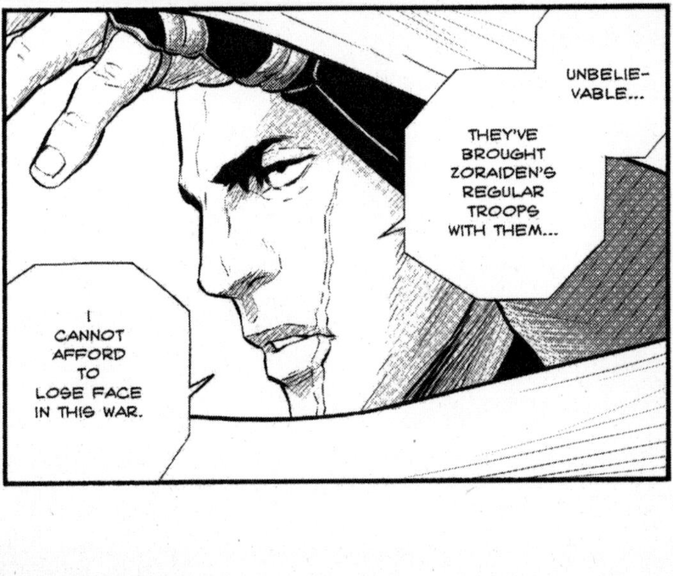
UNBELIEVABLE...
THEY'VE BROUGHT ZORAIDEN'S REGULAR TROOPS WITH THEM...
I CANNOT AFFORD TO LOSE FACE IN THIS WAR.

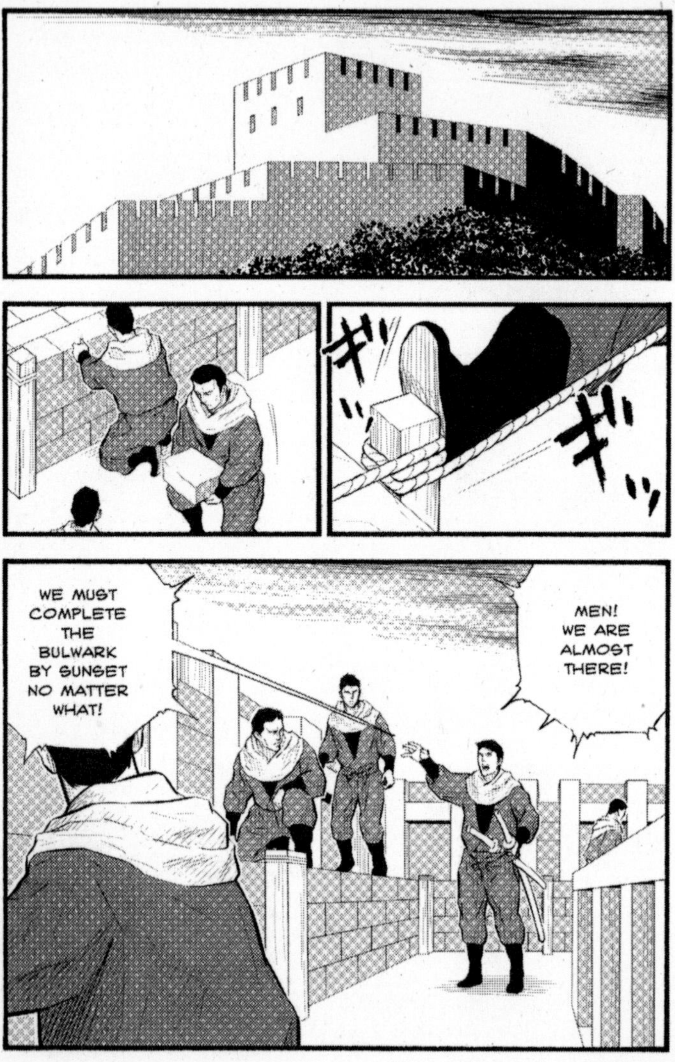
ギッ
MEN! WE ARE ALMOST THERE!
WE MUST COMPLETE THE BULWARK BY SUNSET NO MATTER WHAT!

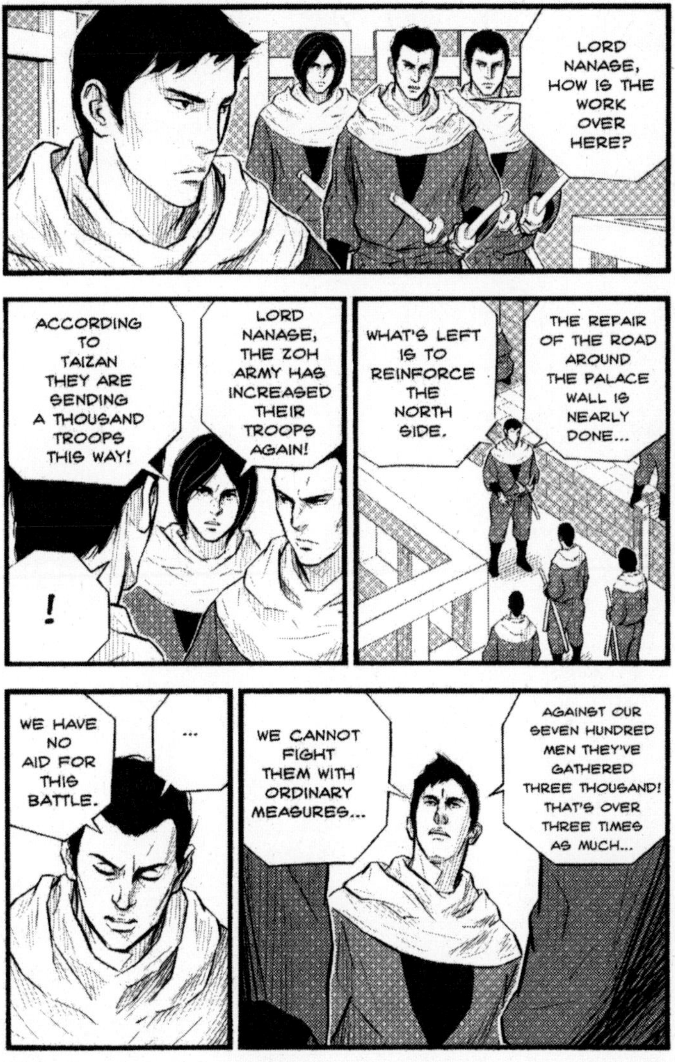
LORD NANASE, HOW IS THE WORK OVER HERE?
THE REPAIR OF THE ROAD AROUND THE PALACE WALL IS NEARLY DONE...
WHAT'S LEFT IS TO REINFORCE THE NORTH SIDE.
LORD NANASE, THE ZOH ARMY HAS INCREASED THEIR TROOPS AGAIN!
ACCORDING TO TAIZAN THEY ARE SENDING A THOUSAND TROOPS THIS WAY!
!
AGAINST OUR SEVEN HUNDRED MEN THEY'VE GATHERED THREE THOUSAND! THAT'S OVER THREE TIMES AS MUCH...
WE CANNOT FIGHT THEM WITH ORDINARY MEASURES...
...
WE HAVE NO AID FOR THIS BATTLE.

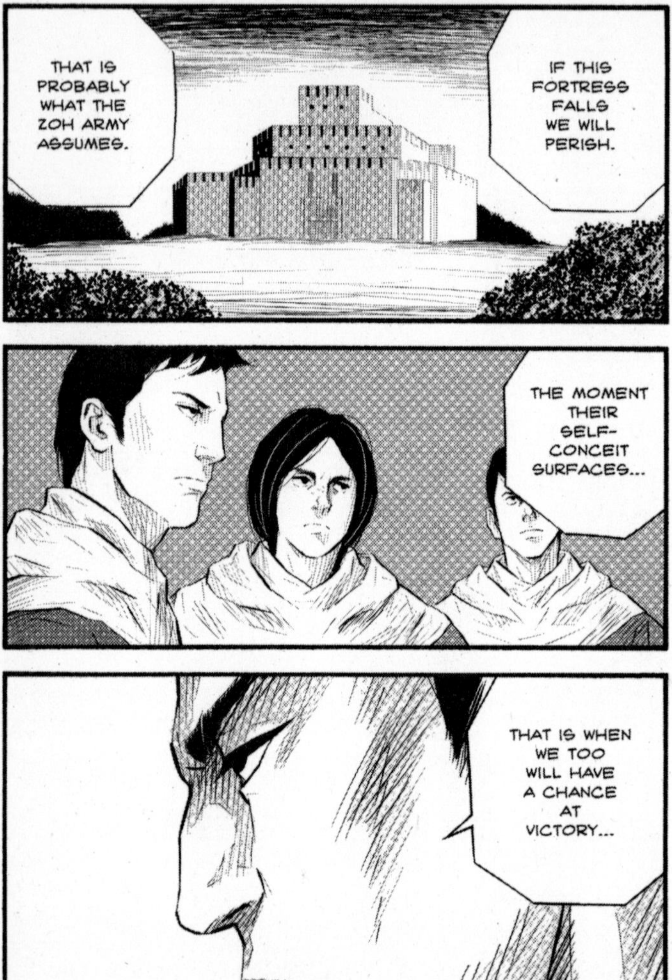
IF THIS FORTRESS FALLS WE WILL PERISH.
THAT IS PROBABLY WHAT THE ZOH ARMY ASSUMES.
THE MOMENT THEIR SELF-CONCEIT SURFACES...
THAT IS WHEN WE TOO WILL HAVE A CHANCE AT VICTORY...

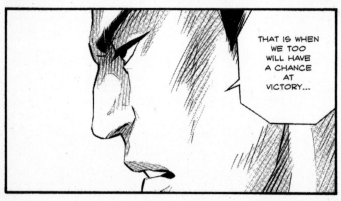

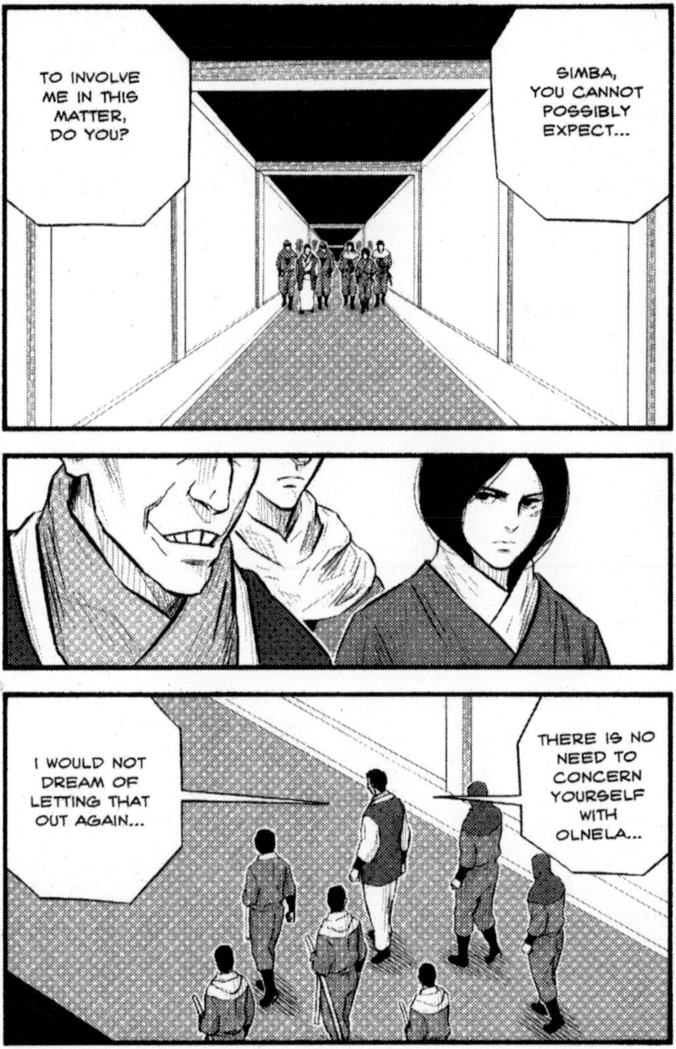
SIMBA, YOU CANNOT POSSIBLY EXPECT...
TO INVOLVE ME IN THIS MATTER, DO YOU?
THERE IS NO NEED TO CONCERN YOURSELF WITH OLNELA...
I WOULD NOT DREAM OF LETTING THAT OUT AGAIN...

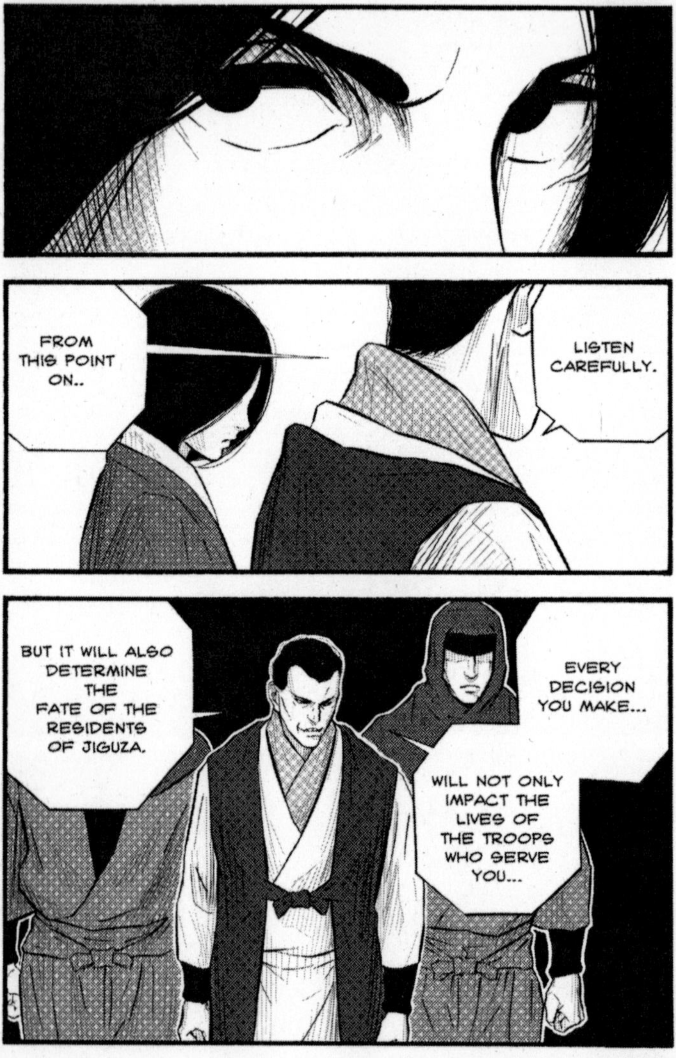
LISTEN CAREFULLY.
FROM THIS POINT ON..
EVERY DECISION YOU MAKE...
WILL NOT ONLY IMPACT THE LIVES OF THE TROOPS WHO SERVE YOU...
BUT IT WILL ALSO DETERMINE THE FATE OF THE RESIDENTS OF JIGUZA.

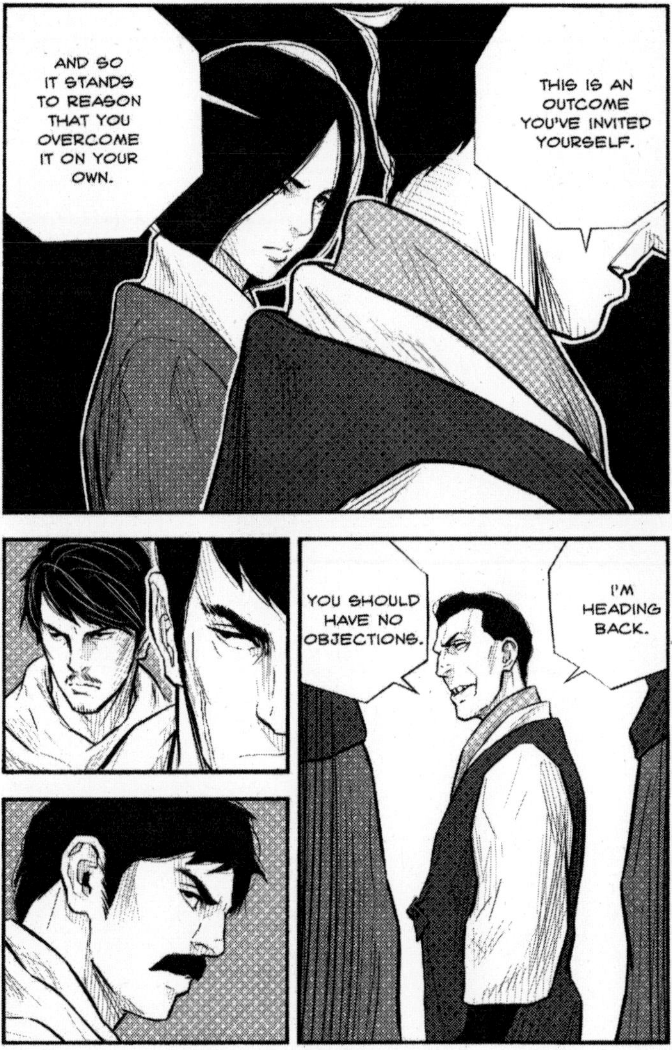
THIS IS AN OUTCOME YOU'VE INVITED YOURSELF.
AND SO IT STANDS TO REASON THAT YOU OVERCOME IT ON YOUR OWN.
I'M HEADING BACK.
YOU SHOULD HAVE NO OBJECTIONS.

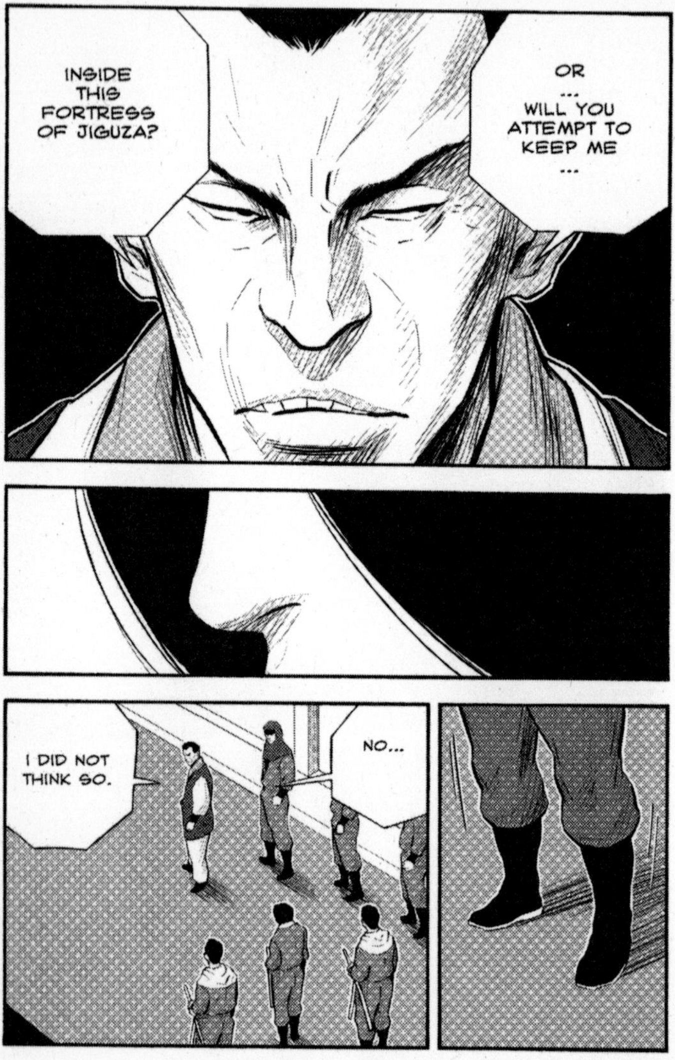
OR ... WILL YOU ATTEMPT TO KEEP ME ...
INSIDE THIS FORTRESS OF JIGUZA?
NO...
I DID NOT THINK SO.

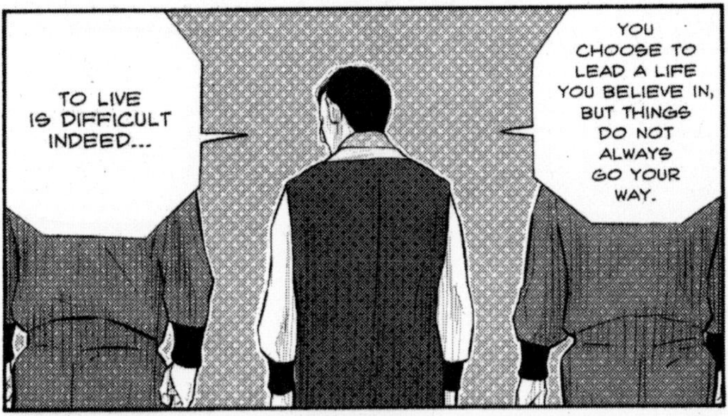
YOU CHOOSE TO LEAD A LIFE YOU BELIEVE IN, BUT THINGS DO NOT ALWAYS GO YOUR WAY.
TO LIVE IS DIFFICULT INDEED...
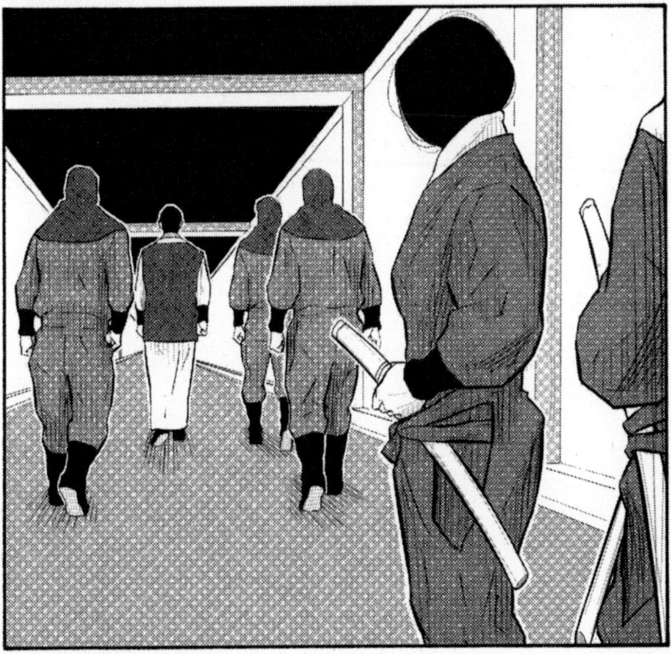

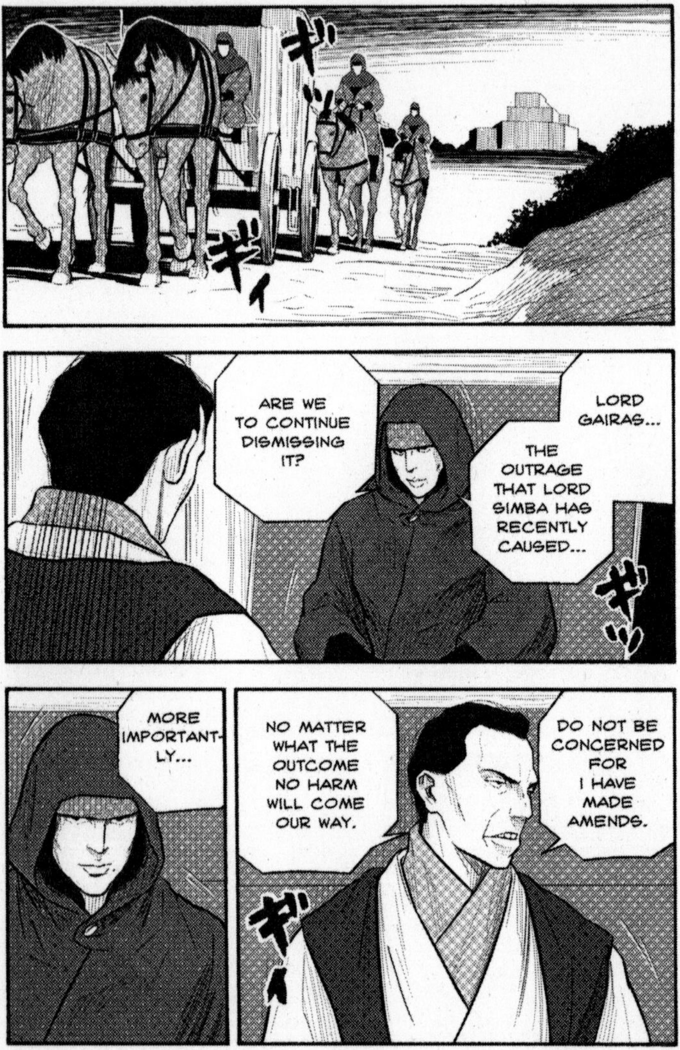
ギッ
ギイ
LORD GAIRAS...
THE OUTRAGE THAT LORD SIMBA HAS RECENTLY CAUSED...
ARE WE TO CONTINUE DISMISSING IT?
ギッ
DO NOT BE CONCERNED FOR I HAVE MADE AMENDS.
NO MATTER WHAT THE OUTCOME NO HARM WILL COME OUR WAY.
ギィ
MORE IMPORTANT-LY...

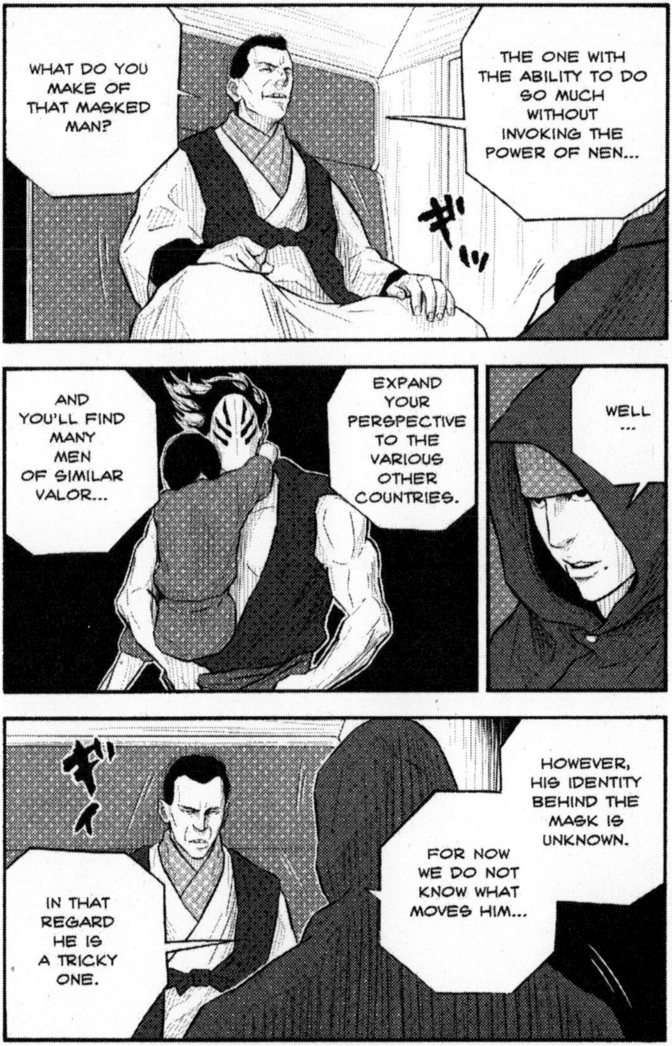
THE ONE WITH THE ABILITY TO DO SO MUCH WITHOUT INVOKING THE POWER OF NEN...
WHAT DO YOU MAKE OF THAT MASKED MAN?
ギッ
WELL...
EXPAND YOUR PERSPECTIVE TO THE VARIOUS OTHER COUNTRIES.
AND YOU'LL FIND MANY MEN OF SIMILAR VALOR...
HOWEVER, HIS IDENTITY BEHIND THE MASK IS UNKNOWN.
FOR NOW WE DO NOT KNOW WHAT MOVES HIM...
ギイ
IN THAT REGARD HE IS A TRICKY ONE.

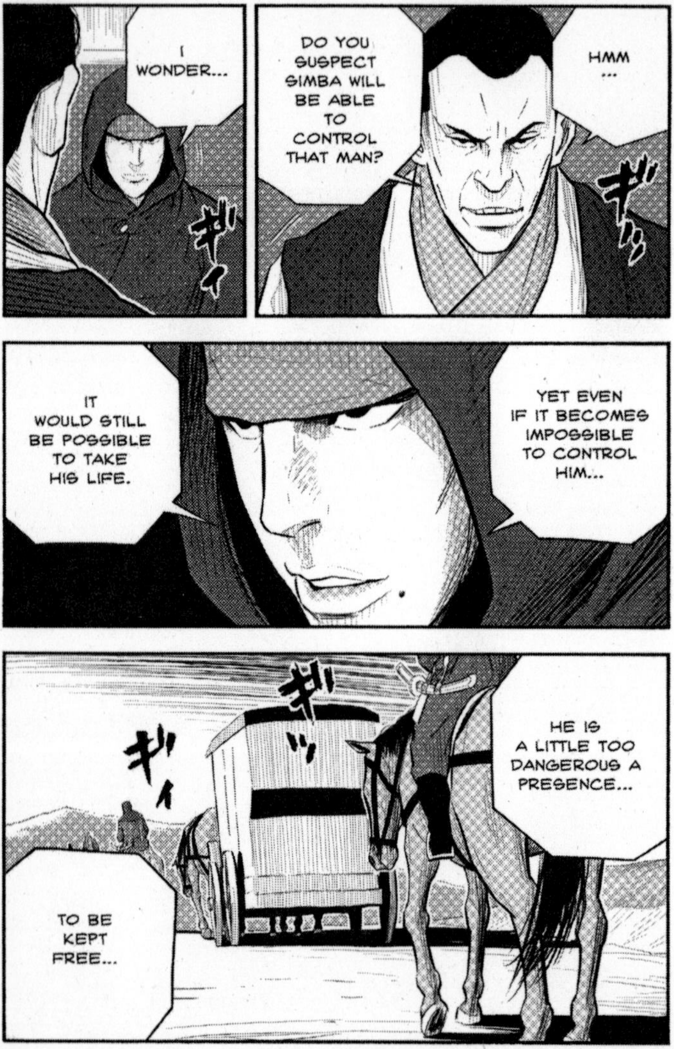
HMM ...
DO YOU SUSPECT SIMBA WILL BE ABLE TO CONTROL THAT MAN?
ギッ
I WONDER...
ギイ
YET EVEN IF IT BECOMES IMPOSSIBLE TO CONTROL HIM...
IT WOULD STILL BE POSSIBLE TO TAKE HIS LIFE.
HE IS A LITTLE TOO DANGEROUS A PRESENCE...
ギッ
ギイ
TO BE KEPT FREE...

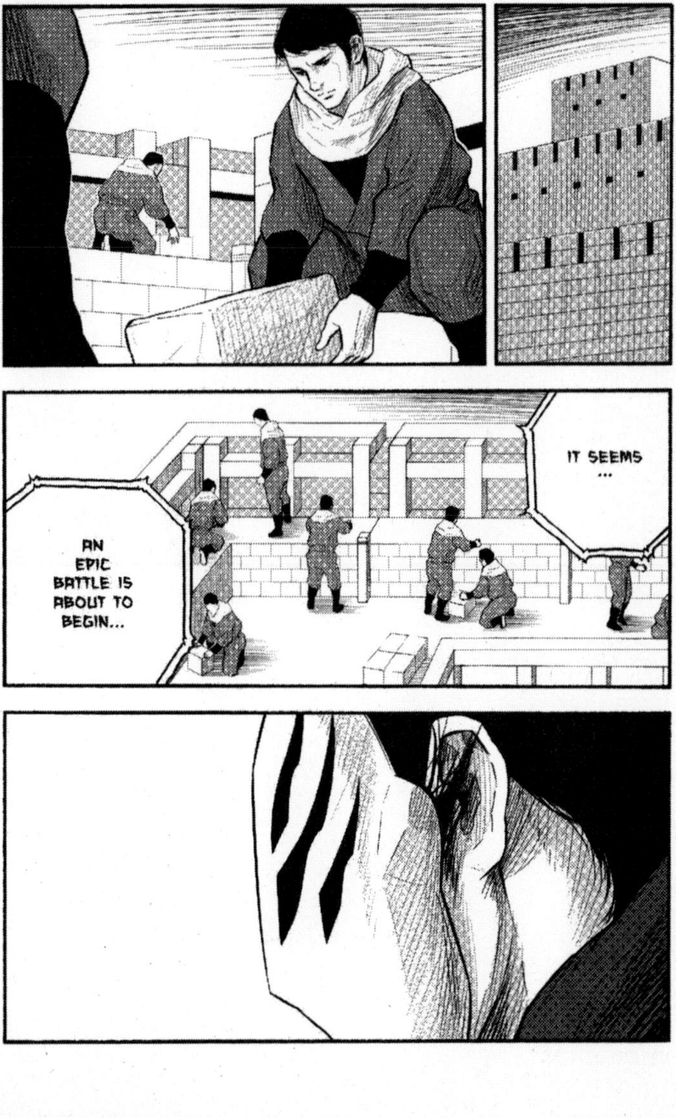
IT SEEMS ...
AN EPIC BATTLE IS ABOUT TO BEGIN...

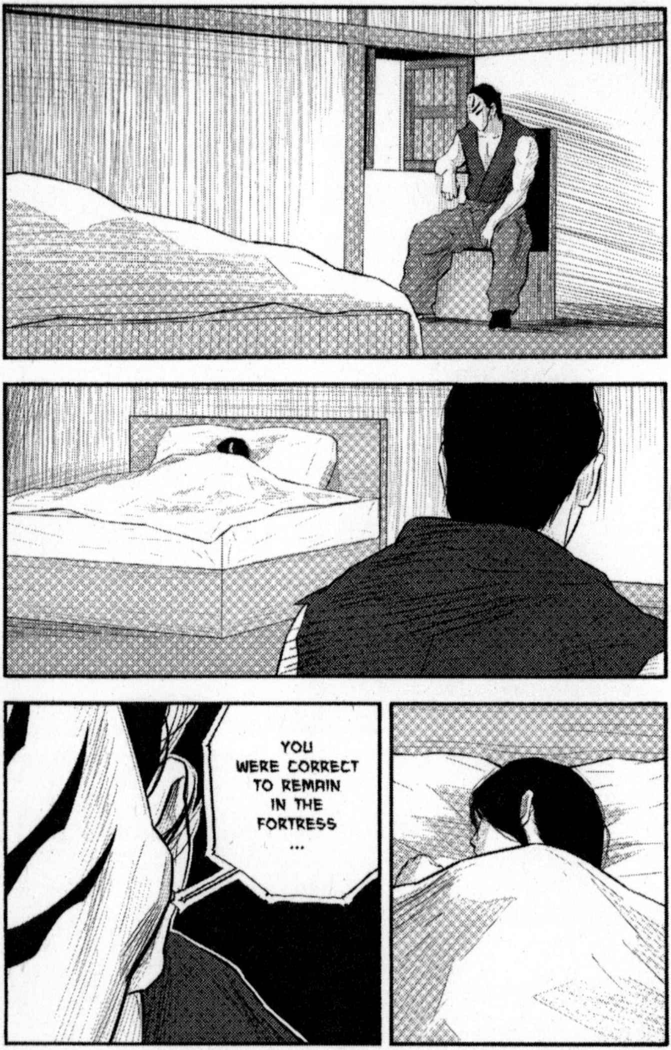
YOU WERE CORRECT TO REMAIN IN THE FORTRESS ...

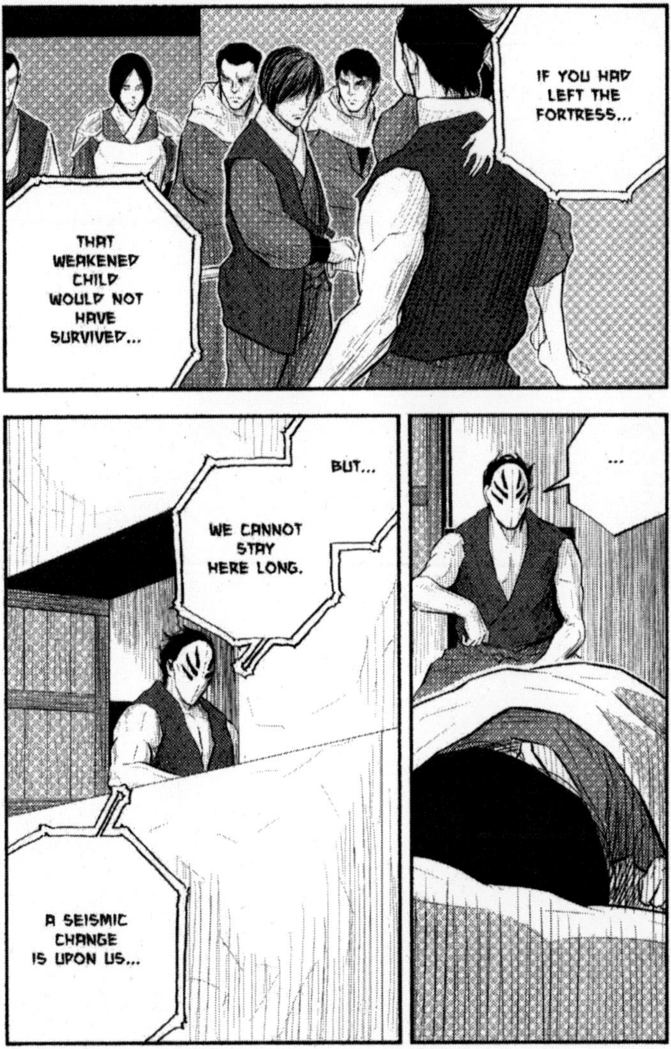
IF YOU HAD LEFT THE FORTRESS...
THAT WEAKENED CHILD WOULD NOT HAVE SURVIVED...
...
BUT...
WE CANNOT STAY HERE LONG.
A SEISMIC CHANGE IS UPON US...

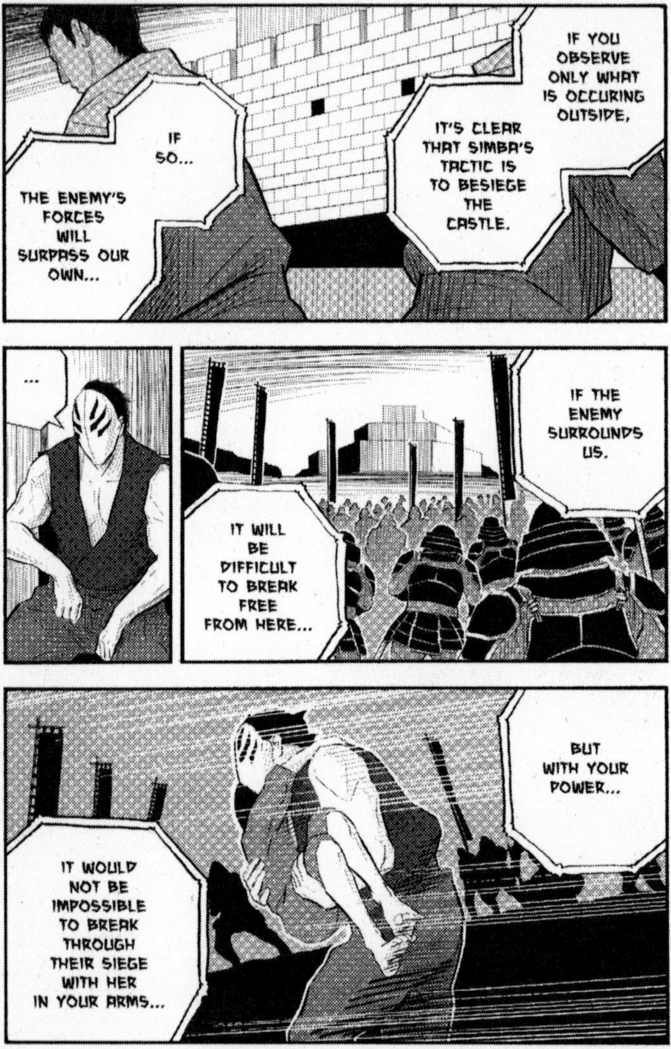
IF YOU OBSERVE ONLY WHAT IS OCCURING OUTSIDE,
IT'S CLEAR THAT SIMBA'S TACTIC IS TO BESIEGE THE CASTLE.
IF SO...
THE ENEMY'S FORCES WILL SURPASS OUR OWN...
IF THE ENEMY SURROUNDS US.
IT WILL BE DIFFICULT TO BREAK FREE FROM HERE...
...
BUT WITH YOUR POWER...
IT WOULD NOT BE IMPOSSIBLE TO BREAK THROUGH THEIR SIEGE WITH HER IN YOUR ARMS...

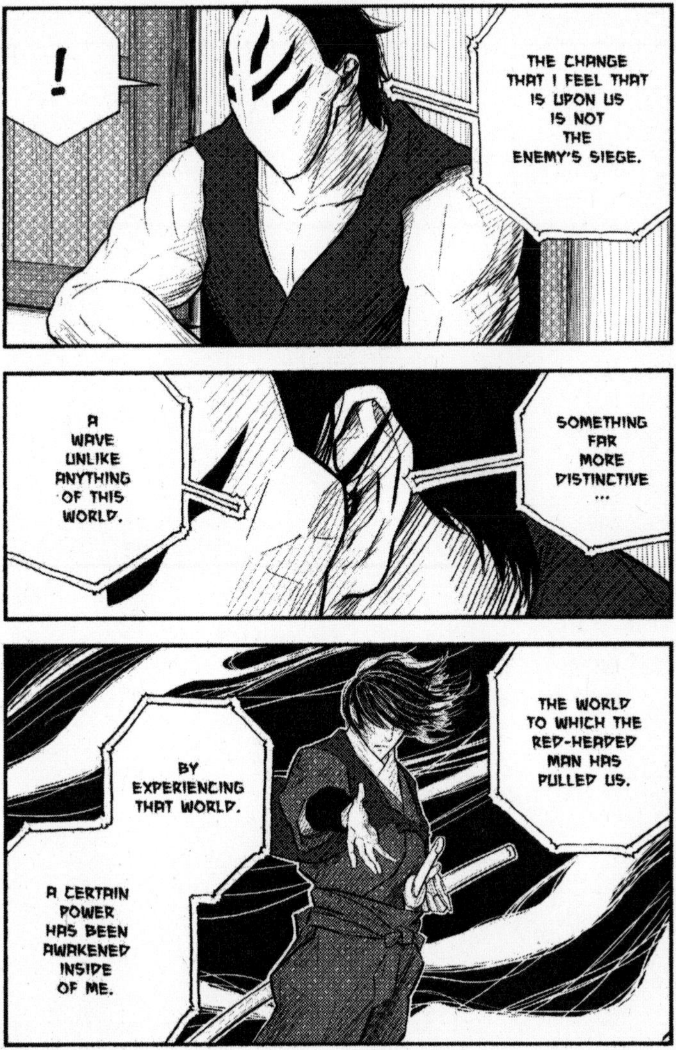
THE CHANGE THAT I FEEL THAT IS UPON US IS NOT THE ENEMY'S SIEGE.
!
SOMETHING FAR MORE DISTINCTIVE ...
A WAVE UNLIKE ANYTHING OF THIS WORLD.
THE WORLD TO WHICH THE RED-HEADED MAN HAS PULLED US.
BY EXPERIENCING THAT WORLD.
A CERTAIN POWER HAS BEEN AWAKENED INSIDE OF ME.

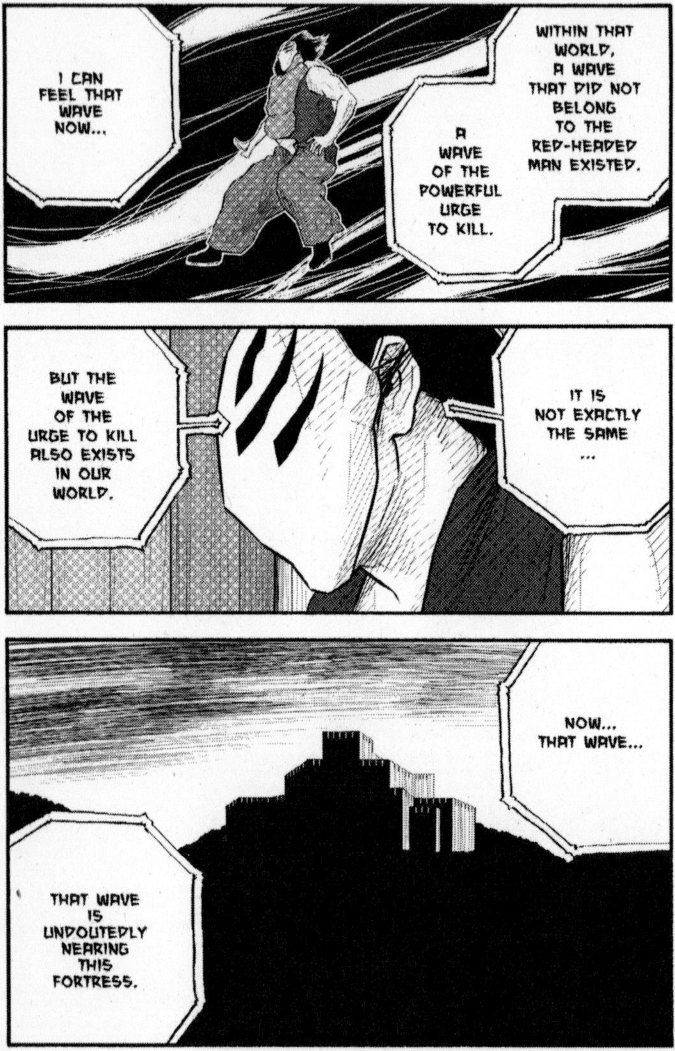
WITHIN THAT WORLD, A WAVE THAT DID NOT BELONG TO THE RED-HEADED MAN EXISTED.
A WAVE OF THE POWERFUL URGE TO KILL.
I CAN FEEL THAT WAVE NOW...
IT IS NOT EXACTLY THE SAME ...
BUT THE WAVE OF THE URGE TO KILL ALSO EXISTS IN OUR WORLD.
NOW... THAT WAVE...
THAT WAVE IS UNDOUTEDLY NEARING THIS FORTRESS.

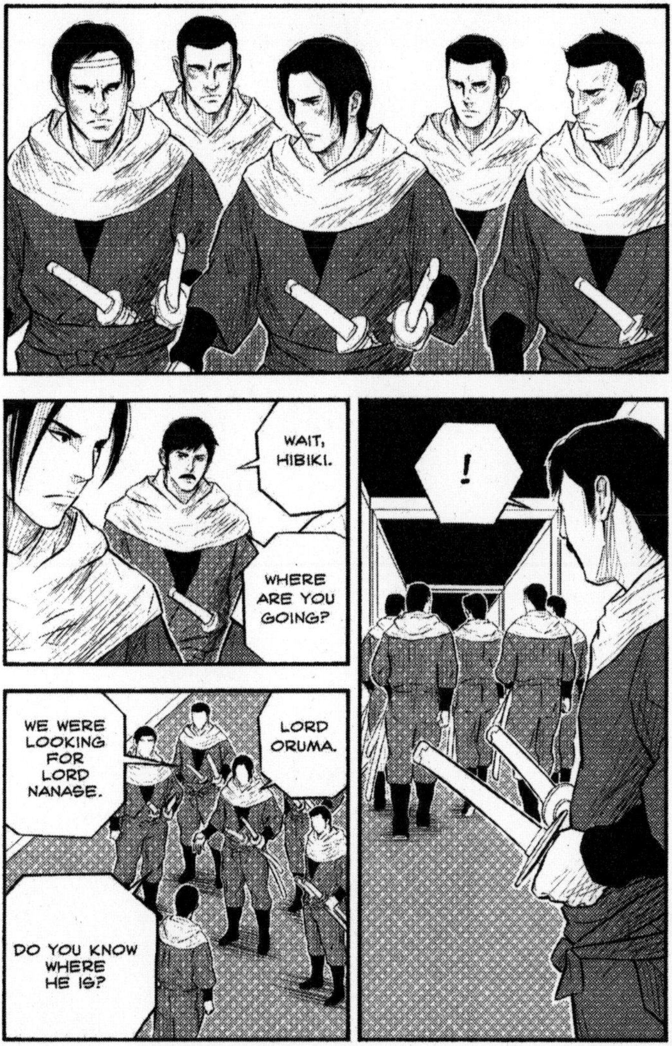
!
WAIT, HIBIKI.
WHERE ARE YOU GOING?
LORD ORUMA.
WE WERE LOOKING FOR LORD NANASE.
DO YOU KNOW WHERE HE IS?

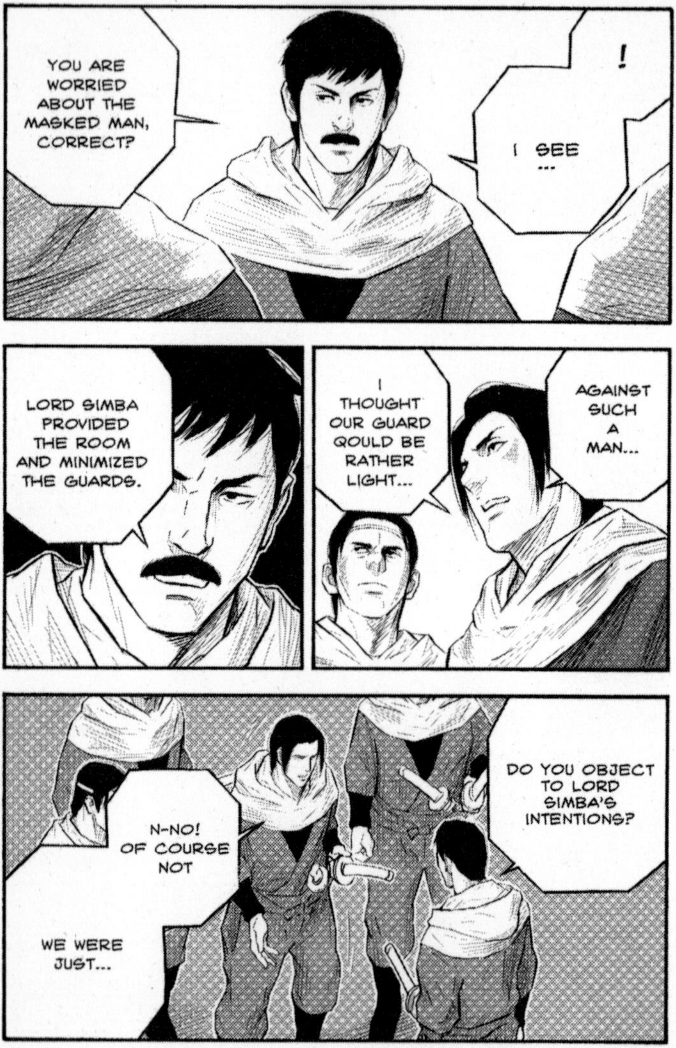
!
I SEE ...
YOU ARE WORRIED ABOUT THE MASKED MAN, CORRECT?
AGAINST SUCH A MAN...
I THOUGHT OUR GUARD QOULD BE RATHER LIGHT...
LORD SIMBA PROVIDED THE ROOM AND MINIMIZED THE GUARDS.
DO YOU OBJECT TO LORD SIMBA'S INTENTIONS?
N-NO! OF COURSE NOT
WE WERE JUST...

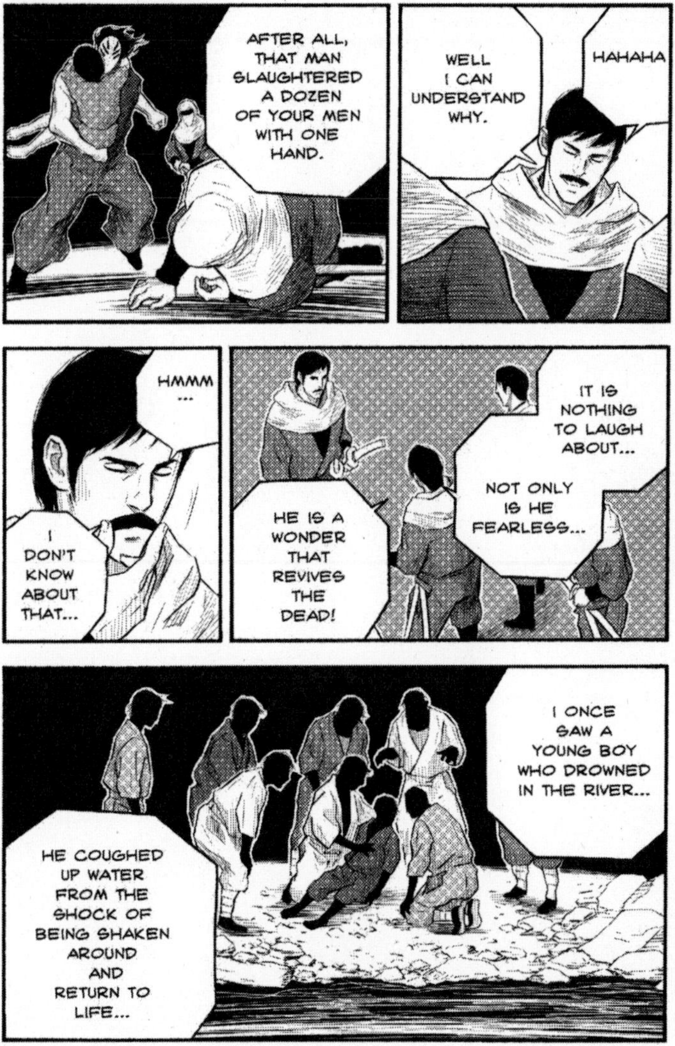
HAHAHA
WELL I CAN UNDERSTAND WHY.
AFTER ALL, THAT MAN SLAUGHTERED A DOZEN OF YOUR MEN WITH ONE HAND.
IT IS NOTHING TO LAUGH ABOUT...
NOT ONLY IS HE FEARLESS...
HE IS A WONDER THAT REVIVES THE DEAD!
HMMM ...
I DON'T KNOW ABOUT THAT...
I ONCE SAW A YOUNG BOY WHO DROWNED IN THE RIVER...
HE COUGHED UP WATER FROM THE SHOCK OF BEING SHAKEN AROUND AND RETURN TO LIFE...

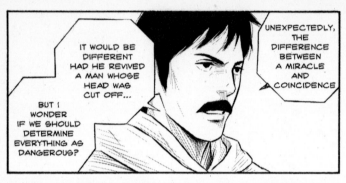

UNEXPECTEDLY, THE DIFFERENCE BETWEEN A MIRACLE AND COINCIDENCE
IT WOULD BE DIFFERENT HAD HE REVIVED A MAN WHOSE HEAD WAS CUT OFF...
BUT I WONDER IF WE SHOULD DETERMINE EVERYTHING AS DANGEROUS?
T-THAT WAS...
THAT WAS NO COINCIDENCE...
REGARDLESS!
WHEN THE ZOH ARMY IS UPON US...
IF HE WERE TO TURN VIOLENT WITHIN THE FORTRESS IT WOULD PROVE FATAL TO US ALL.
IF WE CANNOT INCREASE THE NUMBER OF GUARDS.
THEN WE SHOULD AT LEAST IMPRISION HIM...
HE WILL NOT CAUSE TROUBLE.

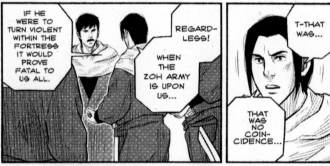

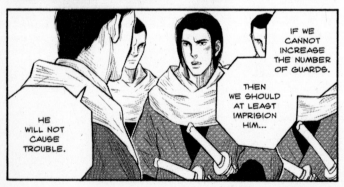

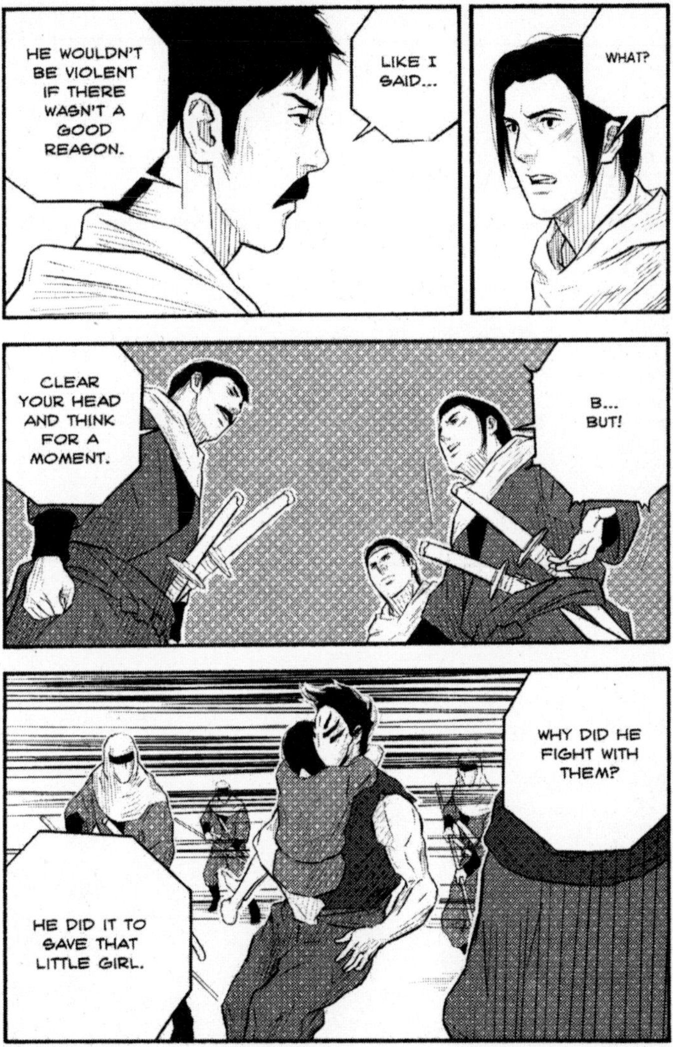
WHAT?
LIKE I SAID...
HE WOULDN'T BE VIOLENT IF THERE WASN'T A GOOD REASON.
B... BUT!
CLEAR YOUR HEAD AND THINK FOR A MOMENT.
WHY DID HE FIGHT WITH THEM?
HE DID IT TO SAVE THAT LITTLE GIRL.

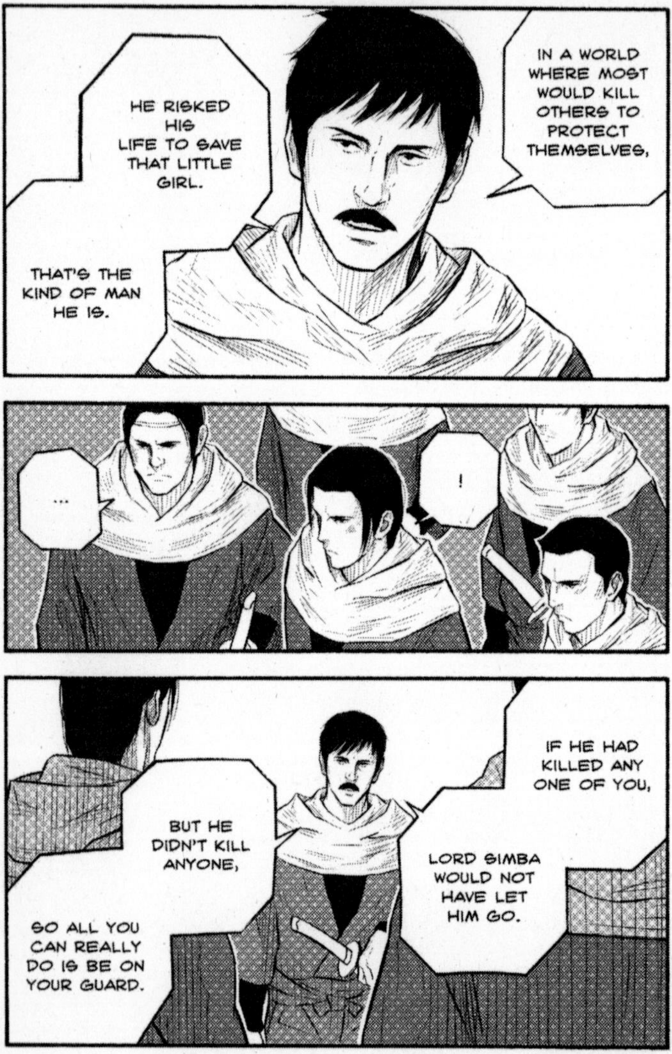
IN A WORLD WHERE MOST WOULD KILL OTHERS TO PROTECT THEMSELVES,
HE RISKED HIS LIFE TO SAVE THAT LITTLE GIRL.
THAT'S THE KIND OF MAN HE IS.
!
...
IF HE HAD KILLED ANY ONE OF YOU,
LORD SIMBA WOULD NOT HAVE LET HIM GO.
BUT HE DIDN'T KILL ANYONE,
SO ALL YOU CAN REALLY DO IS BE ON YOUR GUARD.

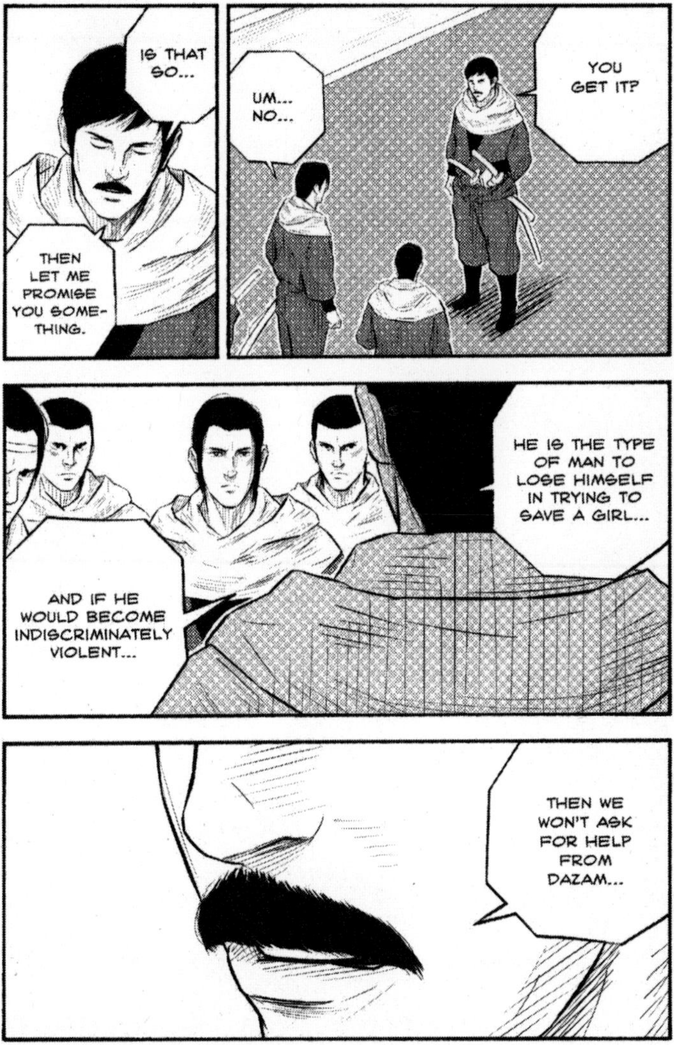
YOU GET IT?
UM... NO...
IS THAT SO...
THEN LET ME PROMISE YOU SOME-THING.
HE IS THE TYPE OF MAN TO LOSE HIMSELF IN TRYING TO SAVE A GIRL...
AND IF HE WOULD BECOME INDISCRIMINATELY VIOLENT...
THEN WE WON'T ASK FOR HELP FROM DAZAM...

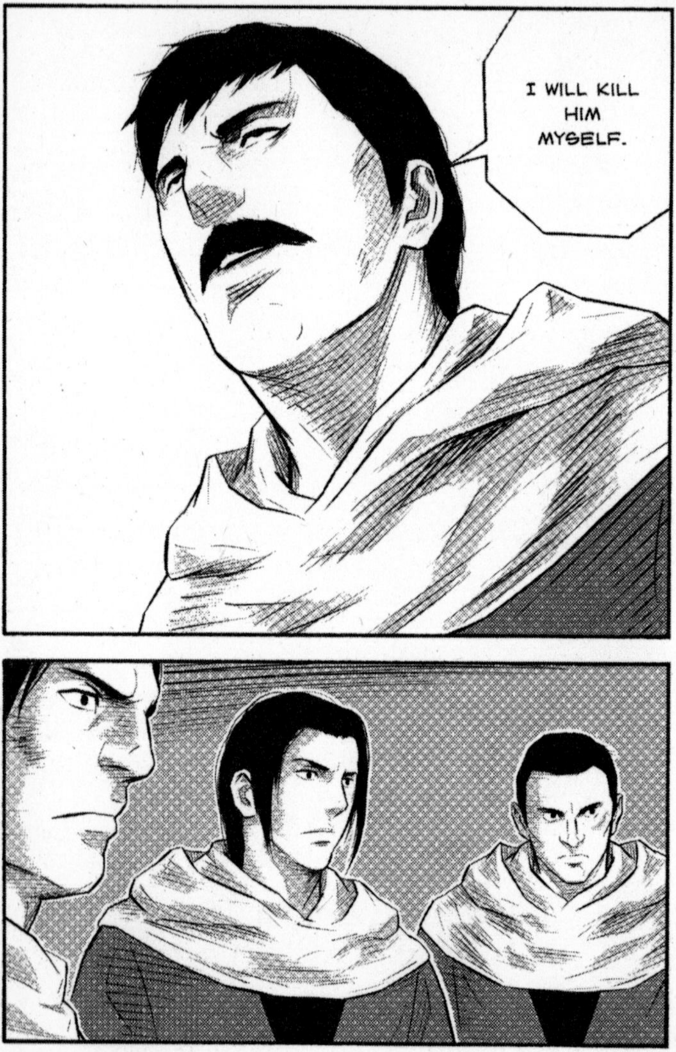
I WILL KILL HIM MYSELF.

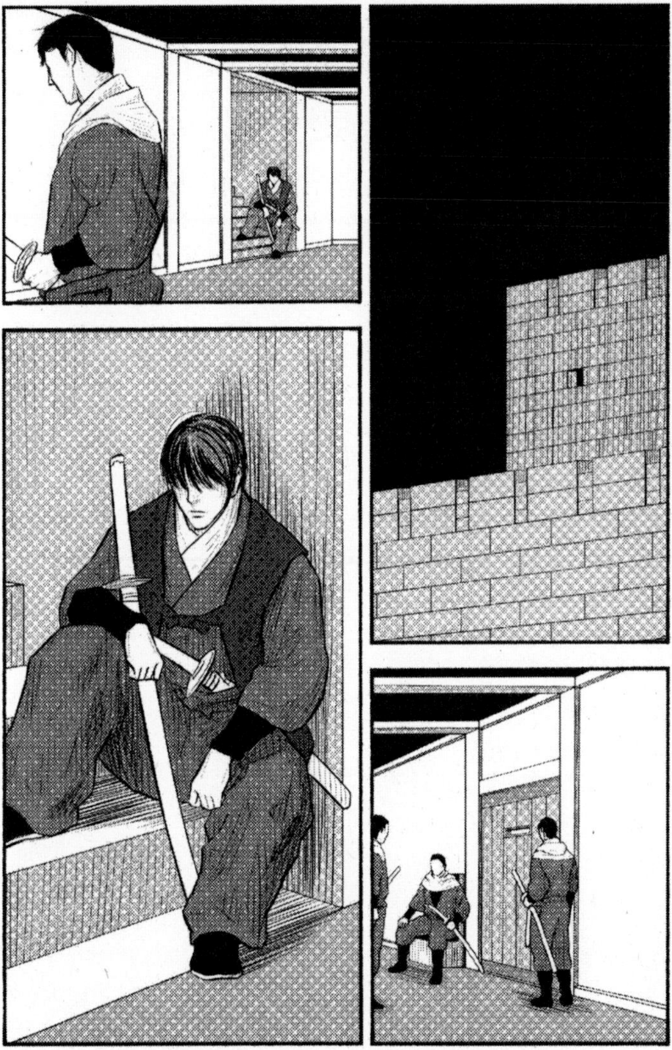

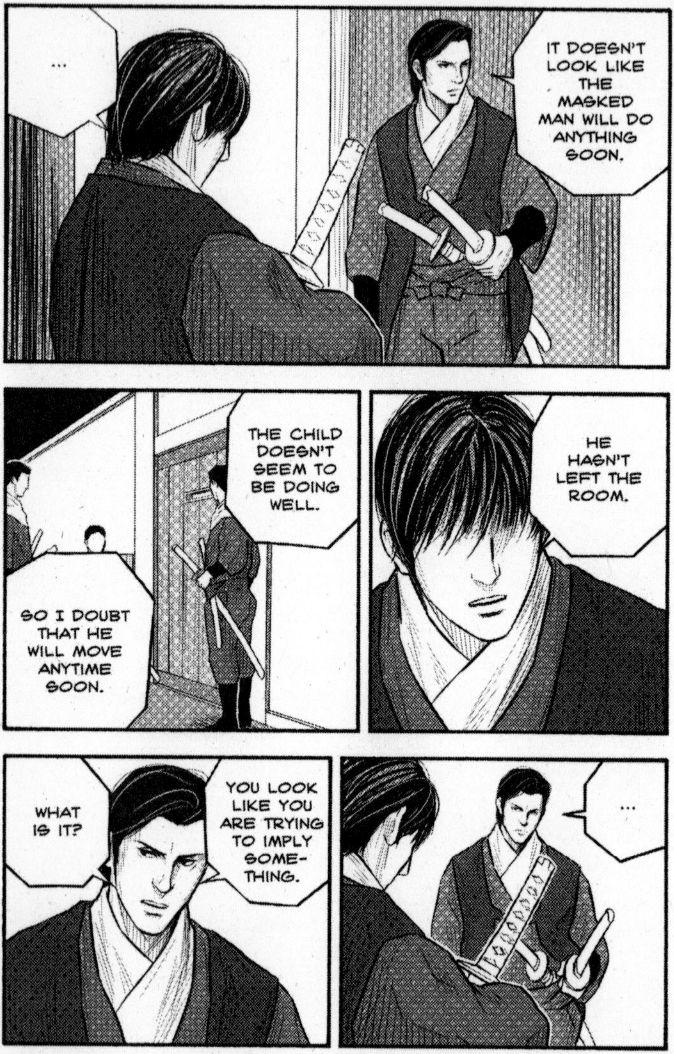
IT DOESN'T LOOK LIKE THE MASKED MAN WILL DO ANYTHING SOON.
...
HE HASN'T LEFT THE ROOM.
THE CHILD DOESN'T SEEM TO BE DOING WELL.
SO I DOUBT THAT HE WILL MOVE ANYTIME SOON.
...
YOU LOOK LIKE YOU ARE TRYING TO IMPLY SOME-THING.
WHAT IS IT?

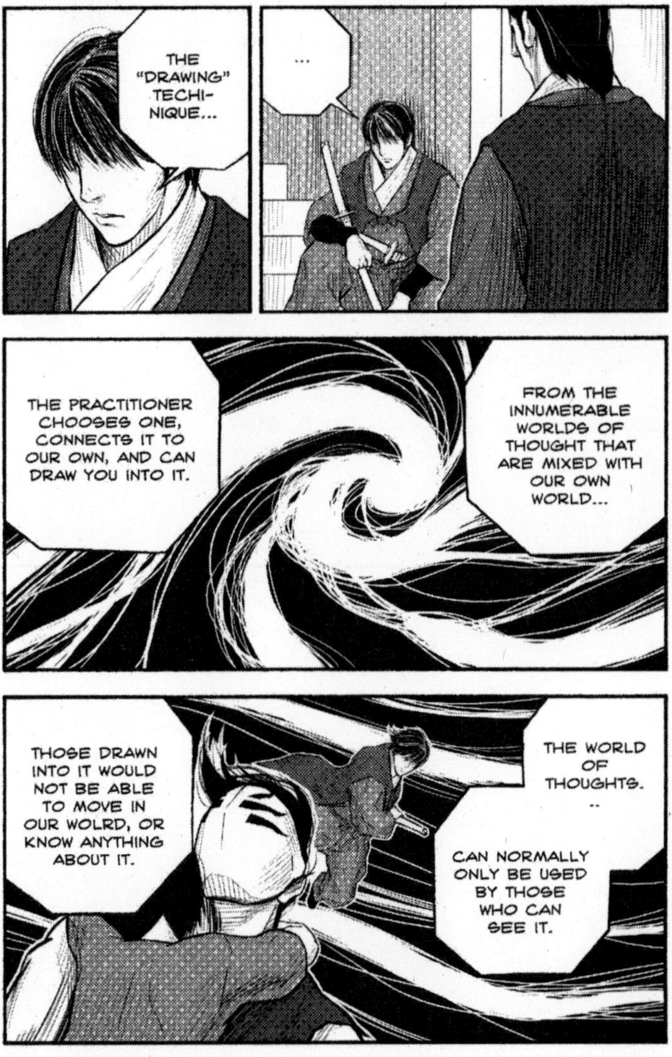
...
THE "DRAWING" TECHI-NIQUE...
FROM THE INNUMERABLE WORLDS OF THOUGHT THAT ARE MIXED WITH OUR OWN WORLD...
THE PRACTITIONER CHOOSES ONE, CONNECTS IT TO OUR OWN, AND CAN DRAW YOU INTO IT.
THE WORLD OF THOUGHTS...
CAN NORMALLY ONLY BE USED BY THOSE WHO CAN SEE IT.
THOSE DRAWN INTO IT WOULD NOT BE ABLE TO MOVE IN OUR WOLRD, OR KNOW ANYTHING ABOUT IT.

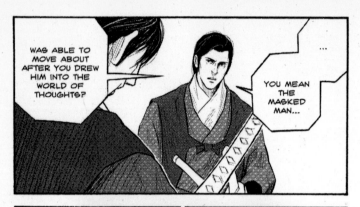

...
YOU MEAN THE MASKED MAN...
WAS ABLE TO MOVE ABOUT AFTER YOU DREW HIM INTO THE WORLD OF THOUGHTS?
NO...
NOT THE MASKED MAN...
!
BUT I SAW IT...

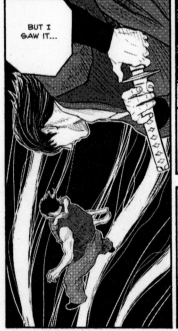

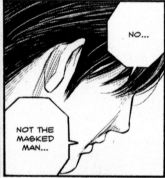

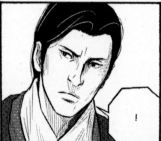

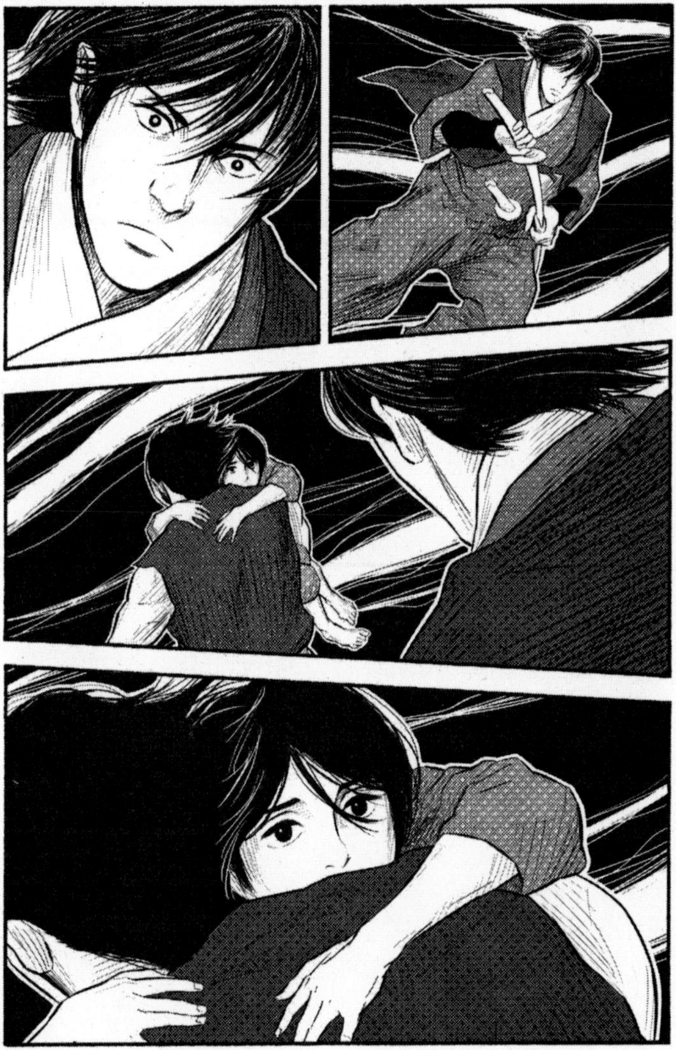

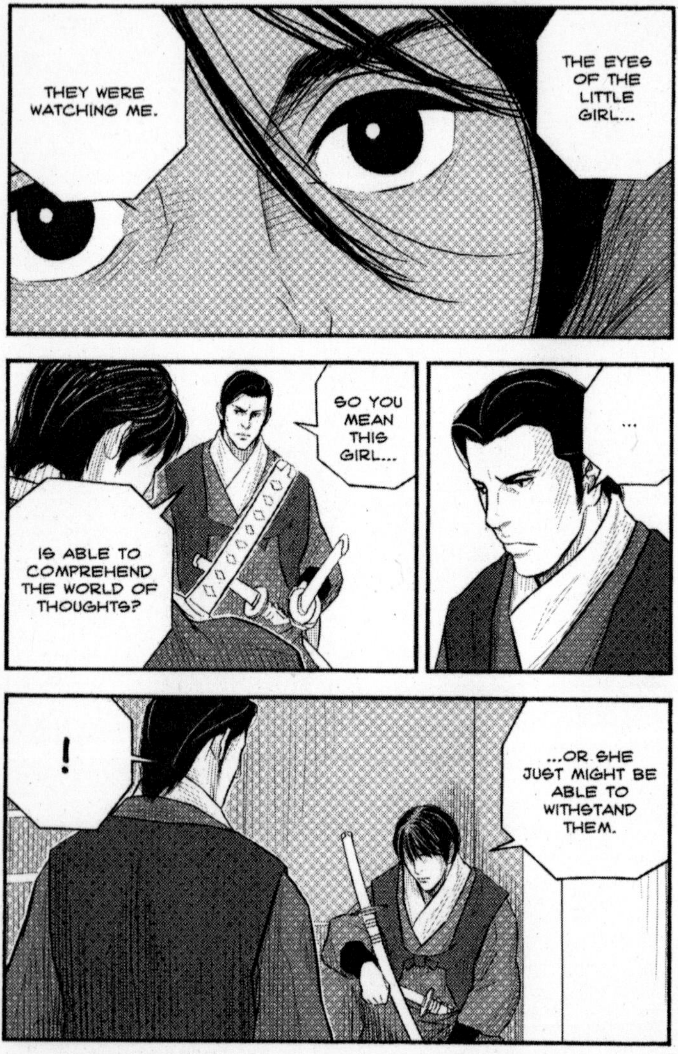
THE EYES OF THE LITTLE GIRL...
THEY WERE WATCHING ME.
...
SO YOU MEAN THIS GIRL...
IS ABLE TO COMPREHEND THE WORLD OF THOUGHTS?
...OR SHE JUST MIGHT BE ABLE TO WITHSTAND THEM.
!

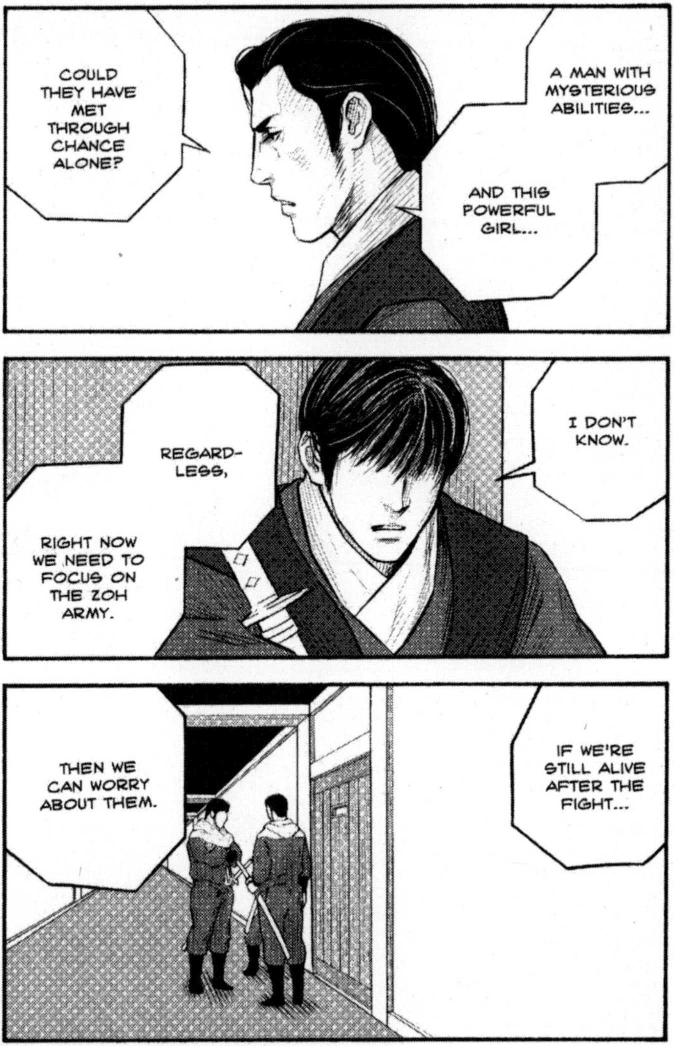
A MAN WITH MYSTERIOUS ABILITIES...
AND THIS POWERFUL GIRL...
COULD THEY HAVE MET THROUGH CHANCE ALONE?
I DON'T KNOW.
REGARDLESS,
RIGHT NOW WE NEED TO FOCUS ON THE ZOH ARMY.
IF WE'RE STILL ALIVE AFTER THE FIGHT...
THEN WE CAN WORRY ABOUT THEM.

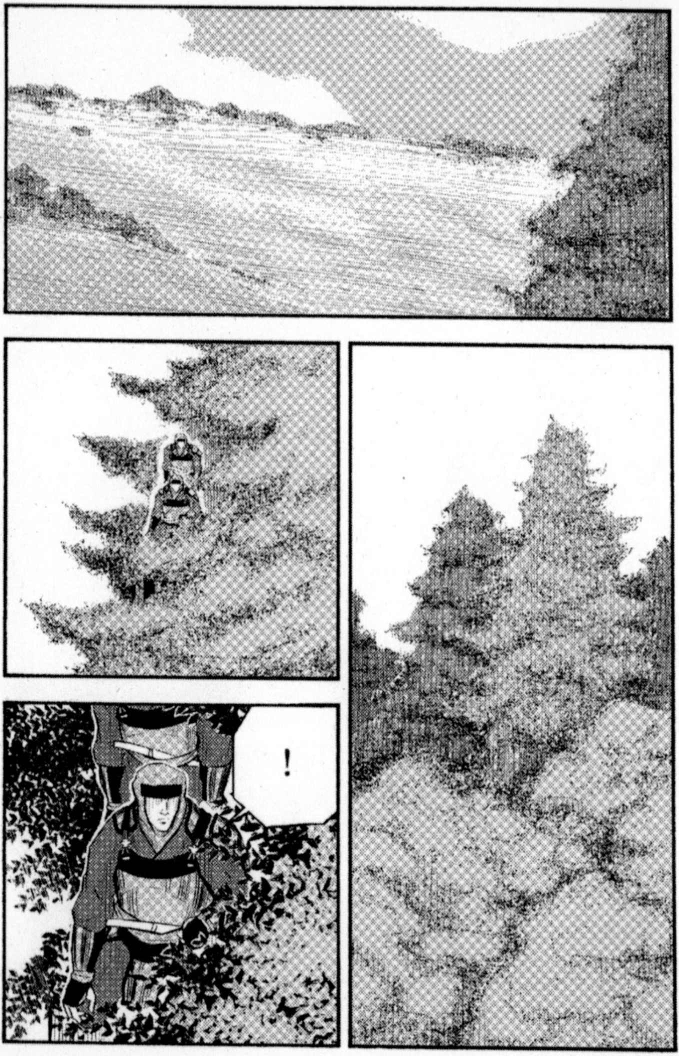
!

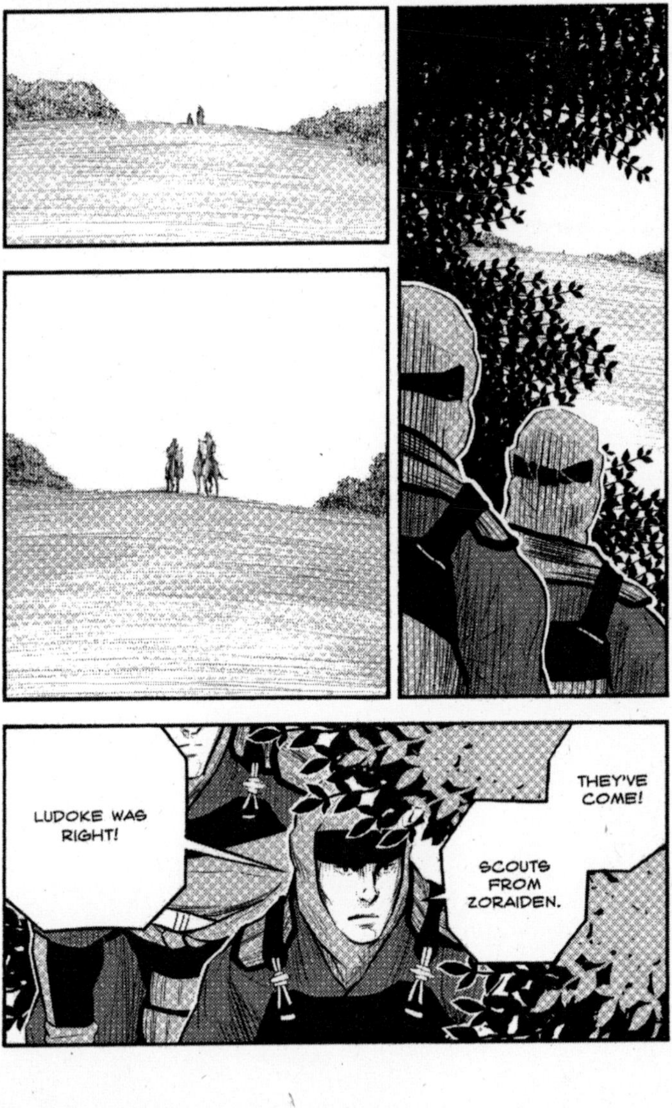
THEY'VE COME!
SCOUTS FROM ZORAIDEN.
LUDOKE WAS RIGHT!

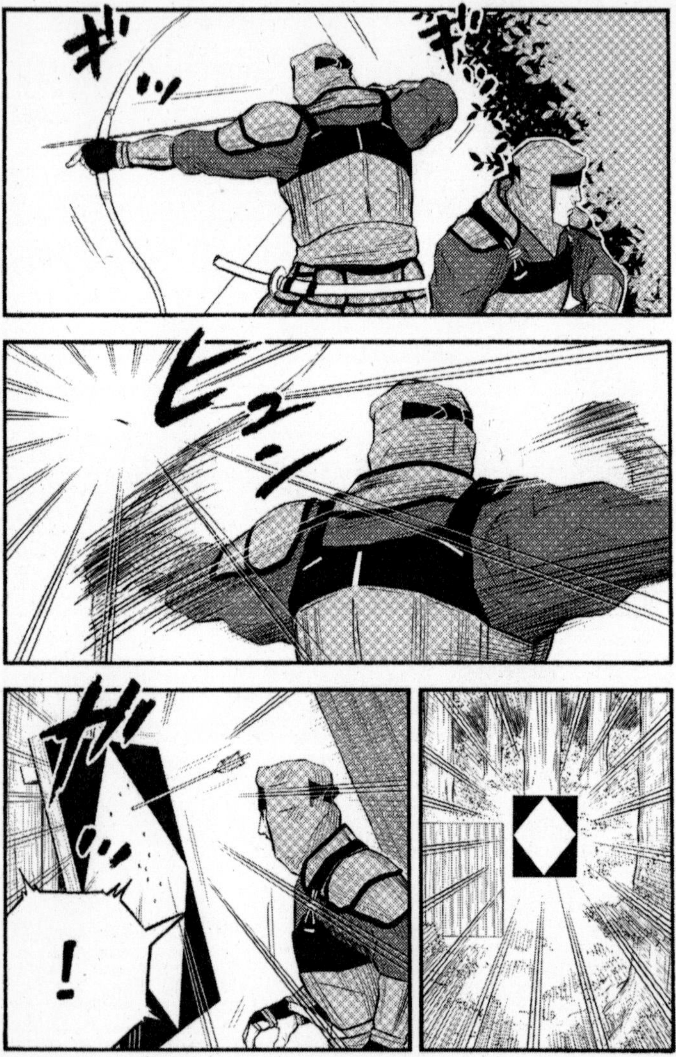

ギリ
ギッ
ヒュン
ガッ
!

THE ZOH ARMY IS COMING UP THE CENTER ROAD!

HURRY AND SPREAD THE WORD!

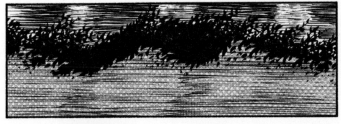

LUDOKE! I HAVE A REPORT!

2000 MEN OF THE ZOH ARMY HAVE BEGUN AN INVASION BY THE CENTER ROAD!

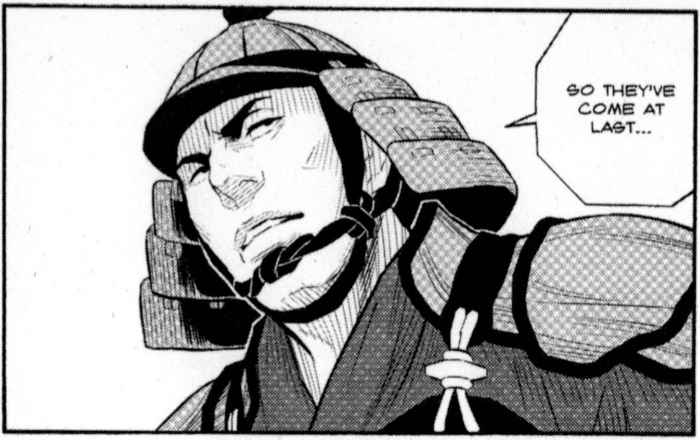
SO THEY'VE COME AT LAST...

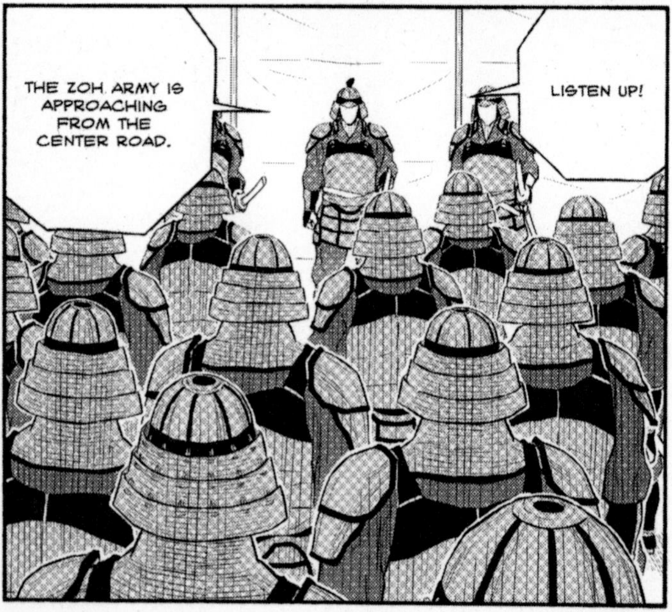
LISTEN UP!
THE ZOH ARMY IS APPROACHING FROM THE CENTER ROAD.

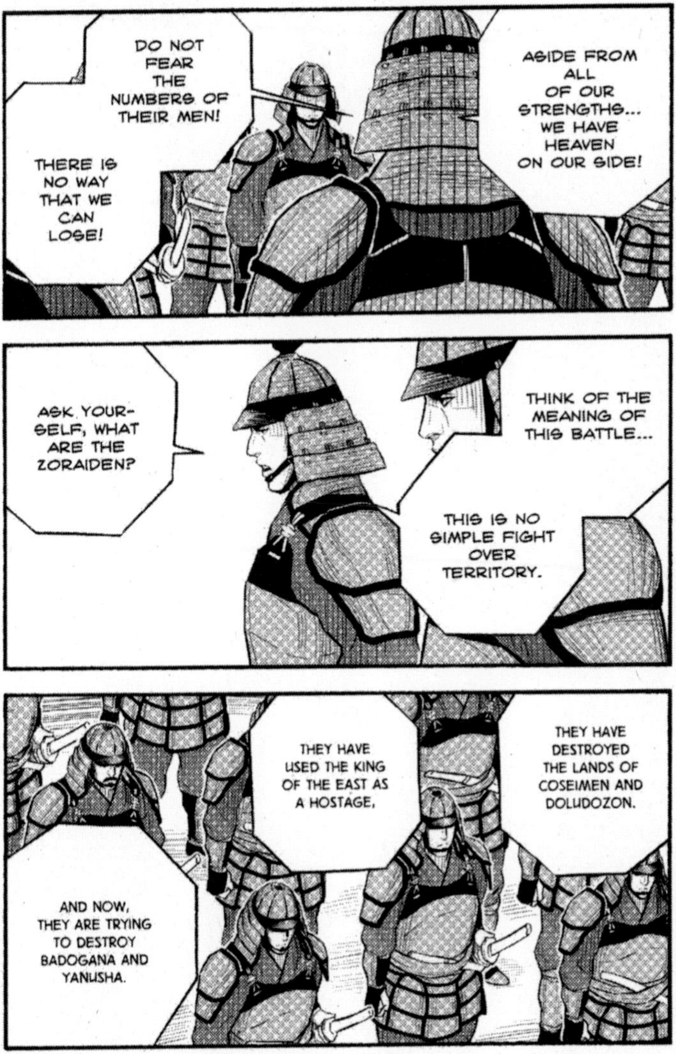
ASIDE FROM ALL OF OUR STRENGTHS... WE HAVE HEAVEN ON OUR SIDE!
DO NOT FEAR THE NUMBERS OF THEIR MEN!
THERE IS NO WAY THAT WE CAN LOSE!
THINK OF THE MEANING OF THIS BATTLE...
THIS IS NO SIMPLE FIGHT OVER TERRITORY.
ASK YOUR-SELF, WHAT ARE THE ZORAIDEN?
THEY HAVE DESTROYED THE LANDS OF COSEIMEN AND DOLUDOZON.
THEY HAVE USED THE KING OF THE EAST AS A HOSTAGE,
AND NOW, THEY ARE TRYING TO DESTROY BADOGANA AND YANUSHA.

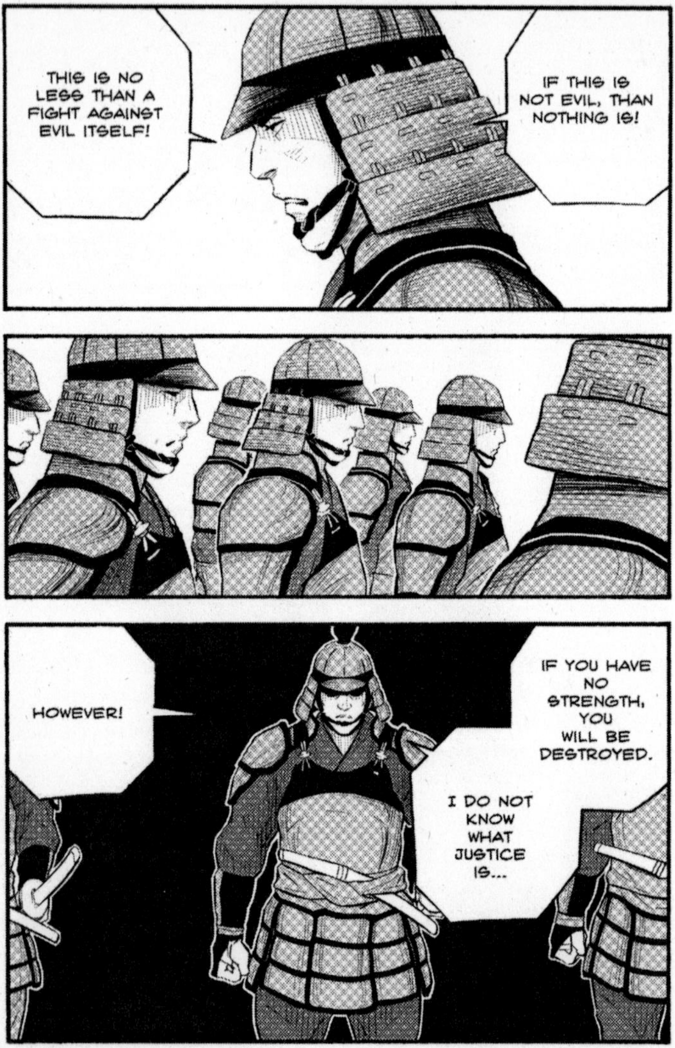
IF THIS IS NOT EVIL, THAN NOTHING IS!
THIS IS NO LESS THAN A FIGHT AGAINST EVIL ITSELF!
IF YOU HAVE NO STRENGTH, YOU WILL BE DESTROYED.
HOWEVER!
I DO NOT KNOW WHAT JUSTICE IS...

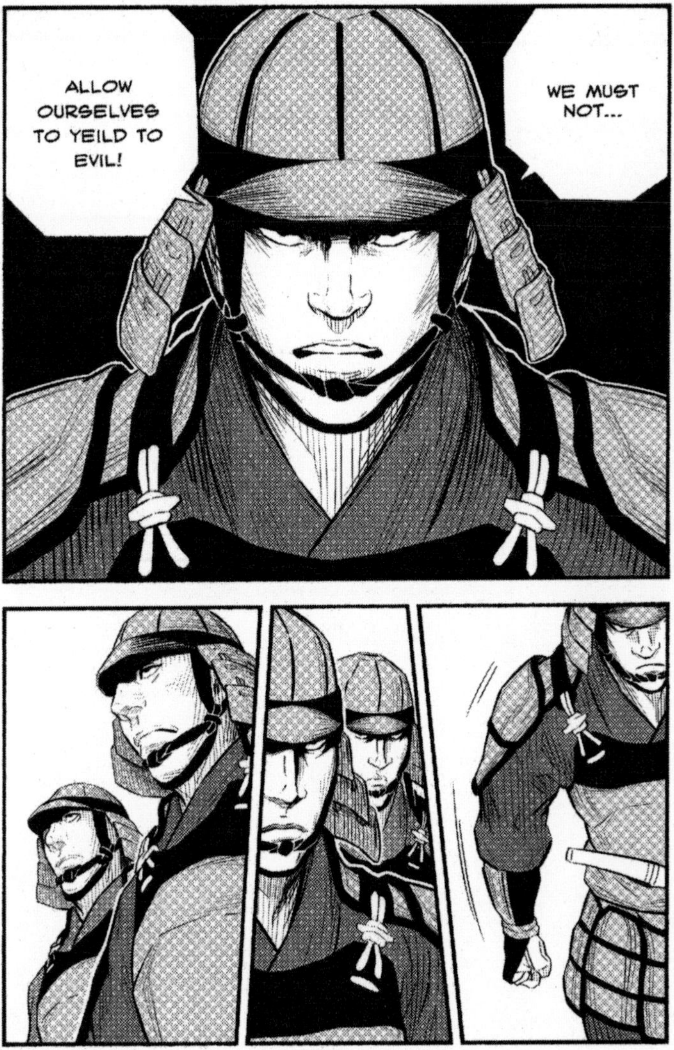
WE MUST NOT...
ALLOW OURSELVES TO YEILD TO EVIL!

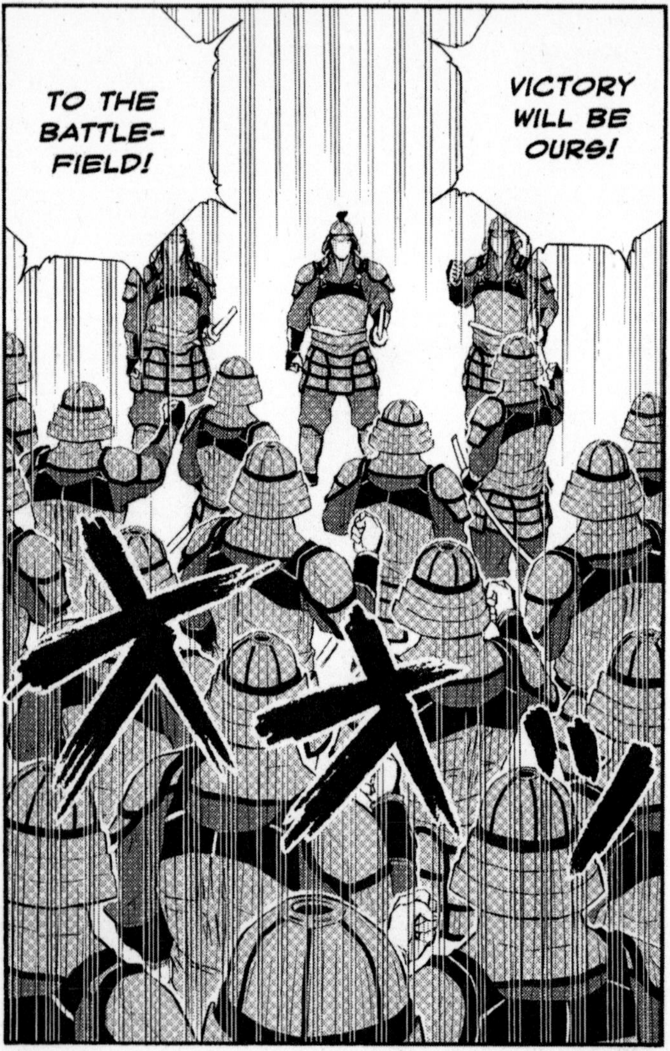
VICTORY WILL BE OURS!
TO THE BATTLE-FIELD!

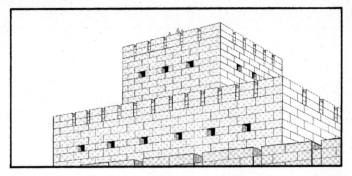

LORD SIMBA...! IT'S FINALLY TIME.

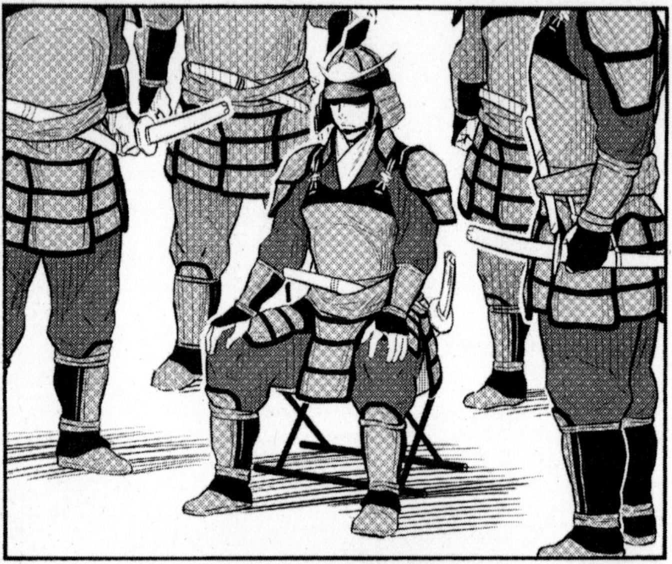
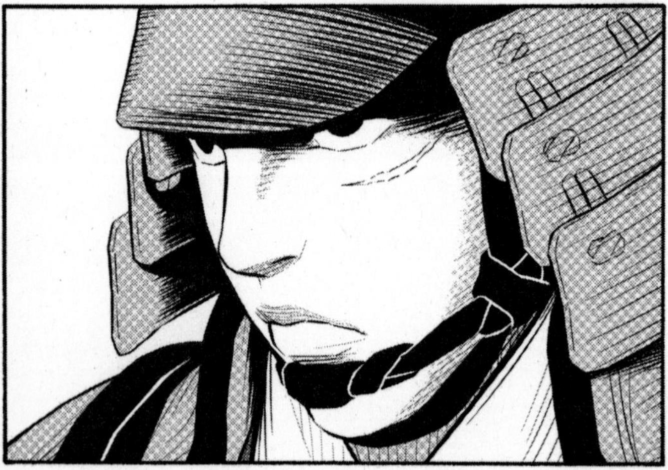

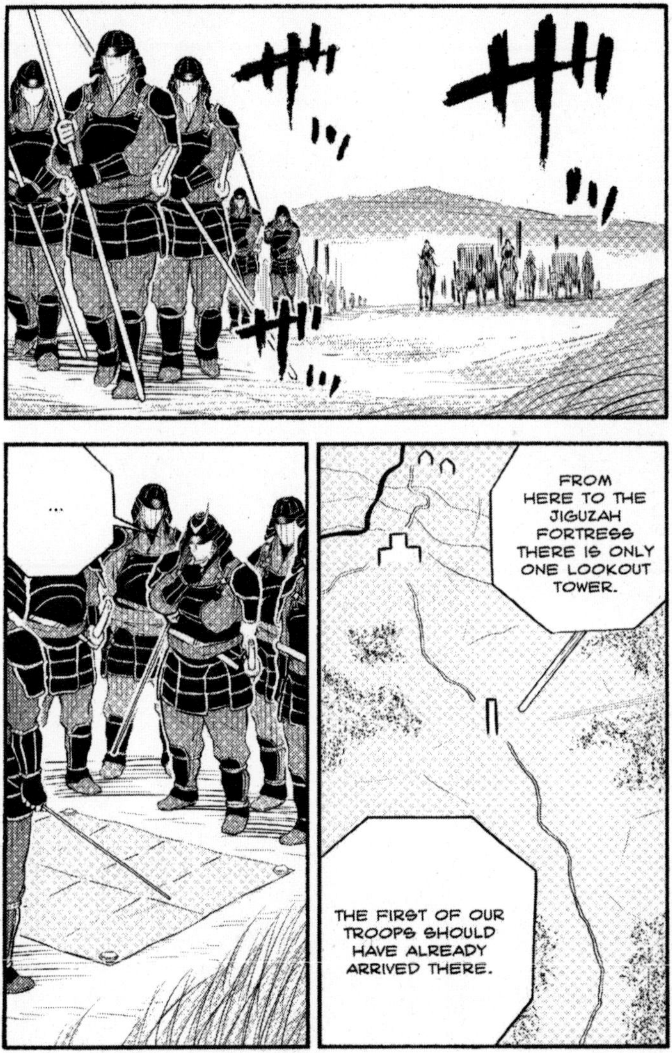
ザッ
ザッ
ザッ
FROM HERE TO THE JIGUZAH FORTRESS THERE IS ONLY ONE LOOKOUT TOWER.
THE FIRST OF OUR TROOPS SHOULD HAVE ALREADY ARRIVED THERE.
...

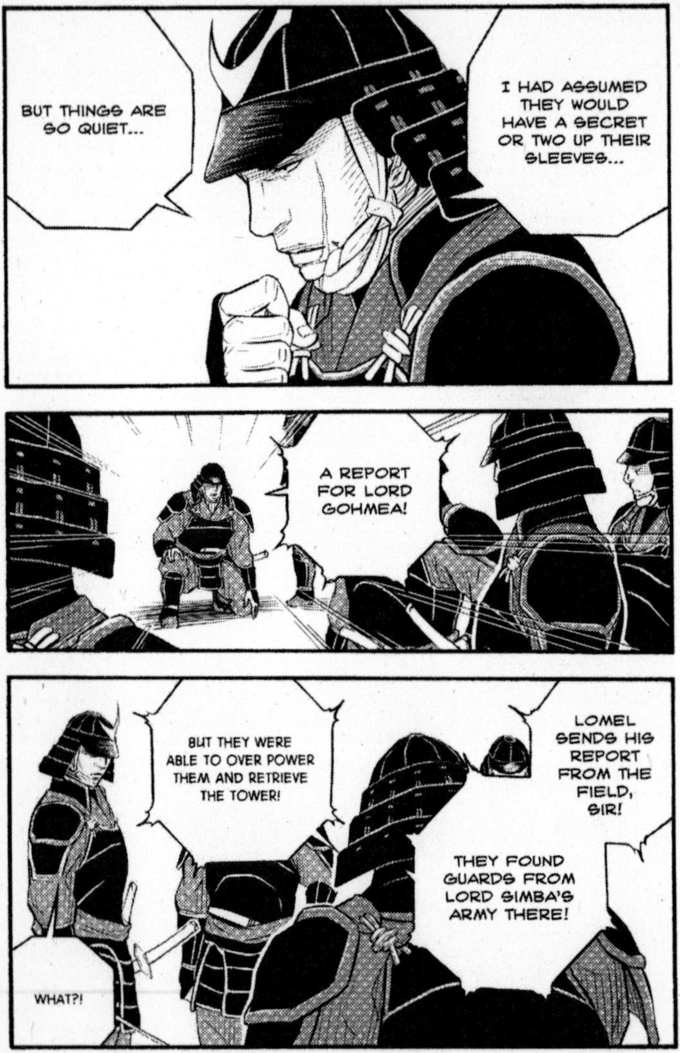
I HAD ASSUMED THEY WOULD HAVE A SECRET OR TWO UP THEIR SLEEVES...
BUT THINGS ARE SO QUIET...
A REPORT FOR LORD GOHMEA!
LOMEL SENDS HIS REPORT FROM THE FIELD, SIR!
THEY FOUND GUARDS FROM LORD SIMBA'S ARMY THERE!
BUT THEY WERE ABLE TO OVER POWER THEM AND RETRIEVE THE TOWER!
WHAT?!

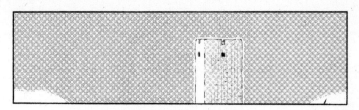

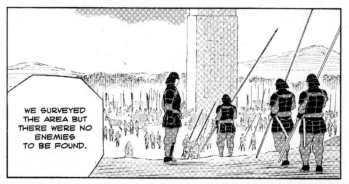

WE SURVEYED THE AREA BUT THERE WERE NO ENEMIES TO BE FOUND.
WE HAVE FORMED OUTPOSTS AROUND THE TOWER, SIR.
THIS WOULD ALSO BE A GOOD PLACE TO PUT A FORMATION.
...
I DON'T GET IT...

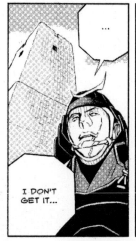

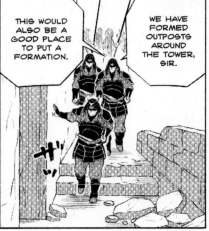

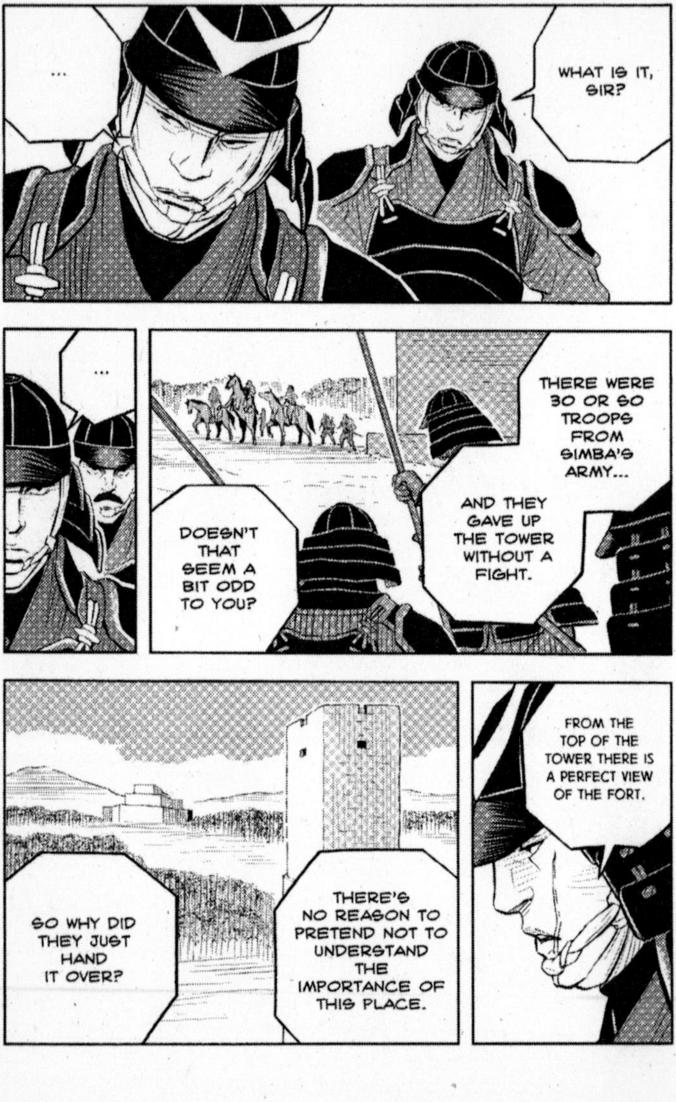
WHAT IS IT, SIR?
...
THERE WERE 30 OR SO TROOPS FROM SIMBA'S ARMY...
AND THEY GAVE UP THE TOWER WITHOUT A FIGHT.
DOESN'T THAT SEEM A BIT ODD TO YOU?
...
FROM THE TOP OF THE TOWER THERE IS A PERFECT VIEW OF THE FORT.
THERE'S NO REASON TO PRETEND NOT TO UNDERSTAND THE IMPORTANCE OF THIS PLACE.
SO WHY DID THEY JUST HAND IT OVER?

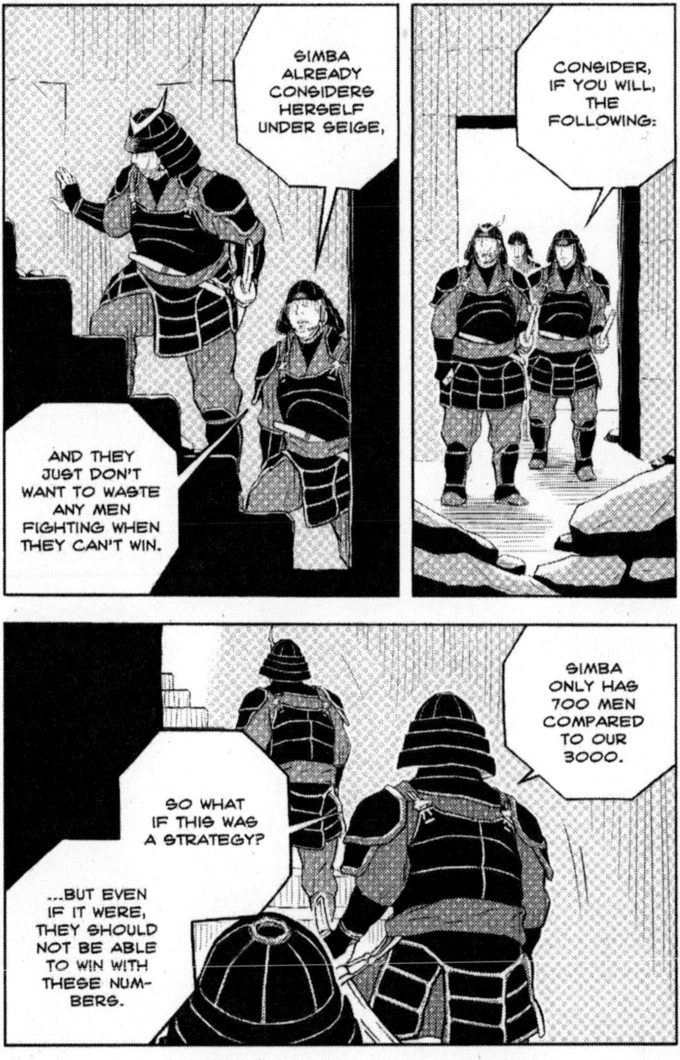
CONSIDER, IF YOU WILL, THE FOLLOWING:
SIMBA ALREADY CONSIDERS HERSELF UNDER SEIGE,
AND THEY JUST DON'T WANT TO WASTE ANY MEN FIGHTING WHEN THEY CAN'T WIN.
SIMBA ONLY HAS 700 MEN COMPARED TO OUR 3000.
SO WHAT IF THIS WAS A STRATEGY?
...BUT EVEN IF IT WERE, THEY SHOULD NOT BE ABLE TO WIN WITH THESE NUM-BERS.

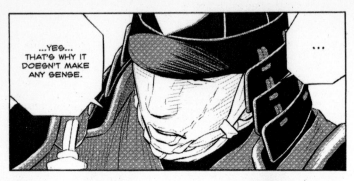

...
...YES... THAT'S WHY IT DOESN'T MAKE ANY SENSE.
...SO... WHAT DO YOU MEAN, SIR?
IF I CAN SURROUND THE FORT FROM HERE,...
THE BATTLE WILL BE DECIDED.
IF WE TAKE THE FORT, THERE WILL BE NO HOPE FOR THEM.
IF OUR INFORMATION IS CORRECT...
THEIR ONE ALLY, LORD GAILAS, HAS NOT COME TO THEIR AID...
THERE APPEARS TO BE NO HOPE FOR SIMBA'S ARMY.

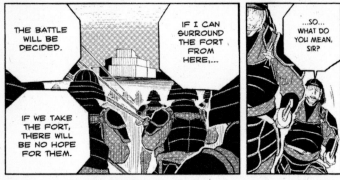

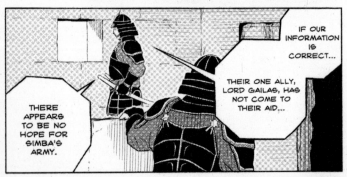

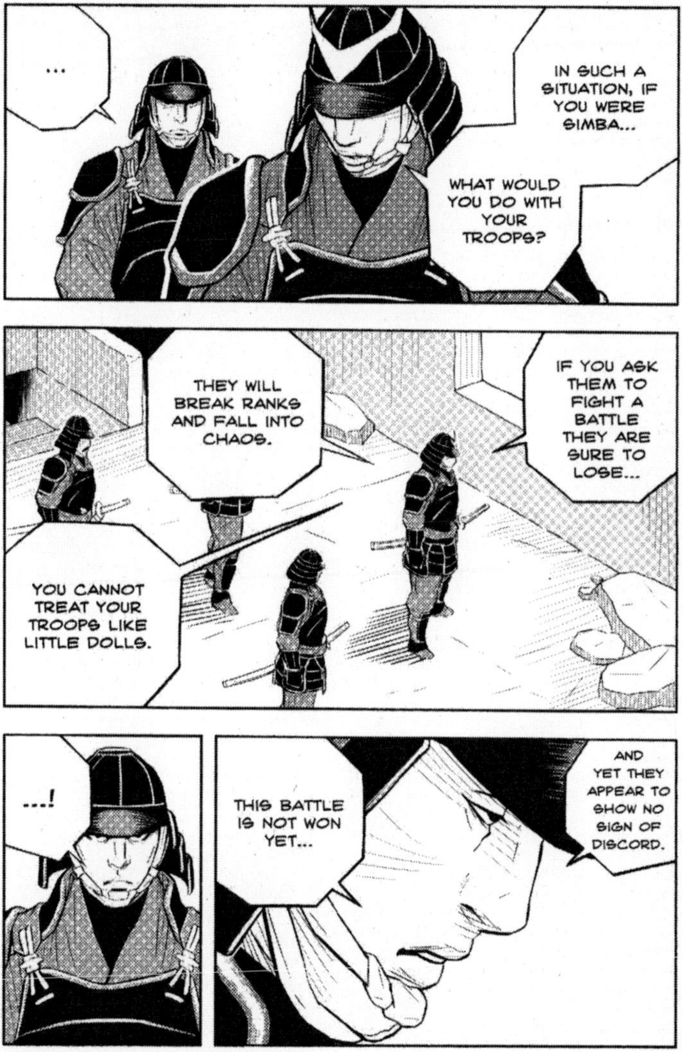
IN SUCH A SITUATION, IF YOU WERE SIMBA...
WHAT WOULD YOU DO WITH YOUR TROOPS?
...
IF YOU ASK THEM TO FIGHT A BATTLE THEY ARE SURE TO LOSE...
THEY WILL BREAK RANKS AND FALL INTO CHAOS.
YOU CANNOT TREAT YOUR TROOPS LIKE LITTLE DOLLS.
AND YET THEY APPEAR TO SHOW NO SIGN OF DISCORD.
THIS BATTLE IS NOT WON YET...
...!

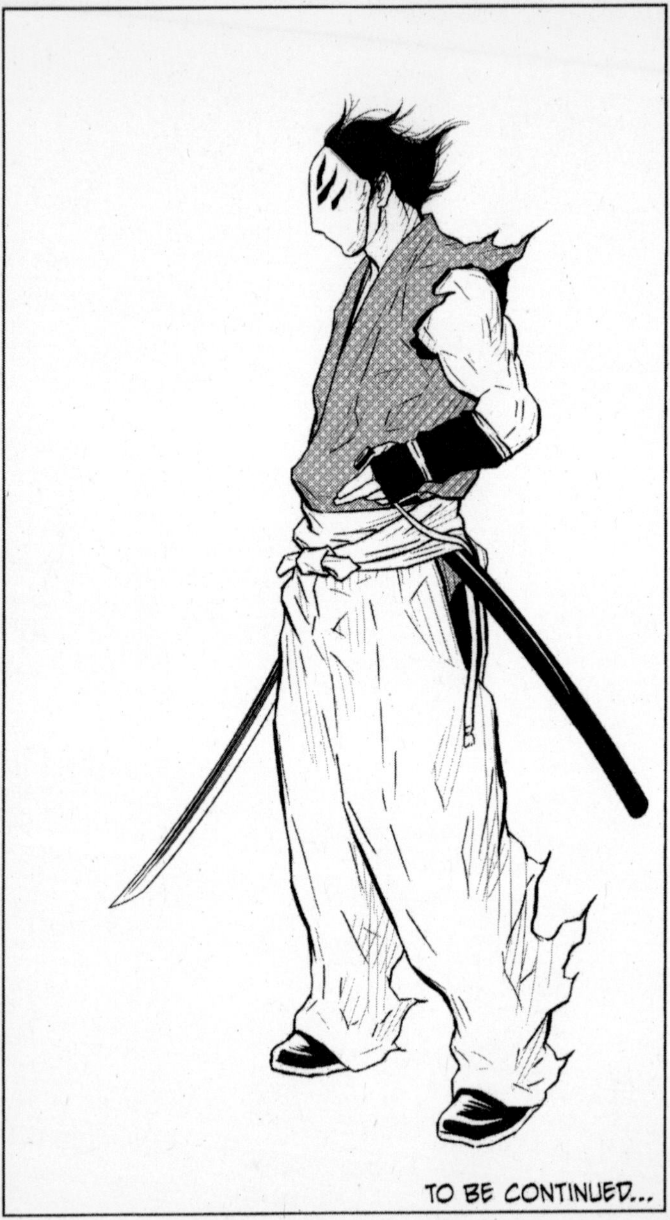
TO BE CONTINUED...

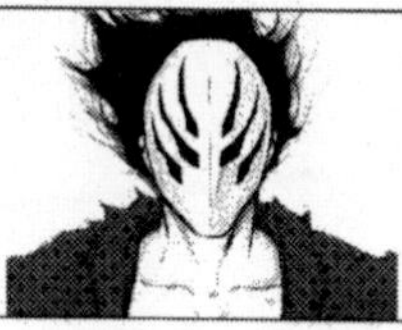

THE MASKED MAN
EVERYTHING ABOUT HIM, INCLUDING HIS AGE AND HIS PAST, IS UNKNOWN.
POSSESSING STRANGE ABILITIES AND CONCEALING HIS FACE BEHIND A SENTIENT MASK, HE APPEARED IN THESE LANDS SUDDENLY.

NAIOMI
A GIRL FROM BADOGANA WHOSE PARENTS WERE KILLED IN THE ZORAIDEN ARMY (ZOH ARMY) INVASION. SHE SEEMS TO HAVE MYSTERIOUS POWERS.

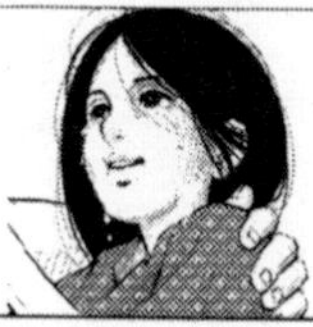

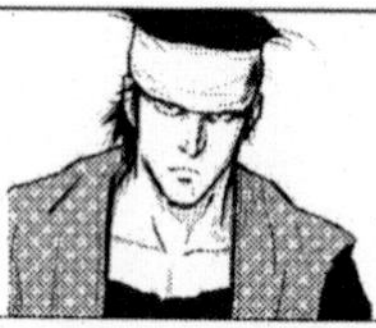

SYBAN
A YOUNG SAMURAI WHO IS INTERESTED IN SIMBA. HE HAS SKILL IN CONTROLLING THE FORBIDDEN WORLD, AND MAY HAVE SOMETHING TO DO WITH COMMANDER LYHAON.

SIMBA ZELBAIN
THE SEVENTEEN-YEAR-OLD FEMALE GENERAL WHO TOOK CONTROL OF THE JIGUZAH REGION IN EIZOS. UNWILLING TO ACCEPT THE SLAUGHTER BEING CARRIED OUT BY THE ZORAIDEN, SHE BROKE HER ALLIANCE WITH THEM AND WENT TO WAR.

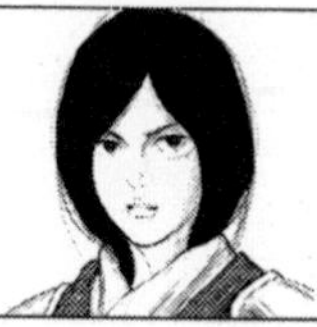

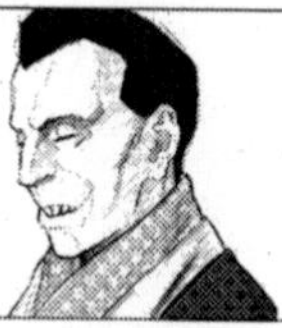

GAILAS ZELBAIN
SIMBA'S UNCLE, THE YOUNGER BROTHER OF HER DECEASED FATHER ORION. HE IS TRYING TO HOLD SIMBA BACK IN ORDER TO PROTECT THE ZELBAIN CLAN.

LUDOKE
ONE OF THE COMMANDERS OF JIGUZAH WHO SERVE UNDER SIMBA. A CAPABLE AND EXCEEDINGLY RESOURCEFUL MAN, HE HAS SAVED HIS YOUNG LEADER FROM DANGER MANY TIMES.

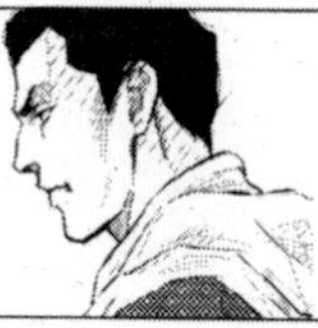

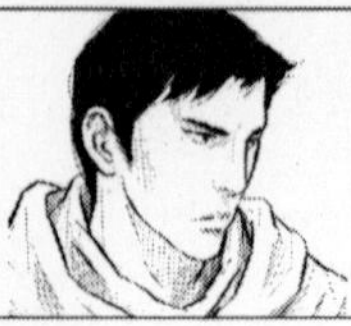

NANASE

ONE OF THE COMMANDERS OF JIGUZAH WHO SERVE UNDER SIMBA. SIMBA HAS GREAT CONFIDENCE IN HIM, AND HE IS IN CHARGE OF MANAGING JIGUZAH FORTRESS WHEN SHE IS NOT THERE.

ORUMA

ONE OF THE SAMURAI WHO SERVE UNDER SIMBA. A TALENTED SWORDSMAN, HE IS OFTEN RESPONSIBLE FOR KEEPING SIMBA SAFE. HE IS AMONG HER STRONGEST WARRIORS.

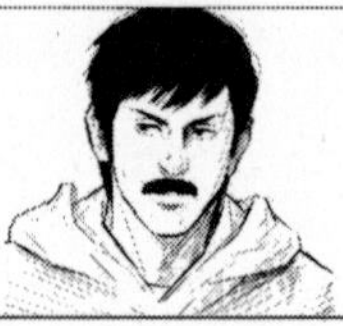

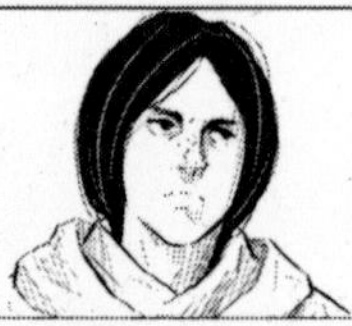

KAGURA

ONE OF THE YOUNG SAMURAI WHO SERVE UNDER SIMBA. INEXPERIENCED AND LACKING IN FORESIGHT, HE IS PURE OF HEART AND WILLING TO SACRIFICE HIS LIFE IF IT IS FOR THE SAKE OF HIS BELIEFS.

DAZAM

A RED-HAIRED SAMURAI WHO SERVES UNDER SIMBA. HE IS ABLE TO USE THE SECRET "NEN ARTS." PEOPLE OF HIS KIND, KNOWN AS "NEN MASTERS," ARE FEW. BECAUSE OF THEIR TALENTS, MANY NEN MASTERS ARE UNDER THE CONTROL OF A LORD.

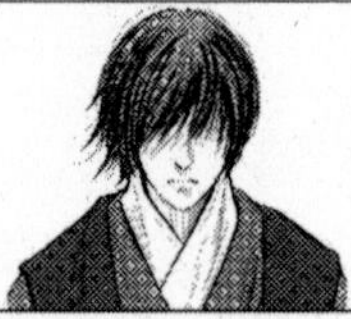

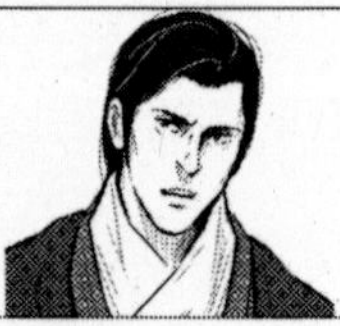

LAIRYUU

A RESILIENT MASTERLESS SWORDSMAN WHO ACCOMPANIES DAZAM. DAZAM'S TRUST IN HIM IS DEEP, AND SIMBA HAS GREAT FAITH IN HIM AS WELL. IT LOOKS AS THOUGH HE CAN ALSO USE THE NEN ARTS, BUT HIS ABILITIES ARE SEALED AWAY FOR SOME REASON.

GOHMEA

A COURAGEOUS ZORAIDEN ARMY COMMANDER. HE WAS ONCE A SAMURAI IN THE KASKAZON REGION, SERVING UNDER THE KING OF THE EAST. AFTER THE ZORAIDEN MADE THE KING INTO THEIR PUPPET, HE EASILY ROSE TO A POSITION OF POWER.

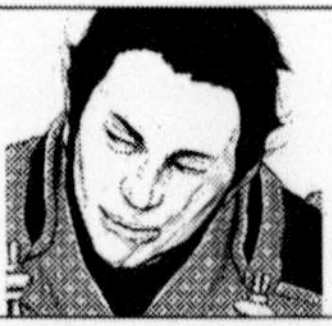

INDIE MANGA FROM THE TOKYO UNDERGROUND

GEN STORIES ARE PUBLISHED NOWHERE ELSE IN THE WORLD. THEY COME STRAIGHT FROM THE ARTISTS IN JAPAN TO YOU. WE TRANSLATE THE STORIES AND PUT THEM OUT AS THEY ARE CREATED.

GEN
MANGA